In Translation

In
TRANSLATION

TRANSLATORS ON THEIR WORK
AND WHAT IT MEANS

Edited by

ESTHER ALLEN *and* **SUSAN BERNOFSKY**

Columbia University Press   *New York*

Columbia University Press
Publishers Since 1893
New York   Chichester, West Sussex
cup.columbia.edu
Copyright © 2013 Columbia University Press

Library of Congress Cataloging-in-Publication Data
In translation : translators on their work and what it means / edited by Esther Allen
and Susan Bernofsky.
p.   cm.
Includes index.
ISBN 978-0-231-15968-5 (cloth : alk. paper) — ISBN 978-0-231-15969-2 (pbk. : alk. paper) —
ISBN 978-0-231-53502-1 (electronic)
1. Translating and interpreting.   2. Literature—Translations—History and criticism.
3. Language and culture.   I. Allen, Esther, 1962-   II. Bernofsky, Susan.
PN241.I45   2013
418'.04—dc23

2012031223

Columbia University Press books are printed on permanent and durable acid-free paper.
This book is printed on paper with recycled content.
Printed in the United States of America

COVER DESIGN: Julia Kushnirsky

References to websites (URLs) were accurate at the time of writing. Neither the author nor
Columbia University Press is responsible for URLs that may have expired or changed since
the manuscript was prepared.

Contents

Contents

Contents

Acknowledgments

We would like to express our utmost gratitude to the contributors whose essays appear here; their achievements as translators and as thinkers about translation were what inspired us to create this anthology.

In addition, the support, engagement, and advice of many other friends, colleagues, and institutions has helped immeasurably to make this volume possible.

Esther Allen would like to thank translators *extraordinaires* Michael Scammell, Brian Nelson, and Bill Johnston, for guidance, inspiration, and prodding; Damion Searls for pointing the way to Murakami's essay on translating Fitzgerald; and Regina Galasso for helping to develop the essay Allen contributed to this volume. She is grateful to Larry Siems and Caro Llewellyn, former colleagues at the PEN American Center, and to Carolyn McCormick and Carles Torner, former colleagues at International PEN and the Institut Ramon Llull, respectively, for friendship, good will, and exemplary leadership. Alma Guillermoprieto, Roberto Tejada, and Francisco Goldman have contributed more than they know by sharing their friendship, mirth, experience, insight, and wisdom. Gabriela Adamo and the Fundación TyPA offered the valuable experience of the Semana de Editores en Buenos Aires, and Susanna Seidl-Fox, Peter Bush, and John Balcom organized the wonderful Session 461 of the Salzburg Global Seminar, while Ivor Indyk and Chris Andrews of the Writing and Society Research Group of the University of Western Sydney did excellent work putting together the wide-ranging Sydney Symposium on Literary Translation—all three forums had considerable impact on this volume. Jean Strouse and the 2009–2010 class of Fellows at the Cullman Center for Scholars and Writers at the New York Public Library provided invaluable support and resources during the inception of this book. And thanks, most of all, to Nathaniel Wice—for love, a kind and attentive ear, editorial expertise, and happiness.

Susan Bernofsky would like to thank some of the mentors and colleagues who guided and accompanied her on her forays into the field of translation studies: her teacher, friend, and colleague William Weaver; Rainer Schulte, who invited her to an American Literary Translation Association conference when she was only a young student; the Alexander von Humboldt Foundation for supporting her research on the history of translation; Breon Mitchell for hosting her at the American Translation Center in Bloomington; Jürgen Jakob Becker of the Literarisches Colloquium Berlin, which invited her to workshops on several occasions; acclaimed German translator Christa Schuenke, with whom she co-taught her first graduate translation workshop; the Goethe Institut for its Translator Study Trips; Linda Gaboriau and Susan Ouriou of the Banff International Literary Translation Centre; Peter Utz and Irene Weber Henking of the Centre de Traduction Littéraire at the University of Lausanne; William Martin and Sal Robinson of the Bridge Series; Chad Post for writing about translation on his blog Three Percent and founding the Best Translated Book Award; translation scholar Bella Brodzki of Sarah Lawrence College; Peter Connor of Barnard College, who hosted the Pedagogies of Translation conference in May 2012 together with Lawrence Venuti; fellow translators John Biguenet, Russell Valentino, Becka McKay, Sean Cotter, and Aron Aji; her Queens College translator colleagues Roger Sedarat and Ammiel Alcalay; her predecessor as chair of the PEN Translation Committee, Michael Moore; writing group members Elizabeth Denlinger and Fiona Wilson; and Cathy Ciepiela for recommending the essay by Clare Cavanagh.

Both of us are grateful to Rosanna Warren, founder of Boston University's legendary Literary Translation Seminar, who has long been a great beacon to many. We are also immensely thankful for the gift of Edith Grossman's work, example, and friendship. Susan Harris of Words Without Borders is a major support and inspiration to translators everywhere. Amy Stolls and the late Cliff Becker, in their work for the Translation Fellowship program of the National Endowment for the Arts, have contributed greatly to the field of literary translation in the United States.

And the biennial Graduate Students National Translation Conference has been a continual source of new ideas and attitudes, energy and uplift; we particularly benefited from its inaugural session at the University of California at Los Angeles in 2004; its 2008 iteration at Columbia University, organized by Idra Novey; and the 2010 session at the University of Michigan.

We are grateful to Amazon.com for a generous grant in support of the publication costs for this volume. We are thankful, as well, to Philip Leventhal of Columbia University Press, whose vision helped bring this book into existence, and to Alison Alexanian, Whitney Johnson, and Leslie Kriesel for their valuable assistance throughout the editorial process.

Finally, we would both like to express our enormous debt and gratitude to Michael Henry Heim, translator, scholar, and activist, whose shining example, extraordinary energy, single-minded devotion, and unfailing friendship meant more to us than we can say. This volume is dedicated to his memory.

Esther Allen & Susan Bernofsky

Introduction

A Culture of Translation

In Canto XXXI of the *Inferno,* as Dante and his guide Virgil approach the edge of the Ninth and final circle of Hell—where traitors meet their eternal punishment—Dante hears a blast louder than the loudest thunderclap and catches sight in the distance of something that to the contemporary reader may seem a description of the Manhattan skyline: *"me parve veder molte alte torri"* or, in Robert and Jean Hollander's translation, "I saw what seemed a range of lofty towers."[1]

Virgil, who's been here before, sympathizes with Dante's misconstrual of the hazy shapes and explains that his eyes have been deceived: these are not towers but the giants that ring the pit within which lies the Ninth Circle. The first giant's grotesque features soon loom into better view, and as the two travelers through Hell draw closer, the giant blows furiously on his horn and shouts these strange words at them: *"Raphel mai amecche zabi almi."*

"You muddled soul, stick to your horn! Vent yourself with that when rage or passion takes you," Virgil shouts back. He then identifies this horn-blower:

> . . . He is his own accuser.
> This is Nimrod, because of whose vile plan
> The world no longer speaks a single tongue.
> Let us leave him and not waste our speech,
> For every other language is to him as his
> To others, and his is understood by none.[2]

Medieval tradition associated Nimrod, grandson of Noah, with the building of the Tower of Babel and hence the demise of monolingual unity and the sad, plurilingual confusion that became mankind's destiny. The words Nimrod bellows—*"Raphel mai amecche zabi almi"*—belong to the lost language of Babel, of which he is the only remaining speaker. In every translation of the *Commedia*, this one line remains identical, for it represents untranslatability itself: a dead language "understood by none."

Dante's Virgil deplores the linguistic plurality Nimrod inflicted upon mankind. The historic Virgil wrote in Latin, the language that, for Dante and many centuries of educated European men who came before and after him, held the greatest claim to universality, transcending temporal and spatial differences and rendering all learned men, whatever their local vernacular, mutually intelligible. Among all European languages, Virgil's was the one that came closest to overcoming the punishment at Babel. Meanwhile, the figure of Dante at Virgil's side says nothing either to or about Nimrod; once he's been apprised of the giant's identity, he simply heeds Virgil's advice to remain silent and move on.

How can we translate that silence? We know that Dante, author of the *Commedia*—as distinct from the character who appears within it—was an accomplished linguistic theorist who, in his incomplete Latin treatise *De Vulgari Eloquentia*, evinced a fully developed and startlingly modern understanding of the fact that linguistic diversity arises out of the plurality of human contexts. Dante knew that human beings in different professions, social classes, places, and times speak different languages, and that these languages are living entities that ceaselessly evolve. Furthermore, Dante himself was a kind of translator, who sought to transfer meaning between these distinct linguistic entities; his avowed ambition for the *Commedia* was to translate the power and scope of the epic poems of classical antiquity into his own vernacular. Small wonder that his literary alter ego fails to chime in when Virgil castigates Nimrod.

And indeed, later on in the *Commedia*, Dante the author reveals that he does not view Nimrod as guilty of humanity's polyglot condition. Mankind turns out to have always been multilingual—as Dante's theory of the inevitable emergence of different languages out of differing contexts would suggest. In Canto XXVI of the *Paradiso*, Dante meets Adam, the first soul, who makes clear that the language he spoke was not that of Babel. His words conjure an almost Darwinian sense of linguistic evolution in which many languages are continually being born, evolving, and dying. "The tongue I spoke," Adam says,

Esther Allen and Susan Bernofsky

. . . was utterly extinct
before the followers of Nimrod turned their minds
to their unattainable ambition.[3]

Yet before we embrace Dante too readily as a standard-bearer for linguistic plurality, let's remember one of the primary aims his masterpiece was intended to achieve—and did achieve, in very large measure. Dante wrote passionately in *De Vulgari Eloquentia* of the need for an "illustrious vernacular" that would replace the "cacophony of the many varieties of Italian speech" with a single, enlightening, exalting, and unifying language.[4] Viewed within the context of the domination of European thought by Latin, the *Commedia* constitutes a bold argument for the vernacular, for linguistic plurality. Viewed in the context of the many competing dialects out of which modern Italian emerged, the *Commedia* is a work of consolidation and unification, a step toward monolingualism of a different sort.

That monolingualism has reached an apogee centuries later with a quite different language: English. Its rise was foreseen as early as 1780 by John Adams, who wrote, "English is destined to be in the next and succeeding centuries more generally the language of the world than Latin was in the last or French is in the present age."[5] Adams was prescient: English is now indisputably the dominant global lingua franca, and this puts the contemporary English-language translator in a peculiar position. Certainly, translators into English can be said to labor in the service of monolingualism, as translation consolidates the global domination of English by increasing the degree to which the culture of the entire globe is available through English. At the same time, translation works to strengthen the pluralism of world languages and cultures by giving writers in all languages the opportunity to reach English's global audience while still writing in their native tongues. Sheldon Pollock has compellingly summed up "the single desperate choice we are now offered: between, on the one hand, a national vernacularity dressed in the frayed period costume of violent revanchism and bent on preserving difference at all costs and, on the other, a clear-cutting, strip-mining multinational cosmopolitanism that is bent, at all costs, on eliminating it."[6] In the sphere of literature, at least, translation offers an alternative, a way beyond these mutually exclusive extremes.

In the current phase of linguistic globalization, second- or third-language acquisition (second, if the student's native language is English;

third, if it is something other than English) occupies an embattled place in universities in many parts of the world, which are seeing language departments other than those that teach English targeted for cuts. Lawrence H. Summers, former president of Harvard University, has openly questioned the usefulness of investing educational resources in the study of any language other than English, declaring in an article published in the *New York Times* (January 20, 2012): "English's emergence as the global language, along with the rapid progress in machine translation and the fragmentation of languages spoken around the world, make it less clear that the substantial investment necessary to speak a foreign tongue is worthwhile."[7] (Summers is less vehement than his predecessors on an early nineteenth-century Harvard University committee, who weighed in on the hotly debated subject of allowing modern languages into the curriculum—as opposed to Greek and Latin—by proclaiming that "the simplistic grammatical structures and base literature of modern languages would irreparably harm a student's capacity for disciplined learning."[8])

A long list of intellectual, literary, socio-cultural, political, diplomatic, and neurobiological arguments could be adduced to counter the idea that foreign language study is not worth the investment, but that is not our subject here. In short, people benefit enormously in a number of ways from learning languages and should learn as many as they can. But no one can or will learn all languages, and that irrefutable fact must not be a barrier to the circulation of literature and culture. Those Nabokovian linguistic purists who turn up their noses at translations are inadvertently adopting a stance oddly similar to "English only," the rallying cry of citizens' groups in the United States who want to block the use of languages other than English in government communications and public schools. Denying the intellectual and artistic value of translation closes off English to other languages and leads to a situation in which books not written in English are undervalued or ignored, even as students in the English sphere are less and less likely to acquire a second language over the course of their education: "English only," indeed.

For the great German translation theorist of the early nineteenth century, Friedrich Schleiermacher, the fact that no one can learn all the world's languages makes translation crucial. In his view, the exceptional linguistic finesse of the best translations transports the reader to the author's social and cultural sphere, "transplant[ing] . . . entire literatures into a single tongue."[9] The preservation of cultural specificity through

Esther Allen and Susan Bernofsky

the translator's skill is also implied in Johann Wolfgang von Goethe's description of the aim of what he called the third and highest epoch of translation (after paraphrase and loosely appropriative translation): "to achieve perfect identity with the original, so that the one does not exist instead of the other but in the other's place."[10] While the ultimate feasibility of either theorist's goal can be debated, without translation to engage people with literatures written in languages other than their own, Goethe's sublime notion of *Weltliteratur* (world literature) could not exist. To be sure, in the era of the global book market, *Weltliteratur* may seem just another name for globalization, a thing to be resisted in the name of preserving local values. But Goethe had in mind something other than global best-sellerdom for Dan Brown, J. K. Rowling, and Stieg Larsson. In his view, it was precisely the constant traffic among the literatures of the world in all their plurality that kept each of them alive: "Left to itself, every literature will exhaust its vitality if it is not refreshed by the interest and contributions of a foreign one."[11]

Today, the English-language translator occupies a particularly complex ethical position. To translate is to negotiate a fraught matrix of interactions. As a writer of the language of global power, the translator into English must remain ever aware of the power differential that tends to subsume cultural difference and subordinate it to a globally uniform, market-oriented monoculture. *Weltliteratur* is no longer (and may never have been) politically, culturally, or ethically neutral. At the same time, the failure to translate into English, the absence of translation, is clearly the most effective way of all to consolidate the global monoculture and exclude those who write and read in other languages from the far-reaching global conversation for which English is increasingly the vehicle.

Nevertheless, contemporary discussions of translation's role—particularly in the English-speaking world—sometimes attest to a stance that barely differs from that of Dante's Virgil, mourning for a lost prelapsarian oneness and concomitant frustration with the affliction of linguistic diversity. This attitude, as David Bellos observes, portrays translation as little more than "a compensatory strategy designed only to cope with a state of affairs that falls far short of the ideal."[12] All translation, in this view, is invariably an inadequate substitute for an original text that can only be legitimately apprehended in the purity of its original language.

To say of translation—as is so often said—that "the original meaning is always *lost*" is to deny the history of literature and the ability of any text to be *enriched* by the new meanings that are engendered as it enters new contexts—that is, as it remains alive and is read anew. The ability to speak and be understood, to write and be read, is one of the great desiderata of the human spirit. Meaning is a slippery fish, but all of us—and translators and writers more than most—prefer to live in a world where people make an effort to be intelligible to one another. This makes it hard to deplore the global rise of a lingua franca. Communication is never easy, but having a common language unquestionably makes it easier. The problem arises when those whose lives are made more convenient by the predominance of this lingua franca forget translation's vital role in most sorts of intercultural communication. A view of translation as loss and betrayal—the translator's presence a "problematic necessity," as one of the contributors to this volume, Eliot Weinberger, once saw himself described—stubbornly persists, supported at one extreme of the intellectual spectrum by those who would have everyone read works only in their original languages, and at the other by those who would have everyone read and write in a single, global language, thus potentially advancing what Michael Cronin has described as the "dystopian scenario of the information-language nexus [that] would see everyone translating themselves into the language or languages of the primary suppliers of information and so dispensing with the externality of translation."[13]

Our purpose in putting together this anthology is simple. We believe that there is much to be found in translation, and much to celebrate. Translation not only brings us the work of those who write in other languages; it simultaneously reveals the limits of our own language and helps us move beyond them, incorporating new words, concepts, styles, structures, and stories. Thinking about translation means thinking about the gaps in our literature and our ability to communicate, revealed by comparison with the capacities of other languages and traditions of thought. It also means thinking about the gaps in our political and cultural discourses, asking ourselves what and who has been left out. And finally, as Clare Cavanagh so beautifully demonstrates in the essay on relations between Polish and American poetry in the twentieth century that concludes this volume, it means thinking about the ways the literatures of different languages are perpetually enriched and revitalized by translation.

Anuvad, the Hindi word for translate, means "to tell again," as Christi A. Merrill notes. When you tell a story, you become part of that story,

Esther Allen and Susan Bernofsky

xviii

and the translator too becomes part of the stories he or she tells. Yet translation inevitably involves guises and masks that can make this truth difficult to perceive; translators, like actors, appear to us under a persona, speaking to us with words that both are and are not their own. In the contemporary Anglophone world this fact does not keep us from appreciating actors. Often, however, it keeps us from even noticing the work of translators. To perceive the translator as endowed with agency, intent, skill, and creativity is to destabilize the foundations of the way we read, forcing us to take in both a text and a literary performance of that text, to see two figures where our training as readers, our literary upbringing, has accustomed us to seeing only the author.

This new century has shown itself to be an age of translation. A world once bifurcated by superpowers has become a place of new pluralities, with different parts of the globe continually coming to prominence. The Internet has given us an entirely new source of access to cultures not our own. We no longer wait for media purveyors to decide what to show us, but can instead go in search of content that interests us without leaving our homes. The Internet has affected every aspect of the translator's work, from the process of producing a translation to the mode of publication, the scope of the audience, and the depth and complexity of the preexisting relationship between source and target languages and texts, particularly when the target language is English. It has also made various forms of machine translation available to everyone, thereby encouraging the belief that soon all translation will be effected by computers. At a point in the history of globalization when literary translation strikes some as on the verge of being definitively outmoded—the translator a scrivener about to be left behind by technological progress—the essays in this book, all written by translators, address the vital necessity of literary translation not only as a subject for theoretical pronouncements but also as an ongoing *practice*.

A paradigm shift in the translator's role is under way in the Anglophone world. There is a generational move toward an image of the translator as an intellectual figure empowered with agency and sensibility who produces knowledge by curating cultural encounters. This shift has come about for a number of reasons, including the rise of the Internet and the power it can confer on individuals who attract an audience; a surge of interest and energy around the issue of translation into English since September 11, 2001; and an increased willingness within the Anglophone academy to view translation as a form of scholarship, as attested by the Executive Council of the Modern Language Association's 2011 issuance of a set of guidelines for evaluating translation as scholarship.[14] A burgeoning in recent years of smaller publishing houses and magazines focused on translation—some of which have cultivated large followings among younger readers in particular—has meant that both the production and reception of literatures not written in English have become less monolithic, less dependent on the tastes and marketing engines of the world's publishing behemoths (some of the largest of which are owned by Dutch, German, and French corporations, which seem no more eager to foster translation into English than their U.S. and UK-based competitors). What we are seeing now, and what we hope to see more of, is a more horizontal process of reception and connoisseurship, a more directly representative and inclusive scenario by which the literatures of many languages have more diverse points of access into the global literary culture that exists in English.

In this anthology, literary translators from widely varying backgrounds, languages, fields, and genres are summoned into the spotlight to speak of the part they play in the works they have translated. If most of their stories were originally written in English, that is because our avowed purpose is to underscore the significance of the translator and translation in the English-speaking world. At the same time, we reject the global tendency so often seen in the social sciences, following behind the hard sciences, toward the universal use of English as the language of research. The translated essays included here—Haruki Murakami's preface to his translation of *The Great Gatsby* into Japanese, and José Manuel Prieto's essay about translating a poem by Osip Mandelstam from Russian into Spanish—invite further inquiry into cultures of translation that exist outside of English and may furnish alternate models for the further development of a translation culture within English.[15]

This volume's first part, "The Translator in the World," explores attitudes toward translation as seen in a variety of ethical, cultural, political, historical, and even legal contexts and offers a number of perspectives on the understanding and self-understanding of translators in the literary and critical arena. The essays by Peter Cole and Eliot Weinberger address ethical and political concerns, while David Bellos interrogates the ways translation engages with "the foreign." Michael Emmerich describes the construction of the concept of translation within the Japanese language. Catherine Porter, former president of the Modern Language Association, addresses the place of translation in the contemporary North American university and its status as a form of scholarship. Alice Kaplan reports as both translator and translated author on some of the legal complications to which the art of translation is subject, while Esther Allen assesses a 150-year history of translation between Latin American Spanish and English.

The second part, "The Translator at Work," focuses on questions of craft and considers specific acts of translation from various points of view. Forrest Gander raises the question of bilingualism in his translations of contemporary Mexican poetry. Maureen Freely describes the challenges of negotiating Western preconceptions of Turkey in translating the work of Orhan Pamuk and shows how a translator's political engagement with a text continues long after it is published. Christi A. Merrill connects translation with ethnography and oral storytelling traditions from Rajasthan to the Mitteleuropa of the Brothers Grimm. Jason Grunebaum writes of the distinctions between the English of the United States and that of India and the dilemmas they pose for the translator of a contemporary Hindi novel. Haruki Murakami's essay on the challenges of translating *The Great Gatsby* into Japanese describes the work as the culmination of a lifetime of literary preparation, while Ted Goossen translates and contextualizes Murakami's essay within the literary culture of contemporary Japan. Lawrence Venuti offers a defense of theory as an antidote to "belletristic commentary" in his exploration of the use of intertexts in translating the archaic Italian religious poet Jacopone da Todi. Richard Sieburth demonstrates how the musicality of the sixteenth-century French poet Maurice Scève can be performed in contemporary English. José Manuel Prieto, translated by Esther Allen, ponders Stalinist totalitarianism and the relationship between translation and commentary. Susan Bernofsky strategizes the revision of literary translations into and out of German, inviting us to consider translation itself a space of writing. Finally, Clare Cavanagh meditates on the "art of loss" in the translation of contemporary Polish poetry and the riches to be found in a practice so widely associated with impoverishment and failure.

Against the hegemony of a single language whose literature, governed to an ever-greater extent by marketing considerations, is exported across the globe, translators interpose joyful multiplicity and a richness of cultural content and linguistic interplay; they invite us to engage in a more genuinely cosmopolitan literary and cultural conversation. Translators are writers and curators of cultural interaction who transport us between linguistic spheres, making their languages listen as well as speak and transforming them into vehicles for a wide range of literary traditions. Such is the culture of translation this book seeks to advance.

Esther Allen and Susan Bernofsky

Notes

1. Dante, *Inferno,* trans. Robert and Jean Hollander (New York: Doubleday, 2000), 567.

2. *Inferno,* 571.

3. Dante, *Paradiso,* trans. Robert and Jean Hollander (New York: Doubleday, 2007).

4. Dante, *De Vulgari Eloquentia,* trans. Steven Botterill (Cambridge: Cambridge University Press, 1996), 27.

5. This line from John Adams's letter to the President of Congress (September 5, 1780) is cited by David Crystal in his valuable work on the role of English in globalization, *English as a Global Language* (Cambridge: Cambridge University Press, 2003), 74.

6. Sheldon Pollock, "Cosmopolitan and Vernacular in History," in *Cosmopolitanism,* ed. Carol A. Breckenridge, Sheldon Pollock, Homi K. Bhabha, and Dipesh Chakrabarty (Durham: Duke University Press, 2002), 17.

7. For perceptive analysis of Summers' comment by several leading American translators, see Mary Hawthorne, "Language Is Music," *The New Yorker Online Only,* posted August 13, 2012, http://www.newyorker.com/online/blogs/books/2012/08/david-bellos-arthur-goldhammer-and-lydia-davis-on-translation.html?mobify=0.

8. Cited by Lino Pertile in his introduction to Dante, *Inferno,* trans. Henry Wadsworth Longfellow (1867), ed. Matthew Pearl (New York: Modern Library, 2003), xii.

9. Friedrich Schleiermacher, "On the Different Methods of Translating," trans. Susan Bernofsky, in *The Translation Studies Reader,* 2nd ed., ed. Lawrence Venuti (New York and London: Routledge, 2004), 55.

10. Johann Wolfgang von Goethe, "Translations," trans. Sharon Sloan, in *The Translation Studies Reader,* 2nd ed., 65.

11. Goethe, "Some Passages Pertaining to the Concept of World Literature" (from *Weltliteratur,* 1827), in *Comparative Literature: The Early Years,* no trans. credited, ed. H. J. Schulz and P. H. Rhein (Chapel Hill: University of North Carolina Press, 1973), 7. For a useful discussion of Goethe's notion of *Weltliteratur* and contemporary literary globalization, see David Damrosch, "Goethe Coins a Phrase" in his *What Is World Literature?* (Princeton: Princeton University Press, 2003), 1–36.

12. David Bellos, *Is That a Fish in Your Ear? Translation and the Meaning of Everything* (New York: Farrar, Straus & Giroux, 2011), 326.

13. Michael Cronin, *Translation and Globalization* (New York: Routledge, 2003), 16.

14. "Evaluating Translations as Scholarship: Guidelines for Peer Review," http://www.mla.org/ec_guidelines_translation.

15. For more on the issue of translation in the social sciences, see Michael Henry Heim and Andrzej W. Tymowski, *Guidelines for the Translation of Social Science Texts* (New York: American Council of Learned Societies, 2006).

PART I

The Translator in the World

Making Sense in Translation

Toward an Ethics of the Art

PETER COLE

Three hundred years after the publication of Pope's *Iliad*, which Samuel Johnson called "the noblest version of poetry which the world has ever seen . . . a performance which no age or nation can pretend to equal," and close to a century after Pound's invention of a China for his time in Cathay, we know more or less, or think we know, what is meant by "the art of translation," even as we argue over tactics and taste. ("You like Plotzkin?! Plotzkin stinks! I like Motzkin!" "Motzkin?! Motzkin's tone deaf!"—as a conversation I once heard between two poets went, around English renderings of a classic work by veteran contemporary translators, whose names I change to protect their innocence.)

But what do we mean when we speak of "the *ethics* of translation"?

Interest in the ethical dimension of literary translation has swelled over the past several decades—ostensibly yet another boon to a field that has begun to gather about it, almost like a halo, a serious theoretical and practical literature. But since there's so often an abyss between theory and practice in this discipline, perhaps it's best at the outset to ask: Can ethics really account for an art in any way that matters? The result of the study of ethics is, traditionally, action, not just knowledge; we study ethics in order to improve our lives (to alter our behavior). Do we study the ethics of translation in order to improve our renderings? To affect the way a culture responds to them? Does the theoretical examination of ethics help—as many theorists claim—jar us out of unexamined assumptions about the art of translation and the role of the foreign in our lives, or do the doctrine and abstraction of ethical inquiry render us deaf and numb to the material realities of actual translations and make it harder to recognize excellence? In other words, does the desire for ethical clarity and consistency all too often reflect an inability to accept the elusive essence of the art?

For we are in translation always defined by relation, and throughout the history of its art we come upon a wide variety of strategies and tacks. Accounting for "foreignness," for instance, is one part of being-in-relation—and a vital one: but the doors of perception in translation's restaurant swing both ways, and waiters who serve there had best watch their heads, and what's on their trays, as translation exists, too, always in relation to its *own* tradition—its predilections and expectations, its trajectory and demands.

❋ ❋ ❋ ❋

Take an almost never discussed set of ethically relevant considerations. How clearly does a translator hear or see or grasp the goal ahead, the tone to be struck or the shape to be molded? And, since action generally arises from perception, *what will he do about it*—about that hearing and grasping, or *not* being able to hear and to grasp? What sort of effort, in other words, will a translator be willing to exert to reach a given goal, and what should that exertion consist of? To what degree will desire and patience—under the stress of a somehow chronic state of both physical and metaphysical frustration—combine in a translator's craft to realize the vision of translation's highest good, an afterlife for the literature in question? There's negative *capability* and then there's *negative* capability. Clearly it's critical to develop a high tolerance for "being in uncertainties, mysteries, doubts," without too much in the way of "any irritable reaching after fact and reason"; but it's also vital to move through these uncertainties and on to the hundreds and sometimes hundreds of thousands of hard decisions the translation of poetry and prose alike entails. Each stage of the process involves discomfort and pleasures of a kind. To remain in bilingual or even polyglot mysteries is to enjoy the full resonance of literary possibility—to be tortured by its pleasures, if not always to be pleased by its torture; to decide is to find oneself—for a while—blessedly free of those doubts, but also hemmed in by one's choices, possibly forever.

Under those pressures, what kind of knowledge will stubbornness and talent lead a translator toward, and will that knowledge serve as a conduit to effective translation or, as so often happens, will knowledge eventually become an obstacle to it? And, even less fashionably, what sort of training and attunement, what kind of artistic or intellectual and, forgive me, spiritual preparation is called for in order to bring about the transformation that translation is? What, to put it differently, will the quality of our translator's devotion to this ever-hungry and restless god be?

❊ ❊ ❊ ❊

At this point the "s" falls away from our ethics, like a spent booster rocket, and the ethic attending to one's labor becomes central. Ethical excellence, says Aristotle or one of his students (in *Magna Moralia*), is not something that develops naturally; it is the result of what he calls "accustoming." As the Greek word for custom or habit (*êthos*) produces *êthike*, or ethics, so our English mores or habits are developed by a person, over time and through experience, into what is moral. At the heart of this fossil poem in the making is the question of character—that Heraclitean determiner of a person's fate, and, if that person happens to translate, of the fate of his translation. For the habits and customs a translator develops in his reading, listening, writing, and learning run like nerves and veins toward every syllable he'll render.

We often hear, from Chapman's "with poesie to open poesie" and on, that the translator of a work of art must at some level be an artist. And that is true. But artists are notorious for their (necessary) egoism. And strong artists are distinguished, well, by their strength—which consists, in part, of their resistance to possession by the spirit of another artist. How will the translator-artist's character bear up, let alone thrive, under the strain of all that subordination? How much of his so-called own work—as if there were a real difference, and the translator's creation were not *owned*—will he give up to make room for these foreign voices? (When it comes to the translator's soul, let's call it, translation can both nourish and drain, strangle and sustain.) What ethical currents inform—and lend form to—the delicate give-and-take translation is? And how will our translator fare on the tightrope of his art, where one wrong move can topple him from an ethically desirable and even critical humility directly into humiliation? How will he manage in a vocation and sometimes a profession where success is often marked by silence and notice reserved largely for failure?

Or, to cast it in more concrete terms: When one of my translations came out a few years ago—a book of fiery political poetry about Israel/Palestine—I sent it to my mild-mannered and politically middle-of-the-road

Making Sense in Translation: Toward an Ethics of the Art

5

retired lawyer-father, now of blessed memory, who, though he almost never read poetry, picked it up and was at once taken in. Struggling to find a way to talk about something he rarely experienced—being moved by poetry, and *in translation*—he went on one morning at the breakfast table while I was visiting about how powerful he thought the poetry was, how much he'd come to admire the poet and his courage, and then, as a wave of guilt washed across his face, and as though suddenly remembering that the offspring of his loins had something to do with it all, he said: "And you . . . you had a difficult job there, I mean, you coulda botched it. . . . But you didn't."

As the laurel descended on my head.

❀   ❀   ❀   ❀

And then there's the question of accounting in ethical fashion for the mercurial aspects of Time in translation. That is, how might one responsibly factor in the centuries between the composition of a given literary artifact from the distant past and the instant of translation? Is it ethically more appropriate to call attention—through register, cadence, and the like—to the passage of time and the difference of cultural context; or, when push comes to translational shove, is it ultimately more honest to create an illusion of immediacy—to account for the way a story or poem *might* have been heard by its original audience? And what about the nagging awareness that, as each generation retranslates the classics, one's rendering will most likely become obsolete? Should that be factored into the ethical calculus? If so, how?

With all this in mind, it's worth pausing for a moment over the word "responsibly." One needs in translating, and especially in translating works from the distant past, to respond and be responsible not only to the original poem or passage of prose but also to the body of knowledge that has accrued around it, around the would-be reader of the translation, and around the two (and sometimes three or more) languages and literary traditions involved. The responsible response will inevitably encode a complex, integrated sense of duration—syllable by syllable, word by word, and line by line. Because translation takes time. Actually, and seriously. When it comes to the rendering of poetry, it takes a lot of time. And in crossing centuries, languages, and cultural galaxies, factoring in the thousands of elusive elements that come into play, the straightforward algebra of equivalence won't do: if we want to approach it in scientific fashion (as some are wont to), we'll need to look in the direction of postquantum physics, or the nature of scientific study itself.

Along the lines of the latter, Max Weber reminds us in "Science as a Vocation" that each realized work of art is its own fulfillment and can never be surpassed or antiquated. (Edwin Denby expresses something similar when he writes that there are in art "as many first prizes as contestants, even if so very few ever win one.") Not so with science, where a worker engages, if not selflessly, then with the self as a vehicle for something much greater, in the production of a kind of knowledge he *knows* will become outdated—taking a strange if complicated delight in that knowledge and the process of production. Weber then asks: "Why does one engage in doing something that in reality never comes, and never can come, to an end?" To do so with passionate devotion, he implies, is to stand "in a service of moral forces."

❖ ❖ ❖ ❖

"The genuine translator," says Friedrich Schleiermacher in a classic statement (translated by André Lefevere), "wants to bring those two completely separated persons, his author and to his reader, truly together, and to bring the latter to an understanding and enjoyment of the former as correct and complete as possible without inviting him to leave the sphere of his mother tongue."

Driving Schleiermacher's desire for "understanding and enjoyment" is that most maligned of phenomena in discussions of translation—sympathy. As the Earl of Roscommon put it in his 1684 poetic "Essay on Translated Verse":

> Examine how your humour is inclined,
> And which the ruling passion of your mind;
> Then seek a poet who your way does bend,
> And choose an author as you choose a friend:
> United by this sympathetic bond,
> You grow familiar, intimate, and fond;
> Your thoughts, your words, your styles, your souls agree,
> No longer his interpreter, but he.

Which is very beautiful and all well and good; but what about needing or wanting to translate someone to whom your spirit or humor does *not* incline? Are there ethical and possibly artistic advantages in that? Does it necessarily guarantee failure? What about the power of assuming someone else's skin, for a moment, or a month, or a year, and trying to form something from that point of view that will last perhaps longer than you will?

If ethics in the Aristotelian sense involve the study of traits that human beings need in order to realize their nature and live well in the noblest sense, in the pursuit and practice of the happiness that is the highest good, then the study of ethics in the context of literary translation should concern the ways to best realize translation's true nature as a carrier or embodiment of the highest *literary* good. Our ethical goal in this vision of what literature has to tell us should be to enter a place of integration, where emotion, thought, and sensation come together to produce a made-thing-that-will-matter. As virtuous living, again, for Aristotle, entails the blending of temperance, courage, humility, a sense of justice, self-discipline, generosity, a feeling for action's consequence, and the capacity for certain kinds of pleasure (including friendship), among other things, so too translational ethics should call for a combination of—among other things—temperance, courage, humility, a sense of justice, self-discipline, generosity, modesty, a feeling for action's consequence, and the capacity for certain kinds of pleasure (including friendship). The vices in both cases might also be thought of as overlapping: recklessness, cowardice, vanity, self-indulgence, dishonesty, and, in the end, injustice.

That's on the Hellenistic side of the ledger. The Hebraic version of this vision might reduce all of translation ethics to two precepts: "Do unto [the work of] others as you would have them do unto [work by] you," and, of course: "Thou shalt not kill."

In this translational scheme, sympathy involves not a matter of parallel personal feeling so much as what I think of as *making sense*—though I should note, at this point, that by "sense" I'm talking not only about "meaning" and "common sense," or even "sense for sense" renderings (as opposed to "word for word" translations, as the classic formulation has it), but something that happens along, or under, the skin: a tangential sensation, one that is rooted not in ideology, not even in good will or fellow feeling, but in syntactical, rhythmic, and acoustic experience, as well as the ambient aspects of a given culture.

The difference is critical.

For what I'll call a lesser-order or simply flimsier sympathy often lies behind the worst sort of distortion in translation and the greatest ethical violation. Hostile Orientalism, to take one easy example, is an indication of condescension and lack of sympathy at every level; but there are also seemingly benign forms of Orientalism that impede translation: the overly infatuated, if well-intentioned outsider who possesses a heartfelt sympathy for, say, Palestinian literature that depicts the oppressed and their oppressors but does not feel the cadences and timbre of a given story or poem across his skin and in his being will not enter sufficiently into the physical or sensory dimension of the text, and his translation will not do it "justice." Nor will an "insider" translator of Hebrew whose ethnic pride or nationalism substitutes for experience of the specific surface of the work in both languages. In socially charged literary situations such as these it is even possible to be ideologically *un*sympathetic to the politics behind a given literary composition and still translate in ethically responsible fashion with the sort of sympathy I have in mind.

Along the same lines, we should also note that there is an often invisible, or at any rate hard to detect, political dimension to the consideration of ethics in translation, beginning with the choice of texts to be translated and deciding how a given literature or even a single poet will be represented. Choices of this sort are made every day by both translators and publishers, or editors—sometimes together, sometimes not. This backstage dynamic has shaped our American view of the Middle East, for instance, though the reading public knows almost nothing of it, and, for that matter, neither do most of the publishers. Political sensitivities of the readership and the publishing industry, dull questions of funding in both the commercial and nonprofit hemispheres of the translation globe, chemistry and temperament extending to the bonds among translator, author, and editor—all play a central role in the development and dissemination of translations from a given culture. Which mouths will the time and money move toward? This, too, is part of the ethical equation.

Sympathy of the sort I'm trying to describe, complex sympathy grounded in sense, involves the preparation of the self for the reception and registration of an actual other, and as such its ethic is technical, and its technique is ethical. Though it does not initially involve a rendering into another visible or audible language, this preparation-for-reception and the reception itself comprise, as I see it, the most important stage of the translation process, and the quality of that reception will to a large extent determine the quality and even the content of what one represents. And as the translation itself unfolds, it is crucial that the translator (and the translation itself) continue to listen to, and sense, not only the sounds of the original work being registered but also the shape, pitch, and timbre of what is produced. An economy of pleasure, in other words, is part and parcel of this literary justice.

But pleasure of this sort is hardly possible without its contrary; and pain, too, is part of the elusive sympathy at the heart of sense. For the ongoing preparation of the self is hard, as is the hosting of that second soul of the foreign text. Both call for constant vigilance, and their reward is the ability to absorb something that will disturb and to a certain extent hurt you as it alters the way you see or hear or speak. Something that will shift the muscles around your mouth and chest, and, instant by instant, revise the way you relate to the world. If this sounds a little like a kind of surrogacy, it is perhaps worth noting that the kabbalistic term for the beneficent transmigration of a meritorious soul from one generation to another is *ibbur*—impregnation. Moreover, fourteenth-century kabbalists sometimes called this transmigration *ha'ataqah,* or transference, which also happens to be a term Hebrew uses to mean—*translation.*

There is, in short, no serious afterlife for a given poet or writer of prose that does not re-embody (as it reimagines) the sensory dimensions at the heart of an art.

So how is that sort of re-embodiment brought about?

A start might be made by avoiding talk of "inscription" and "translemes," "decomposition of the source message," "invariant transfer," and "the release of domestic remainders"—all of which are the product of an academic industry run seriously amok. Reading late twentieth- or twenty-first-century translation theory, one often gets the sense that many of the principal theorists simply resent the imagination, if not the English language itself. For the fact is that the best translators I've read, worked with, and known, even those who are well versed in theory, ultimately rely as they translate on instinct, not ideology. Trained by long apprenticeship to attention in language, they let themselves be led by a feel for the words before them in an asymptotic rehearsal and performance involving desire, denial, vision, revision, imagination, and regret—nearing, perhaps, but never achieving something we choose to call perfection. Though the perfect translation, as Borges knew, is not a translation at all.

Bad translation, then, is senseless; it is (often, when closely examined) unreasonable in some basic way, but more important, it lacks tactility, or produces tactility that we find merely tacky, and so it ends up just getting in the way. The "tact" at tactility's heart is the one we find in George Steiner's comment that "Tact intensified is moral vision."

Part I: The Translator in the World

Good translation, on the other hand, is translation that both makes and discovers sense. It is reasonable, and coheres emotionally, but it also and more importantly engages the senses as it embodies, in a physical manner, what the translator recognizes as the salient properties or qualities of the original and its artfulness. And in taking on the *responsibility* for another work of art in a different language—for the particular pressure, pleasure, texture, tension, and tone of its constituent parts—the translator also (if he is up to the task) becomes more *responsive* to these same constituent qualities; and so he will in the passage to a new language try to account for them as live elements, to preserve them through transformation rather than salting or pickling them through superficial mimicry.

Call it the recognition of a dignity.

Vital transformation of this sort will not be brought about by focusing on discrete one-to-one equivalence, what Dryden called "tedious transfusions," as so many translators and certain kinds of scholars like to do, especially when they take us "into the workshop." Make no mistake about it, the choice of individual words is extremely important; but far more important to a translation's chances for success—if one looks back across the history of English—is attending to the way words in a row, their shapes in the mouth and their echoes in the body, come together as a whole.

When they do coalesce, something extraordinary occurs: "Three or four words in exact juxtaposition," Pound tells us, "are capable of radiating . . . energy at a very high potentiality: . . . [These words] must augment and not neutralize each other. This peculiar energy which fills [them] is the power of tradition."

❀ ❀ ❀ ❀

Last in the ethical precept department (though for most it's first) is the injunction that in many ways relates to Frost's semiapocryphal isolationist aphorism, namely, that the honest translator acknowledge the loss—and some would say the essential loss—inherent in his transfer. Clearly the translator must always, at some level, be aware of this loss; and translation does, again, require a firmly moored sense of humility. But it also requires a potent sort of presumption—one that is akin to the belief that lies behind fictional creation. Although the vast majority of poems in translation are no better or worse than the vast majority of original poems, the former and not the latter almost invariably lead to the sort of warning issued by the poet and essayist Donald Hall, who cautions poets against imbibing too much translation, since "almost always a

translation omits the oldest and most primitive sources of eros in poetry," what he calls "the intimacies of sound form." But it is precisely
those mysteries of sound, that eros of cadence and linkage, that intimate
aspect of breath and articulation, that translators are, in the scheme I'm
sketching, ethically obliged to embody anew. When they are successful, rare or partial as that success is, they manage to do what Hall says
real poems do (however rarely or partially they do that). In fact, the
description he offers of that doing is one I recognize as the ethical art of
translating: "By the *studious* imagination, by continuous connection to the
sensuous body, and by spirit steeped in the practice and learning of
language," poets, Hall tells us, "say the unsayable."

❊ ❊ ❊ ❊

So much for some of the eye-and-ear level ethical questions a translator
lives with on a daily basis. There is also a transcendental aspect to the
ethical dimension of the enterprise. Dedicated practitioners begin their
days at the desk knowing full well, or at least deep down, that translation
has traditionally been thought of as a curse or a necessary evil: the shame
of knowing in Eden is matched by the frustration of having to translate
after Babel (or talk about translation after Steiner). This too is part of
translation's moral makeup: that it is, at root, hubristic, delusional, even
sinful. (Think of what has been said and done to translators in the name of
religion: Wycliffe's bones were exhumed and torched, and the great Tyn-
dale was hanged and then burned, to take just two of the most prominent
English examples.) And the Talmud, lest we forget, reports that even after
the translation of the Greek Septuagint, or "translation of the seventy
(two)," which has been called "the most important translation ever made,"
three days of darkness descended upon the world—and that for a translation produced by divine inspiration, a kind of prophetic spirit that passed
through all seventy-two translators in seventy-two days, so that each
emerged from his solitary and wholly independent labor bearing a translation of Scripture that was identical to that of the other seventy-one.

But where some see hubris, a very different moral approach envisions
translation as "a radically generous" enterprise, one that's rooted in a
desire *to bestow*—to offer others access to the Truth (especially where
Scripture is involved), or merely to the splendors of art and maybe the
larger global conversation. Seen in that strong light, translation implies a
common humanity that might take us—in spirit, and however tenuously—
beyond difference. Moreover, it has been argued that the very possibility

of getting beyond that difference posits the existence of a mystical universal language. And some, as we'll see, go so far as to suggest that the act of translation responds, imperceptibly, to the gravitational field of that inaudible universal tongue.

For, as it were, moral support, and since we've already touched on theology, let's up the ante and note, apropos translation's more sanguine aspect, that Franz Rosenzweig, Martin Buber's partner in the German translation of the Old Testament, announced their project by declaring that "every translation is a messianic act." While even the agnostics among us will understand what he means, this theologian-translator went still further and claimed—brows will furrow—that the messianic act of translation "brings redemption nearer."

Brings redemption nearer. Certainly, when it's working, it brings the foreign author or culture nearer. But redemption?

And yet, if we think of it, translation does embody longing for a kind of fulfillment, a restoration of worth, and possibly even deliverance from loss and suffering—of being partial and apart, of not knowing, or not quite being able to say something. Moreover, it *is* a matter of life and death—of reprieve (extended life for the work and possibly its translator) or of execution (again, of the work and possibly its translator). And when that work is from an earlier era, it leads to either profanation or resurrection of the dead.

❋ ❋ ❋ ❋

Lest we get too self-righteous about it, a slippery question that theorists do not like: What is the role of falseness and the fictional in translation? And how might an ethics of translation account for it?

Writing in the eleventh century, the great Hebrew poet of Muslim Spain, Shmuel HaNagid, said:

> He'll bring you trouble with talk like dreams,
>   invoking verse and song to cheat you.
> But dreams, my son, aren't what they seem.
>   Not all the poet says is true.

Of course my sentence preceding his poem is also a kind of fiction, as HaNagid wrote no such thing, since he wrote in Hebrew, and in a mode that involves what we might as well call a deep translation from Arabic, collaged from a biblical vocabulary. In fact, the poem may involve the loose translation of specific lines of Arabic verse. The English translation is mine, and it is believed or not because a compelling fictional (or false) surface has or hasn't been built up within it, in the way that we continually build up our worlds and vocabularies and the relationships in which we use these words and pass them back and forth, mostly managing to understand one another, inexplicably, it often seems.

"Tell all the truth," scrawled Dickinson, "but tell it slant," since "the truest poetry," as Shakespeare noted, "is the most feigning." Precisely in this claim for an essential falseness to poetry's particular way of getting at the truth there is also something reassuring. "Yea though I walk through the valley of the shadow of death, I will fear no evil," . . . for the translation comforteth me. For the translation—and in the case of the 23rd Psalm, the *mis*translation (of an archaic word for "deep darkness" as "the shadow of death")—endows us with a strong and almost conscious sense that we are not entirely alone in that valley and darkness.

If a translator doesn't make use of that fictional dimension, in which truth and falseness are more than conventional moral badges, then won't he create a lesser thing? Won't he betray the art he is obliged to account for, to re-present? Is honesty in this scheme unethical? Can the fiction of essence precipitate essence, or at least partake of it? Is the lie really what ethical understanding requires? And is there anything wrong with the analogy of the Latin husband, who is faithful in his way as he strays (so as not to appear overly slavish)? Why isn't that really appropriate? Because vows were taken and the straying is illicit? Doesn't the translator tacitly take a vow as well (to honor, cherish, and—for the most part—obey)? And isn't there always something illicit about the fictional? The metaphor of course breaks down with the very real pain of the betrayed wife and the absence of mutual enhancement—that most reliable mark of successful translation.

Note that I've said *mutual* enhancement. In giving the original new life, a translation sheds new light on it as well. And in the process, the language of the translation is also renewed. But the presence of the foreign body of sounds in the texture of the translator's language need not be that of a freakish or distorting implant shouting, "Look at me, I'm different, foreign, *unusual*!" Presence does not equal conspicuous distortion. At times the specific nature of a particular foreign text will alter the language of the translation and perhaps bring it into peculiar territory; but more often than not the presence should be an animating force within the range of what Schleiermacher called "the malleable material" of one's own language.

So whether you believe, with Scripture, that the matrix from which language emerges in the created world is sacred; or with Tolstoy trust that art through language links us in a critical bond; or if you simply feel that it is the writer's job to be precise about the most elusive and critical dimensions of human experience—then, however unconsciously, you accept that literary translation partakes of something central to our existence, or is at the very least a transmitter of that central something. And that, like literature at its best, and *as* literature at its best, it extends our sense of what it means to be alive in the world as a user of words. For translation involves a binding back that leads us forward. It leaves us bound—recalling the Latin *religare*, or the binding that gives us "religion." In a similar manner, Church relics "bind" as they are "translated," or moved from one shrine to another, which must be consecrated, or invested with their presence and with belief in their power to transform. In each of these analogues, as in the word "translation" itself—which etymologically suggests a "ferrying or carrying across" (as does the root of the word "metaphor")—investment, surrender, and belief lead to a place where alignment is sought between souls.

Gershom Scholem tells us something similar. Scholem is widely regarded as one of the major scholars of the twentieth century—the man who turned the study of Jewish mysticism into a serious discipline. Few, however, even among those who are familiar with his masterful prose, know that early in his career Scholem harbored thoughts of becoming a literary translator. He translated the stories of S. Y. Agnon (who would go on to become Hebrew's only Nobel Prize winner), and in a letter to Rosenzweig while the latter was translating Scripture with Buber, Scholem—who in fact didn't like the Buber-Rosenzweig Bible—wrote that "translation is one of the greatest miracles . . . leading into the heart of the sacred orders from which it springs."

Rosenzweig responded in characteristic fashion: "All life beyond one's own soul is conditioned by the possibility of this miracle," which elsewhere he calls a Holy Wedding between two languages.

In the previous sentence Rosenzweig had readied the ethical ground: "Only one who is profoundly convinced of the impossibility of translation can really undertake it."

❊ ❊ ❊ ❊

And finally, a word from the rabbis, who—in nearly vaudevillian fashion—manage to sum up the translator's predicament and possibly also his feeling about how art and ethics in his efforts might be one:

Making Sense in Translation: Toward an Ethics of the Art

In the tractate known as—curiously—Consecration (again, as in marriage), and in the course of a chapter treating the conditions of binding betrothal, the Talmud surprises us with the following: "If one translates a verse literally," says Rabbi Judah, "he is a liar; if he adds thereto, he is a blasphemer and a libeler. Then what is meant by translation?" Judah asks, and answers, not quite ethically: "Our translation!"

*T*wo

Anonymous Sources

(On Translators and Translation)

ELIOT WEINBERGER

Some years ago, Bill Moyers did a PBS series on poetry that was filmed at the Dodge Festival in New Jersey. Octavio Paz and I had given a bilingual reading there, and I knew that we would be included in the first program. The morning of the broadcast, I noticed in the index of that day's *New York Times* that there was a review of the show. This being my national television debut, I naturally wondered if their TV critic had discovered any latent star qualities, and quickly turned to the page. This is what he wrote: "Octavio Paz was accompanied by his translator,"—no name given, of course—"always a problematic necessity."

"Problematic necessity," while not yet a cliché about translation, rather neatly embodies the prevailing view of translation. I'd like to look at both terms, beginning with the one that strikes me as accurate: necessity.

Needless to say, no single one of us can know all the languages of the world, not even the major languages, and if we believe—though not all cultures have believed it—that the people who speak other languages have things to say or ways of saying them that we don't know, then translation is an evident necessity. Many of the golden ages of a national literature have been, not at all coincidentally, periods of active and prolific translation. Sanskrit literature goes into Persian which goes into Arabic which turns into the translation of Ovid. German fiction begins with imitations of the Spanish picaresque and *Robinson Crusoe*. Japanese poetry is first written in Chinese; Latin poetry is first an imitation of the Greek; American poetry in the first half of this century is inextricable from all it translated and learned from classical Chinese, Greek, and Latin; medieval Provençal and modern French; in the second half of the century, it is inextricable from the poetries of Latin America and Eastern Europe, classical Chinese again, and the oral poetries of Native Americans and other indigenous groups. These examples could, of course, be multiplied endlessly. Conversely, cultures that do not translate stagnate, and end up repeating the same things to themselves. Classical Chinese poetry, perhaps the best literary example, is at its height during the T'ang Dynasty, an age of internationalism, and then becomes increasingly moribund for almost a millennium as China cuts itself off from the world. Or, in a wider cultural sense of translation: the Aztec and Inkan empires, which could not translate the sight of some ragged Europeans on horseback into anything human.

But translation is much more than an offering of new trinkets in the literary bazaar. Translation liberates the translation language. Because a translation will always be read as a translation, as something foreign, it is freed from many of the constraints of the currently accepted norms and conventions in the national literature.

This was most strikingly apparent in China after the revolution in 1949. An important group of modernist poets who had emerged in the 1930s and early 1940s, greatly under the influence of the European poets they were translating, were now forbidden to publish and were effectively kept from writing. All the new Chinese poetry had to be in the promoted forms of socialist realism: folkloric ballads and paeans to farm production and boiler-plate factories and heroes of the revolution. (The only exceptions, ironically, or tragically, were the classical poems written by Mao himself.) Yet they could continue to translate foreign poets with the proper political credentials (such as Eluard, Alberti, Lorca, Neruda, Aragon) even though their work was radically different and not social realist at all. When a new generation of poets in the 1970s came to reject socialist realism, their inspiration and models were not the erased and forgotten Chinese modernists—whose poems they didn't know, and had no way of knowing—but rather the foreign poets whom these same modernists had been permitted to translate.

Translation liberates the translation language, and it is often the case that translation flourishes when the writers feel that their language or society needs liberating. One of the great spurs to translation is a cultural inferiority complex or a national self-loathing. The translation boom in Germany at the turn of the nineteenth century was a response to the self-perceived paucity of German literature; translation became a project of national culture-building: in the words of Herder, "to walk through foreign gardens to pick flowers for my language." Furthermore, and rather strangely, it was felt that the relative lack of literary associations in the language—particularly in contrast to French—made German the ideal language for translation, and even more, the place where the rest of the world could discover the literature it couldn't otherwise read. Germany, they thought, would become the Central Station of world literature precisely because it had no literature. This proved both true and untrue. German did become the conduit, particularly for Sanskrit and Persian, but it also became much more. Its simultaneous, and not coincidental, production of a great national literature ended up being the most influential poetry and criticism in the West for the rest of the century. (And perhaps it should be mentioned that, contrary to the reigning cliché of Orientalism—namely that scholarship follows imperialism—Germany had no economic interests in either India or Persia. England, which did, had no important scholars in those fields after the pioneering Sir William Jones. Throughout the nineteenth century, for example, Sanskrit was taught at Oxford exclusively by Germans.)

In the case of the Chinese poets, their coming-of-age during the Cultural Revolution meant that they had been unable to study foreign languages (or much of anything else) and thus were themselves unable to translate. But to escape from their sense of cultural deficiency, they turned to the translations of the previous generation, and began to discover new ways of writing in Chinese, with the result that Chinese poetry experienced its first truly radical and permanent change in centuries.

Among American poets, there have been two great flowerings of translation. The first, before and after the First World War, was largely the work of expatriates eager to overcome their provinciality and to educate their national literature through the discoveries made in their own self-educations: to make the United States as "cultured" as Europe. The second, beginning in the 1950s and exploding in the 1960s, was the result of a deep anti-Americanism among American intellectuals: first in the more contained bohemian rebellion against the conformist Eisenhower years and the Cold War, and then as part of the wider expression of disgust and despair during the civil rights movement and the Vietnam War. Translation—the journey to the other—was more than a way out of America: the embrace of the other was, in the 1960s, in its small way, an act of defiance against the government that was murdering Asian others abroad and the social realities that were oppressing minority others at home. Foreign poetry became as much a part of the counterculture as American Indians, Eastern religions, hallucinatory states: a new way of seeing, a new "us" forming out of everything that had not been "us." From 1910 to 1970, it is difficult to think of more than a very few American poets who didn't translate at least something, and many translated a great deal. It was one of the things that one did as a poet, both a practice for one's own work and a community service.

By the early 1970s, of course, this cultural moment was over, and the poets became detached from the intellectual and cultural life of the country, as they vanished along career paths into the creative writing schools. There were now more American poets and poetry readers than in all the previous eras combined, but almost none of them translated. The few who continued to do so, with two or three notable exceptions, were all veterans of the 1960s translation boom.

The obvious result was that we were simply not getting the news. In the 1960s—to take only Latin America—works by Neruda, Paz, Parra, and many others were being translated as, or shortly after, they were being written. There was a lively international dialogue among the living. But for the next thirty years or so, the subsequent generations remained invisible. At various times I was asked to edit anthologies of Latin American poetry, but I realized that at least half of the poets I would want to include had never been translated, and there were simply not enough poet-translators to take on the work.

Paradoxically, the rise of multiculturalism may have been the worst thing to happen to translation. The original multiculturalist critique of the Eurocentrism of the canon and so forth did not lead—as I, for one, hoped it would—to a new internationalism, where Wordsworth would be read alongside Wang Wei, the Greek anthology next to Vidyakara's *Treasury*, Ono no Komachi with H.D. Instead it led to a new form of nationalism, one that was salutary in its inclusion of the previously excluded, but one that limited itself strictly to Americans, albeit hyphenated ones. Freshman literature courses began to teach Chinese-American writers, but no Chinese, Latinos but no Latin Americans. In terms of publishing, if you were a Mexican from the northern side of the Rio Grande, it was not very difficult to get published; if you were from the southern side, it was almost impossible. Coincident with an explosion of Chicano Studies departments, Chicano literary presses, special collections at libraries, literary organizations, and so on, readers in the United

States had far less contemporary Mexican literature available to them than they did in the 1960s.

This complacent period—nationalist without overt flag-waving, isolationist without overt xenophobia, and uninformed—came to end with 9/11, the rise of the Cheney–Bush administration, and the wars in Afghanistan and Iraq. Once again, Americans were ashamed to be American, were fed up with America, and began looking abroad just to hear the sound of someone else's voice. The first years of the twenty-first century have seen a boom in new presses that publish translation, grants and prizes, courses in translation, international festivals, websites. Relative to publishing in other countries, the situation is still pathetic: the total number of translated literary books with any sort of national distribution is still in the low hundreds. But an awareness has changed—and, for the first time, there is actually some interest in Arabic literature, an almost entirely unexplored library of wonders. George Bush may be the best thing that happened to literature.

The necessity of translation is evident; so why is it a problem—or, as they now say, problematic? Milan Kundera famously considered the poor translations of himself as—and only a man would write this—a form of rape, and he characterized the bad translations of Kafka as betrayals in a book called *Testaments Betrayed*. All discussions of translation, like nineteenth-century potboilers, are obsessed with questions of fidelity and betrayal. But in the case of a writer like Kundera, who came of age in a society dominated by the secret police, "betrayal" carries an especially heavy weight. We know what a translation is supposedly a betrayal of, but is it unfair to ask to whom the text is being betrayed?

And one can never mention the word "translation" without some wit bringing up—as though for the first time—that tedious Italian pun *traduttore traditore*. Luckily, the Italian-American philosopher Arthur Danto has recently and I hope definitively laid it forever to rest:

> Perhaps the Italian sentence betrays something in the cultural unconscious of Italy, which resonates through the political and ecclesiastical life of that country, where betrayal, like a shadow, is the obverse side of trust. It is an Unconscious into which the lessons of Machiavelli are deeply etched. Nobody for whom English is a first language would be tempted to equate translation and treason.

Anonymous Sources (On Translators and Translation)

The characterization of translation as betrayal or treason is based on the impossibility of exact equivalence, which is seen as a failing. It's true: a slice of German pumpernickel is not a Chinese steam bun which is not a French baguette which is not Wonder Bread. But consider a hypothetical line of German poetry—one I hope will never be written, but probably has been: "Her body (or his body) was like a fresh loaf of pumpernickel." Pumpernickel in the poem is pumpernickel, but it is also more than pumpernickel: it is the image of warmth, nourishment, homeyness. When the cultures are close, it is possible to translate more exactly: say, the German word *pumpernickel* into the American word *pumpernickel*— which, despite appearances, are not the same: each carries its own world of referents. But to translate the line into, say, Chinese, how much would really be lost if it were a steam bun? (I leave aside sound for the moment.) "His body (her body) was like a fresh steam bun" also has its charm—especially if you like your lover doughy.

It's true that no translation is identical to the original. But no reading of a poem is identical to any other, even when read by the same person. The first encounter with our poetic pumpernickel might be delightful; at a second reading, even five minutes later, it could easily seem ridiculous. Or imagine a fourteen-year-old German boy reading the line in the springtime of young Alpine love; then at fifty, while serving as the chargé d'affaires in the German consulate in Kuala Lumpur, far from the bakeries of his youth; then at eighty, in a retirement village in the Black Forest, in the nostalgia for dirndled maidens. Every reading of every poem is a translation into one's own experience and knowledge—whether it is a confirmation, a contradiction, or an expansion. The poem does not exist without this act of translation. The poem must move from reader to reader, reading to reading, in perpetual transformation. The poem dies when it has no place to go.

Translation, above all, means change. In Elizabethan England, one of its meanings was "death": to be translated from this world to the next. In the Middle Ages *translatio* meant the theft or removal of holy relics from one monastery or church to another. In the year 1087, for example, St. Nicolas appeared in visions to the monks at Myra, near Antioch, where his remains were kept, and told them he wished to be translated. When merchants arrived from the Italian city of Bari and broke open the tomb to steal the remains, Myra and its surroundings were filled with a wonderful fragrance, a sign of the saint's pleasure. In contrast, when the archdeacon of the Bishop of Turin tried to steal the finger of John the Baptist from the obscure church of Maurienne, the finger struck him dead. (Unlike dead authors, dead saints could maintain control over their translations.) Translation is movement, the twin of metaphor, which means "to move from one place to another." Metaphor makes the familiar strange; translation makes the strange familiar. Translation is change. Even the most concrete and limited form of translation—currency exchange—is in a state of hourly flux.

The only recorded example of translation as replication, not as change, was, not surprisingly, a miracle: around 250 B.C., seventy-two translators were summoned to Alexandria to prepare, in seventy-two days, seventy-two versions of the Hebrew Bible in Greek. Each one was guided by the Original of all Original Authors and wrote identical translations. Seventy-two translators producing seventy-two identical texts is an author's—or a book reviewer's—dream and a translator's nightmare.

A work of art is a singularity that remains itself while being subjected to restless change—from translation to translation, from reader to reader. To proclaim the intrinsic worthlessness of translations is to mistake that singularity with its unendingly varying manifestations. A translation is a translation and not a work of art—unless, over the centuries, it takes on its own singularity and becomes a work of art. A work of art is its own subject; the subject of a translation is the original work of art. There is a cliché in the United States that the purpose of a poetry translation is to create an excellent new poem in English. This is empirically false: nearly all the great translations in English would be ludicrous as poems written in English, even poems written in the voice of a *persona*. I have always maintained—and for some reason this is considered controversial—that the purpose of a poetry translation into English is to create an excellent translation in English. That is, a text that will be read and judged *like* a poem, but not *as* a poem.

And yet translations continue to be measured according to a utopian dream of exact equivalences, and are often dismissed on the basis of a single word, usually by members of foreign language departments, known in the trade as the "translation police." They are the ones who write—to take an actual example—that a certain immensely prolific translator from the German "simply does not know German" because somewhere in the vastness of *Buddenbrooks*, he had translated a "chesterfield" as a "greatcoat." Such examples, as any translator can tell you, are more the rule than the exception. One can only imagine if writers were reviewed in the same way: "the use of the word 'incarnadine' on page 349 proves the utter mediocrity of this book."

This is the old bugbear of "fidelity," which turns reviewers into television evangelists. Obviously a translation that is replete with semantical errors is probably a bad translation, but fidelity may be the most overrated of a translation's qualities. I once witnessed an interesting experiment: average nine-year-old students at a public school in Rochester, New York, were given a text by Rimbaud and a bilingual dictionary, and asked to translate the poem. Neither they nor their teacher knew a word of French. What they produced were not masterpieces, but they were generally as accurate as, and occasionally wittier than, any of the existing scholarly versions. In short, up to a point, anyone can translate anything faithfully.

But the point at which they cannot translate is the point where real translations begin to be made. The purpose of, say, a poetry translation is not, as it is usually said, to give the foreign poet a voice in the translation language. It is to allow the poem to be *heard* in the translation language, ideally in many of the same ways it is heard in the original language. This means that a translation is a whole work; it is not a series of matching *en face* lines and shouldn't be read as such. It means that the primary task of a translator is not merely to get the dictionary meanings right—which is the easiest part—but rather to invent a new music for the text in the translation language, one that is mandated by the original. A music that is not a technical replication of the original. (There is nothing worse than translations, for example, that attempt to re-create a foreign meter or rhyme scheme. They're sort of like the way hamburgers look and taste in Bolivia.) A music that is perfectly viable in English, but which—because it is a translation, because it will be read as a translation—is able to evoke another music, and perhaps reproduce some of its effects.

But to do so requires a thorough knowledge of the literature *into which* one is translating. Before modernism, poems, no matter from where, were translated into the prevailing styles and forms: the assumed perfection of the heroic couplet could equally serve Homer, Kalidasa, or the Chinese folk songs of the *Book of Odes*. The great lesson of modernism—first taught by Ezra Pound, but learned, even now, only by a few—was that the unique form and style of the original must in some manner determine the form and the style of the translation; the poem was not merely to be poured into the familiar molds. Thus, in Pound's famous example, a fragment of Sappho was turned into an English fragment, ellipses and all, and not "restored" or transformed into rhyming pentameters.

This was based on a twofold, and somewhat contradictory, belief: first, that the dead author and his or her literature were exotic, and therefore the translation should preserve this exoticism and not domesticate it. Second, that the dead author was our contemporary, and his or her poems—if they were worth reading—were as alive and fresh as anything written yesterday. An unrestored Sappho was "one of us" precisely because she was not one of us: a foreign (in the largest sense) poet pointing to a way that our poems could be written today.

Modernism—at least in English—created extraordinary works in translation because they were written *for* modernism: written to be read in the context of modernist poetry. The cliché that the only good poetry translators are themselves poets is not necessarily true: the only good translators are avid readers of contemporary poetry in the translation language. All the worst translations are done by experts in the foreign language who know little or nothing about the poetry alongside which their translations will be read. Foreign-language academics are largely concerned with semantical accuracy, rendering supposedly exact meanings into a frequently colorless or awkward version of the translation language. They often write as though the entire twentieth century had not occurred. They champion the best-loved poet of Ruthenia, but never realize that he sounds in English like bad Tennyson. Poets (or poetry readers) may be sometimes sloppy in their dictionary use, but they are preoccupied with what is *different* in the foreign author, that which is not already available among writers in the translation language, how that difference may be demonstrated, and how the borders of the possible may be expanded. Bad translations provide examples for historical surveys; good translations are always a form of advocacy criticism: Here is a writer one ought to be reading, and here is the proof.

Translation is an utterly unique genre, but for some reason there is a perennial tendency to explain it by analogy. A translator is like an actor playing a role, a musician performing a score, a messenger who sometimes garbles the message. But translation is such a familiar and intrinsic part of almost any culture that one wonders why there is this need to resort to analogies: we do not say that baking is like playing the violin. One analogy, however, is exact: translators are the geeks of literature.

Translators are invisible people. They are often confused with simultaneous interpreters—even at bilingual poetry readings. According to a

Anonymous Sources (On Translators and Translation)

25

survey of my own clippings—which I happen to have, but any translator could tell you the same story—90 percent of book reviews never mention the translator's name, even when they are talking about the author's so-called style. When they do, the work is usually summed up in a single word: *excellent, mediocre, energetic, lackluster*. Discussions of the translation longer than one word are nearly always complaints about the translation of a word or two.

Translators sometimes feel they share in the glory of their famous authors, rather like the hairdressers of Hollywood stars, but authors tend to find them creepy. As Isaac Bashevis Singer said:

> The translator must be a great editor, a psychologist, a judge of human taste; if not, his translation will be a nightmare. But why should a man with such rare qualities become a translator? Why shouldn't he be a writer himself, or be engaged in a business where diligent work and high intelligence are well paid? A good translator must be both a sage and a fool. And where do you get such strange combinations?

"Why shouldn't he be a writer himself?" is the great and terrible question that hangs over the head of every translator, and of every author thinking about his translator. One might say that the avoidance of the question—not the response to it—has been the recent flood of publications in which translators explain themselves.

Some translators now claim that they are authors (or something like authors), which strikes me as a Pirandellesque (or Reaganesque) confusion of actor and role. It began some thirty years ago in the United States as a tiny microcosm of the larger social currents. Translators began to come out of their isolation and anonymity to form groups, such as the Translation Committee of the PEN American Center, where they could share the tales of misfortune of their underpaid, entirely unrecognized, and often exploited occupation. This led to demands, as a group, for thoroughly justified material concessions: the translator's name prominently featured on the book and in all notices of the book, a share in the author's royalties and subsidiary rights (rather than a flat fee—degradingly known as "work for hire"—with no subsequent rights or income), and some sort of "industry standard" for translation fees. Simultaneous to the slow acceptance of these demands was a proliferation of conferences and lectures on translation as an art. This in turn coincided with the rise of so-called theory in the universities, and there is, perhaps, no subject in literature more suited for theoretical rumination in its current modes than translation: the authority of the author, the transformation of the sign, the tenuousness of signifier and signified, the politics of what is/isn't translated and how it is translated, the separation of text and author, the crossing (or impossibility of crossing) cultural barriers, the relativism of the translation as discourse, the translator as agent of political/cultural hegemony, and so on. All of which are sometimes interesting in themselves, but generally unhelpful when one actually translates. (As Borges said, "When I translate Faulkner, I don't think about the problem of translating Faulkner.")

With this preoccupation with the translator—and the self-evident and now excessively elaborated corollary that everything is a form of translation—the translator has suddenly become an important person, and explaining translation a minor but comfortable academic career and a source of invitations to conferences in exotic climes. Small wonder, then, that the advance guard of translators and their explainers are now declaring that the translator is an author, that a translated and original text are essentially indistinguishable (because an original text is a translation and/or a translation is an original text) and, most radically, that the sole author of a translation is the translator (who should therefore have 100 percent of the rights and royalties to the books).

This strikes me as presumptuous, if not hubristic; and it may well be time to raise the banner of the translator's essential and endearing anonymity. In the United States, we can no longer use the word "craft," which has been taken over by the so-called creative writing schools, where the "craft" is taught in "workshops." So let us say that translation is a trade, like cabinet-making or baking or masonry. It is a trade that any amateur can do, but professionals do better. It is a trade that can be learned, and should be (though not necessarily institutionally) in order to practice. It is a trade whose practitioners remain largely unknown to the general public, with the exception of a few workers of genius. It is a trade that is essential to a literate society, and—let's raise another banner—whose workers should be better paid.

For me, the translator's anonymity—his role as the Man Without Qualities standing before the scene, a product of the *zeitgeist* but not a direct maker of it—is the joy of translation. One is operating strictly on the level of language, attempting to invent similar effects, to capture the essential, without the interference of the otherwise all-consuming ego. It is the greatest education in how to write, as many poets have learned. It is a prison in the sense that everything is said and must now be re-said, including all the author's bad moments—the vagaries, the repetitions, the clichés, the clinkers—while strictly avoiding the temptation to explain or improve. It is a prison, or a kind of nightmare, because one is in a dialogue with another person whom you must concede is always right. But it is also a liberation. It is the only time when one can put words on a page entirely without embarrassment (and embarrassment, it seems to me, is a greatly underrated force in the creation of literature). The introspective bookworm happily becomes the voice of Jack London or Jean Genet; translation is a kind of fantasy life.

Translators are often asked to talk about their relationships with the authors they translate, and they tend to reply with sometimes amusing intertextual anecdotes. Authors, however, never talk about their translators, beyond a few passing complaints. This is because the author-translator relationship has no story. Or more exactly, the story has only one real character: the author. The translator, as translator, is not a fully formed human being; the translator, in the familiar analogy, is an actor playing the role of the author. Sometimes we, the audience, are aware of the actor "doing" the role brilliantly or poorly, sometimes we forget he is an actor at all (the "invisibility" that is often still considered the translation ideal, particularly for prose). But in either case, reflections on that role remain one-sided: Olivier may write a memoir of his Hamlet, but Hamlet, if he existed, would never write of his Olivier.

Translation is the most anonymous of professions, yet people die for it. It is little known that the *fatwa* against Salman Rushdie and its subsequent global mayhem, riots, and deaths were the result of a mistranslation. Rushdie's book was named after a strange legend in Islamic tradition about the composition of the Quran, which was dictated to Muhammad by Allah Himself through the angel Jibril. According to the story, Muhammad, having met considerable resistance to his attempt to eliminate all the local gods of Mecca in favor of the One God, recited some verses that admitted three popular goddesses as symbolic Daughters of Allah. Later he claimed that the verses had been dictated to him by Satan in the voice of Jibril, and the lines were suppressed. The nineteenth-century British Orientalists called these lines the "Satanic verses," but in

Arabic (and its cognate languages) the verses were known as *gharaniq*, "the birds," after two excised lines about the Meccan goddesses: "These are the exalted birds / And their intercession is desired indeed." In Arabic (and similarly in the cognate languages) Rushdie's title was literally translated as *Al-Ayat ash-Shataniya*, with *shaytan* meaning Satan, and *ayat* meaning specifically the "verses of the Quran." As the phrase "Satanic verses" is completely unknown in the Muslim world—which Rushdie apparently didn't know—the title in Arabic implied the ultimate blasphemy: that the entire Quran was composed by Satan. The actual contents of the book were irrelevant.

Translators were among those who paid for this mistake: in July of 1991, the Italian translator of *The Satanic Verses*, Ettore Caprioli, was stabbed in his apartment in Milan, but survived. Days later, the Japanese translator, Hitoshi Igarashi, an Islamic scholar, was stabbed to death in his office at Tsukuba University in Tokyo.

As far as I know, Rushdie has never made any extended comment on Hitoshi Igarashi. It would take another kind of novelist—Dostoyevsky perhaps—to untangle the psychological, moral, and spiritual meanings and effects of the story of these two: the man who became the most famous writer in the world at the price of what seemed, for some years, to be life imprisonment, and the anonymous man who died for a faithful translation of an old mistranslation, paying for the writer's mistake.

Translation is the most anonymous of professions, yet people—to paraphrase William Carlos Williams on poetry—die from the lack of it. The first World Trade Center bombing, in 1993, might have been averted if the FBI had bothered to translate the boxes of letters, documents, and tapes it had already seized in the course of various investigations, which specifically detailed the plot. But those were in a foreign language—Arabic—and who could be bothered?

After 9/11, however, they began to bother, and there is now something called the 300th Military Intelligence Brigade. Fifteen hundred language experts, most of them Mormons trained for missionary work in heathen lands, housed in six sites in the state of Utah, are frantically trying to translate the mountain of documents that have been gathered by the various agencies. Their commander, Col. Dee Snowball, rallied the troops with these words: "You will not garner the glory that the combat soldier receives, but you will make a huge impact in the defense of your country." It is the military version of what all translators feel.

Translation is an obvious necessity that is somehow considered to be a problem. (There are never conferences on the "pleasures of translation.") Yet it is a problem that only arises in the interstices when one is not casually referring to some translated bit of literature: the Bible, Homer, Kafka, Proust. . . . Could it possibly be that translation essentially has no problems at all? That it only has successes and failures? There is no text that cannot be translated; there are only texts that have not yet found their translators. A translation is not inferior to the original; it is only inferior to other translations, written or not yet written. There is no definitive translation because a translation always appears in the context of its contemporary literature, and the realm of the possible in any contemporary literature is in constant flux—often, it should be emphasized, altered by the translations that have entered into it. Everything worth translating should be translated as many times as possible, even by the same translator, for you can never step into the same original twice. Poetry is that which is worth translating, and translation is what keeps literature alive. Translation is change and motion; literature dies when it stays the same, when it has no place to go.

THREE

Fictions of the Foreign

The Paradox of "Foreign-Soundingness"

DAVID BELLOS

For most of the last century reviewers and laymen have customarily declared in order to praise a translation to the skies that it sounds as if it had been written in English. This is hollow praise indeed, since the selfsame community of reviewers and laymen has often shown itself unable to tell when an alleged translation *was* written in English. All the same, the high value placed on fluency in the "target" or "receiving" language is a strong feature of the culture of translation in the English-speaking world today. But there are contrarian voices. If a detective novel set in Paris makes its characters speak and think in entirely fluent English, even while they plod along the Boulevard Saint-Germain, drink Pernod, and scoff a *jarret de porc aux lentilles*—then something must be wrong. Where's the bonus in having a French detective novel for bedtime reading unless there is something French about it? Don't we want our French detectives to sound French? Domesticating translation styles that eradicate the Frenchness of Gallic thugs have been attacked by some critics for committing "ethnocentric violence."[1] An ethics of translation, such critics say, should restrain translators from erasing all that is foreign about works translated from a foreign tongue.

How then should the foreignness of the foreign best be represented in the receiving language? Jean d'Alembert, a mathematician and philosopher who was also coeditor of Diderot's *Encyclopédie*, came up with an ingenious answer in 1763:

The way foreigners speak [French] is the model for a good translation. The original should speak our language not with the superstitious caution we have for our native tongue, but with a noble freedom that allows features of one language to be borrowed in order to embellish another. Done in this way, a translation may possess all the qualities that make it commendable—a natural and easy manner, marked by the genius of the original and alongside that the added flavor of a homeland created by its foreign coloring.[2]

The risk of this approach is that in many social and historical circumstances the foreign-soundingness of a translation—just like the slightly unnatural diction of a real foreigner speaking French (or English, or German . . .)—may be rejected as clumsy, false, or even worse.

In fact, the most obvious way to make a text sound foreign is to leave parts of it in the original. Such was the convention in Britain in the Romantic era. In the earliest translation of the novel now known in English as *Dangerous Liaisons*, for instance, characters refer to and address each other by their full titles in French (*monsieur le vicomte, madame la présidente*) and use everyday expressions such as *Allez! Parbleu!* and *Ma foi!* within sentences that are in other respects entirely in English.[3] Similarly, in recent translations of the novels of Fred Vargas, the lead character Jean-Baptiste Adamsberg retains his French rank of *commissaire* in charge of a clutch of *brigadiers*, but he talks to them in English.[4] Following the same logic of selective foreignism, German officers in most World War II movies made in Hollywood speak natural English interrupted at regular intervals by *Jawohl, Gott im Himmel*, and *Heil Hitler*.

This device may be taken much further, in popular as well as classical works. The dubbed Italian version of *Singin' in the Rain*, though it performs miracles of lip-synch in the translation of witty patter, leaves the sound track of the title song in the original English. A famous modern production of *King Lear* in Chinese has Cordelia speaking Shakespeare's lines— she speaks the truth to her father in the true language of her speech.[5]

In general, however, translations only simulate the foreign-soundingness of foreign works. In fact, the challenge of writing something that sounds like English to speakers of other languages can even be met by not writing English at all.

English is heard around the world in pop songs, commercials, TV news broadcasts, and so on by millions of people who do not understand the words of the lyrics, jingles, and reports. As a result, there are large numbers of people who recognize the phonology of English—the kinds of sounds English makes—without knowing any English vocabulary or grammar. Some forty years ago, an Italian rock star performed a musical routine in which he pretended to be a teacher of English showing his class that you do not need to understand a single word in order to know what English sounds like. Sung to a catchy tune, Adriano Celentano's "Prisencolinensinainciusol ol rait" is witty and surprising simulation of what English sounds like—without being in English at all. However, the transcription of its "anglogibberish" in textual form represents English-soundingness only when it is vocalized (aloud, or in your head) according to the standard rules for vocalizing *Italian* script. "Prisencolinensinainciusol ol rait," which can be found on many currently available websites, in some cases with one of its possible transcriptions, is a specifically Italian fiction of the foreign.

It is equally possible to produce gibberish that sounds foreign to English ears. A famous example is the song sung by Charlie Chaplin in *Modern Times* (1936). Having got a job as a singing waiter, the hapless fellow finds himself on the restaurant dance floor with the band thumping out a French music-hall tune, *Je cherche après Titine*—but he does not know the words! Chaplin dances, mimes, looks perplexed. Pauline Goddard, in the wings, mouths the word "Sing!" Our lip-reading is confirmed by the intertitle: "Sing! Never Mind the Words!"

Chaplin then launches into a ditty in Generic Immigrant Romance, which *for English-speakers only* can be represented thus:

Se bella giu satore
Je notre so cafore
Je notre si cavore
Je la tu la ti la toi

La spinash o la bouchon
Cigaretto Portabello
Si rakish spaghaletto
Ti la tu la ti la toi

Senora pilasina
Voulez-vous le taximeter?
Le zionta su la sita
Tu la tu la tu la oi

Sa montia si n'amura
La sontia so gravora
La zontcha con sora
Je la possa ti la toit

Je notre so lamina
Je notre so consina
Je le se tro savita
Je la tossa vi la toit

Se motra so la sonta
Chi vossa l'otra volta
Li zoscha si catonta
Tra la la la la la la

That sounds like French—or Italian, or perhaps Spanish—to an English speaker with no knowledge of the languages, only a familiarity with what French (or Italian or Spanish) sounds like. The verses have no meaning, of course, and only a few of the words are actual words of French (Italian, Spanish). The point is this: you do not have to make any sense at all to sound foreign. For the ancient Greeks, the sound of the foreign was the unarticulated, open-mouthed blabber of *va-va-va-*, which is why they called all non-Greek speakers *varvaros*, that is to say, *barbarians*, "blah-blah-ers." To sound foreign is to mouth gibberish, to be dim, to be dumb: the Russian word for "German" is немец, from немой, "dumb, speechless," and in an older form of the language it was used for any non-Russian speaker.

However, since the 1980s a number of modern European classics have been retranslated into English and French by translators whose avowed intention was to make familiar modern classics like *Crime and Punishment* and *The Metamorphosis* sound more foreign—although they certainly did not wish to make them sound dumb.

Nineteenth-century translators frequently left common words and phrases in the original (mostly when the original was French), but this device is rarely used by contemporary retranslators into English, however "foreignizing" they may seek to be. When Gregor Samsa wakes one morning and finds that he has turned into an insect overnight, he does not exclaim *Ach Gott!* in any modern English version; nor does Ivan Fyodorovich say *Это вот как* in any available translation of *The Brothers Karamazov*. Had these novels been written in French and translated into

English by the conventions of the 1820s, we can be fairly sure that Gregor Samsa would have said *Oh mon Dieu!* and Ivan Fedorovich would have said *Alors, voilà* in the English translation.

Things have changed, not in French, German, or Russian, but in English. In the English-language culture of today, readers are not expected to know how to recognize conversational interjections like "Good God!" or "Well, now" when spoken in German or Russian; whereas within the language culture of Victorian and Edwardian Britain, educated readers were familiar with French expressions of that kind.

A genuine educational and social purpose can be served by maintaining items of the source text in the translation. It allows readers to acquire what they had not learned at school, or to refresh their memory of half-forgotten lessons. Retention of the original expression in narrowly delimited and self-explanatory speech situations such as greetings and exclamations provides readers with something they might well want to glean from reading a translated work: the vague impression of having read a novel in French. When reading French was an important mark of cultural distinction, this could be a very satisfying feeling indeed.

Selective or "decorative" foreignism is available only in translating between languages with an established relationship. For many centuries, knowledge of French was a requirement of advanced education in the English-speaking world, and bits of French were therefore part of the educated English speaker's general linguistic resource. What those fragments signified was, simply, "This is French!" together with the pleasing corollary, "I know some French!" The effect on the reader's self-esteem was hardly diminished if the exact meaning of phrases like *parbleu* and *ma foi* was lost. When a mastery of French was the hallmark of the educated classes, part of the point of reading a French novel in translation for those whose education had not been quite so complete was to acquire the cultural goods that the elite already possessed. Thus the more French the translation of a French work left in, the better the reader's needs and wants were served.

You can't do that with Russian or German anymore. These languages are taught to only tiny groups of students nowadays. Knowledge of either or even both has no relation to cultural hierarchies in the English-speaking world—it just means you are some kind of a linguist, or maybe an astronaut or an automobile engineer.

What could represent "Russianness" or "Germanness" inside a work written in English? Conventional solutions to this conundrum are no more than that—cultural conventions, established within the English-language domain by historical contact, patterns of immigration, and popular entertainments such as Cold War dramas like *Dr. Strangelove*. But if we were to take d'Alembert's recommendations as our guide, then we would try to make Kafka and Dostoyevsky sound like the foreigners that they surely were . . . by having them write English "embellished" with features not native to it.

In German and Russian, of course, Kafka and Dostoyevsky, however unique their manners of expression may be, do not sound foreign to native readers of those languages. Foreignness in a translation is necessarily an addition to the original. In Chaplin's gibberish as in retranslations of literary classics, foreignness is necessarily constructed inside the receiving tongue. As a result, the "foreign-soundingness" of a translation seeking to give the reader a glimpse of the authentic quality of the source can only reproduce and reinforce what the receiving culture already imagines the foreign to be.

Friedrich Schleiermacher, a distinguished nineteenth-century philosopher and the translator of Plato into German, hovered around this fundamental paradox in his much-quoted paper "On the Different Methods of Translating." He's usually understood to have taken his distance from fluent, invisible, or "normalizing" translation when he said, "The goal of translating even as the author himself would have written originally in the language of the translation is not only unattainable but is also in itself null and void."[6] But that famous statement can also be understood the other way around: that it would be just as artificial to make Kafka sound like a "stage German" writing English as it would be to make Gregor Samsa sound as if he had turned into a beetle in a bedroom in Hoboken.

Why should we want or need Kafka to sound German, in any case? In German, Kafka doesn't sound "German" at all—he sounds like Kafka. Of course, to the ear of an English speaker who has learned German but does not inhabit that language entirely naturally, everything Kafka wrote sounds German to some degree, precisely because German is not quite that reader's home tongue. Making Kafka sound German in English is perhaps the best means a translator has to communicate to the reader his or her own experience of reading the original.

For Schleiermacher, in fact, apart from "those marvelous masters to whom several languages feel as one," everybody "retains the feeling of foreignness" when reading works not in their home tongue. The translator's task is to "transmit this feeling of foreignness to his readers." But this is a peculiarly hard and rather paradoxical thing to do unless you can call on conventions that the target language already possesses for representing the specific "other" associated with the culture of the language from which the source text comes.

Foreign-soundingness is therefore only a real option for a translator when working from a language with which the receiving language and its culture have an established relationship. The longest and most extensive relationship of that kind in the English-speaking world in general is with French. In the United States, Spanish has recently become the most familiar foreign tongue for the majority of younger readers. English therefore has many ways to represent Frenchness, and American English now also has a panoply of devices for representing Spanishness. To a lesser degree, we can represent Germanness, and, to a rather limited and usually comical degree, Italianness as well. But what of Yoruba? Marathi? Chuvash? Or any one of the nearly seven thousand other languages of the world? There is no special reason why anything within the devices available to a writer of English should "sound just like Yoruba" or give a more authentic representation of what it feels like to write in Chuvash. We just have no idea. The project of writing translations that preserve *in the way they sound* some trace of the work's "authentic foreignness" is really applicable only when the original is not very foreign at all.

On the other hand, translated texts can teach interested and willing readers something about the sound and feel and even the syntactic properties of the original. So can originals—Achebe's *Things Fall Apart* introduces elements of African languages, and Upamanyu Chatterjee's *English, August* gives you a good start on Hindi and Bengali vocabulary. But when foreignness is not thematized—not made the explicit subject of the story—some prior knowledge of the original language is essential for a foreign effect to arise. In order to even notice that this sentence from German a foreignizing translation is have you to know that in German subordinate clauses at the end their verbs put. Otherwise it is comical, clumsy, nonsensical, and so forth—not "German" at all.

Modern Times and Adriano Celentano play entertaining games with foreign-soundingness quite literally, in sung and spoken speech sounds. A recent translation of Kafka's *Metamorphosis* could of course be sounded out in the reader's head in a non-native phonology. Gregor Samsa's first words in direct speech—

"Oh God," he thought, "what a grueling job I've picked! Day in, day out—on the road."

—would then be taken as a written representation of sounds more recognizably transcribed as

"Och Gott," e saut, "vot a kruling tschop aif picked! Tay in, tay out—on ze rote."

This is surely very silly: no serious translator ever intends his work to be sounded out with a stage accent. It nonetheless forces us to ask a real question: If that is not what is meant by foreign-soundingness in the translation of a foreign literary or other text, then what exactly *is* foreign-soundingness? What allows us to judge whether the following passage retains some authentic trace of the Frenchness of Jacques Derrida, or whether it is just terribly hard to understand?

> The positive and the classical sciences of writing are obliged to repress this sort of question. Up to a certain point, such repression is even necessary to the progress of positive investigation. Beside the fact that it would still be held within a philosophizing logic, the ontophenomeno-logical question of essence, that is to say of the origin of writing, could, by itself, only paralyze or sterilize the typological or historical research of *facts*.
>
> My intention, therefore, is not to weigh that prejudicial question, that dry, necessary, and somewhat facile question of right, against the power and efficacy of the positive researches which we may witness today. The genesis and system of scripts had never led to such profound, extended, and assured explorations. It is not really a matter of weighing the question against the importance of the discovery; since the questions are imponderable, they cannot be weighed. If the issue is not quite that, it is perhaps because its repression has real consequences in the very content of the researches that, in the present case and in a privileged way, are always arranged around problems of definition and beginning.[7]

We know that the content of this hard-to-follow extract isn't related to whether it "sounds like" English or not-English—Celentano's song has shown us already that you can make completely meaningless concatenations sound like perfect English if phonetic English-soundingness is all you want to achieve. However, one detail that marks it as a translation *from French* is the anomalous use of the word *research* in the plural, matching a regular usage of a similar-looking word in French, *recherche*. Obviously, that can be seen only by a reader who knows French as well as English: the foreignness of "researches" is not self-evident to an English-only speaker, who may well construct quite other hypotheses to account for it, or else accept it as a special or technical term belonging to this particular author. But if the bilingual reader also has some additional knowledge of French philosophical terminologies, then the word *positive* preceding the first occurrence of *researches* becomes quite transparent. It stands to reason to a bilingual reader that *positive researches* in the English represents *recherches positives* in the source. What that French phrase means is another issue: it is the standard translation of "empirical investigation" into French.

We could say that "positive researches" is a poor translation of a standard French phrase that the translator seems to have treated as something else, or we could see it as a trace of the authentic sound of the original. Indeed, unless an English phrase *is* perceptibly anomalous, we would not be able to see it as containing any trace of not-English. But it is equally clear that we would not be able to see the "Frenchness" of the phrase if we had no knowledge of French.

Back-translation of the foreignism "positive researches" into a number of other languages, among them Modern Greek, would produce the same result, that is to say, would allow its meaning to be identified as "empirical investigation." Without the information that the work in question has been translated from language A, foreignizing translation styles do not themselves allow the reader to identify which foreign language A is.

Foreignizing translation styles bend English into shapes that mirror some limited aspect of the source language, such as word order or sentence structure. But they rely for their foreignizing effect on the reader's prior knowledge of the approximate shape and sound of a foreign language—in the case of Gayatri Chakravorty Spivak's translation of Derrida quoted above, specific items in the vocabulary of the foreign tongue.

Imagine a novel translated from Hindi. Hindi has not one, not two, but three ways of saying "you": *tu, tum,* and *ap,* corresponding to the intimate, the friendly, and the formal. Alternating among the three forms of address is a significant part of the way the characters in our imaginary novel relate to one another. Could a translator create a linguistic anomaly in

English that corresponds to this triple division of "you"? Yes, of course. But would we know that it was a mark of Hindi? Not without a translator's footnote—because we do not know any Hindi.

Since the majority of translations take place between languages spoken by communities that have quite a lot to do with each other, culturally, economically, or politically, formal and lexical borrowings from the source have often been used to represent the foreignness—and the prestige—of texts imported from abroad. In the sixteenth century, for example, many works of literature and philosophy were brought from Italian into French, just as many Italian craftsmen were imported to beautify palaces and castles across the land. The translators of that era wrote French with a wealth of Italian words and turns of phrase, because they felt that their readers either did or really should know the words and phrases they imported. More than that: they thought French would be positively improved by being made a little more like Italian. And in fact the process of making French more like Italian has continued down to the present day. The *caban* (pea jacket) and the *caleçon* (underpants) in your closet, and, if you're lucky, the *cantaloup* and the *caviar* in your refrigerator, like a huge number of other ordinary, scholarly, refined, and delicious things, are all named in French by words taken from Italian, and for the majority of them the taking was first done by translators.[8]

A similar kind of lexical enrichment took place in the nineteenth century when German-speaking peoples sought to constitute themselves as a distinct and increasingly unified nation. German translators consciously imported a quantity of words from Greek, French, and English, not only to make European classics accessible to speakers of German but also to improve the German language by extending its range of vocabulary. The issue as they saw it was this: French and English were international languages already, propped up by powerful states. That was why non-native speakers learned French (and to a lesser extent, English). How could German ever be the vehicle of a powerful state unless non-natives learned to read it? And why should they learn to read it unless it could easily convey the meanings that arise in the transnational cultures held to represent the riches of European civilization?

In today's world translators into "small" languages also often see their task as defending or else improving their own tongues—or both at the same time. Here's a letter I received just the other day from a translator in Tartu:

> My mother language, Estonian, is spoken by about a million people. Nevertheless I am convinced that *Life: A User's Manual* and my language mutually deserve each other. Translating Perec, I want to prove that Estonian is rich and flexible enough to face the complications that a work of this kind brings along.

Translation can clearly serve national purposes—but also their opposite, the cause of internationalism itself. A contemporary writer of French who uses the pen name Antoine Volodine has formulated in striking terms why he wishes to use his native language as if it were a foreign tongue. For Volodine, French is not just the language of Racine and Voltaire. Because translation into French has been practiced for a very long time, French is also the language of Pushkin, Shalamov, Li Bai, and García Márquez. Far from being the privileged vector of national identity, history, and culture, "French is a language that transmits cultures, philosophies, and concerns that have nothing to do with the habits of French society or the Francophone world."[9] It is not that French is by its nature or destiny an international language: on the contrary, only the practice of translation into French has made the language a tool of internationalism in the modern world. Thanks to its long history of translation from foreign languages, French is now a possible vehicle for an imaginary, infinitely haunting literature that Volodine would like to consider absolutely foreign to it.

It would therefore be quite wrong to see the progressive interpenetration of English, French, German, and Italian together with terms and phrases from the ancient source tongues, Latin and Greek, and (in the writings of Volodine) Russian and Chinese too, as the sole product of what is now called globalization. In any case, globalization does not spread only English into other languages and cultures: it could just as well be exemplified by the spread of pizza language and the vocabulary of pasta (along with pizza and pasta as well) into corner stores and fast-food joints the world over. It is also the result of long efforts by translators to raise their national languages to international status. They did not necessarily seek to make their translations sound authentically foreign. Indeed, if that is what they were really trying to do, their success has made mincemeat of their ambition, because the words they imported or mimicked have now become part of the receiving language to such an extent that they are no longer foreign at all.

No less than 40 percent of all headwords in any large English dictionary are imports from other languages. A foreignism—be it a word, a turn of phrase, or a grammatical structure that is brought into our marvelously and infuriatingly malleable tongue by a translator seeking to retain the authentic sound of the original—has its path already mapped out. Either it will be disregarded as a clumsy, awkward, or incomplete act of translation, or it will be absorbed, reused, integrated, and become not foreign at all.

However, contemporary efforts to produce translations into English that keep something authentically foreign about them are not strictly comparable to the kind of translators' campaigns in centuries past that made German more like English, French more like Italian, Syriac more like Greek, and so forth. The foreignizers of today are not struggling to make English an international language, because English *is* the international language of the present. To some degree, they are seeking to enrich English with linguistic resources afforded by languages that are distant from it. "One subliminal idea I started out with as a translator was to help energize English itself," Richard Pevear stated in an interview published in *The New Yorker*.[10] That creative, writerly project rests on a wish to share with readers some of the feelings that Pevear has when reading a Russian novel. He has also often said that he is not a fluent speaker of the language and relies on his partner to provide a basic crib that he then works into a literary version.[11] Something similar may be true of other proponents of awkward and foreign-sounding translation styles. The project of writing translations that do the least "ethnocentric violence" to the original thus runs the risk of dissolving into something different—a representation of the funny ways foreigners speak.

The natural way to represent the foreignness of foreign utterances is to leave them in the original, in whole or in part. This resource is available in all languages, and has always been used to some degree in every one of them.[12] It is not easy to represent the foreignness of foreign languages in complete seriousness. It takes the wit of Chaplin or Celentano to do so for comic effect without causing offense. What translation does is to represent the meaning of a foreign text. And that's quite hard enough.

Notes

1. Lawrence Venuti, *The Translator's Invisibility: A History of Translation* (London: Routledge, 1995), 20 and passim.

2. Jean le Rond d'Alembert, "Observations sur l'art de traduire," in *Mélanges de littérature, d'histoire, et de philosophie* (Amsterdam: Chatelain, 1763), 3:18. My translation.

3. *Dangerous connections: or, letters collected in a society, and published for the instruction of other societies.* By M. C**** de L*** [Choderlos de Laclos, a translation from the French] (London: T Hookham, 1784).

4. Fred Vargas, *Have Mercy on Us All*, trans. David Bellos (London: Harvill, 2003).

5. Directed by David Ka-Shing for the Yellow Earth Theatre and Shanghai Dramatic Arts Center, performed in Stratford-upon-Avon, London, and Shanghai, in 2006.

6. Friedrich Schleiermacher, "Über die verschiedenen Methoden des Übersetzens," a paper read in 1813 to the Royal Academy of Sciences in Berlin, in a new translation by Susan Bernofsky, in *The Translation Studies Reader*, ed. Lawrence Venuti, 2nd ed. (New York: Routledge, 2004). An earlier and more widely available translation by Waltraud Bartscht omits several passages.

7. From Chapter Two of Jacques Derrida's *Of Grammatology* (1967), trans. Gayatri Chakravorty Spivak (Baltimore and London: Johns Hopkins University Press, 1974).

8. Adapted from Mariagrazia Margarito, "Une valise pour bien voyager . . . avec les italianismes du français," *Synergies* 4 (2008): 63–73.

9. Antoine Volodine, "Écrire en français une littérature étrangère," *chaoïd* 6 (2002).

10. David Remnick, "The Translation Wars," *The New Yorker*, November 7, 2005.

11. "Pevear has certainly picked up a great deal of Russian, but not its outlandishly rich vocabulary, the complicated grammar, with its maddening various verb conjugations, shades of tense, reflexivities, cases, endings, gerundial gymnastics." Remnick, "The Translation Wars." For a detailed discussion of the effects of Pevear's retranslations of the Russian classics, see Gary Saul Morton, "The Pevearsion of Russian Literature," *Commentary*, July–August 2010.

12. For a particularly effective use of this technique, see Mariusz Wilk, *The Journals of a White Sea Wolf*, trans. Daniusa Stok (London: Harvill, 2003).

FOUR

Beyond, Between

Translation, Ghosts, Metaphors

MICHAEL EMMERICH

What is translation? Translation is an English word. Translation is, moreover, a somewhat peculiar English word. Peculiar, I would suggest, because it is incapable of definition. It is impossible to define because it is a sort of node—a point of intersection. Translation, used in the most ordinary of its many senses, refers to something that takes place, or at least seems to take place, between two languages. The English word "translation" has meaning only because we know there are other languages besides English from which one might translate into English, or into which one might translate from English. The word "translation" implies, that is to say, the existence of other languages. But it also indicates that other languages can be connected to English: it points to itself as the bridge, the carrying across that occurs between languages. We might say, then, that the word only means anything at all because it can itself cross its own bridge by being translated into other languages. "Translation" is defined, first and foremost, by its own translatability. Saussure would say that "translation" is defined by its difference from, for instance, "interpretation," "adaptation," "transnation," et cetera. But that is only part of the picture. Translation might also be defined by its difference from the French word *traduction*. But that is still only part of the picture. More important is the fact that in order to mean what it does, "translation" must also be a translation of *traduction*, just as *traduction* is a translation of "translation." It is this convergence that defines "translation."

This is fairly easy to grasp when we are talking about French and English, in which the two words are used, as far as I know, in relatively similar ways—though the range of the French word is considerably narrower than the English one. French and English are, after all, similar in many ways: both languages use the Latin alphabet, for instance. But what if we bring in Japanese, about which I know somewhat more? How would we translate "translation" into Japanese? That would depend on the sort of translation we were talking about—even if we limit ourselves to the ordinary sense of the word with which we are presently concerned. And of course "translation" is and has been used in many ways that have very little to do with the ordinary sense of the word. It is also used to describe the movement of living bishops and the relics of dead saints, for instance, and people can be "translated" to heaven, as we see in this entry from Ambrose Bierce's *Devil's Dictionary*: "Gallows, n. A stage for the performance of miracle plays, in which the leading actor is translated to heaven."

Setting these unusual usages aside, the most obvious Japanese translation of the English word "translation" would be 翻訳 *hon'yaku*. But the obviousness of this translation is misleading: it comes to mind first, I would suggest, not because it is a general category like "translation" within which other types of translation are included, but because it is the most nondescript, or the least specific in a series of terms denoting various sorts of translation. "Translation" in English is an overarching category that includes all sorts of translations, the act as well as the product of the act; *hon'yaku* can be used in a way that makes it seem like an overarching term—it can refer both to translation as an act and to a translation of a book, and is used to translate the "translation" in "translation studies"—but it isn't exactly, at least not in the way that "translation" is. This is evident, for instance, in the fact that 現代語訳 *gendaigoyaku* (the rendering of a work in a premodern form of Japanese into a modern form of Japanese, which is unquestionably a form of "translation") is not generally considered a subset of *hon'yaku. Hon'yaku* also has considerably less of the ambiguously theoretical or metaphorical flexibility of the English term: one might classify transliteration as a subset of translation (indeed, Jerome J. McGann uses the term "type-translation" to refer to transliteration), but in Japanese one would simply be using the wrong word for the activity variously known as 翻刻 *honkoku*, 翻字 *honji*, or 翻印 *hon'in. Hon'yaku* refers specifically to translation from foreign (non-Japanese) languages into Japanese (or vice versa), sometimes more specifically still to translations from Europe or the United States, and its usefulness as a general term is thus limited. Those like myself who attempt to translate "translation" with the word *hon'yaku* are, in other words, subtly carrying out the type of translation (if it is a type of translation) known in Japanese as 誤訳 *goyaku*, or "mistranslation."

Japanese has another word, 訳 *yaku*, that might seem at first to serve as a general term with a theoretical/metaphorical inclusiveness similar to that of the English word "translation." *Yaku* appears in numerous multicharacter compounds that correspond to different types of "translation," including *hon'yaku* and *gendaigoyaku*, and can be used to form neologisms: I have seen a recent *manga* translation of *Genji monogatari* (*The Tale of Genji*) by the artist Egawa Tatsuya described more than once as an 絵訳 *eyaku* ("pictorial translation"). But in fact it is only the Sino-Japanese character that has this general meaning; the word *yaku* itself refers to specific translations, as in "the Egawa translation of *Genji*," 『源氏』の江川訳 *Genji no Egawa-yaku*. The general meaning of the character *yaku*, moreover—its theoretical/metaphorical inclusiveness— only arises *through* its use in compounds, and is thus limited by its uses. And so once again we find ourselves having to ask, in order to translate "translation" into Japanese, what particular variety of "translation" we are talking about. It will be useful, I think, to pause and consider a sampling of the answers we might give, if only as an exercise.

What, then, is "translation" in Japanese? If the translation we are discussing is complete, we might call it a 全訳 *zen'yaku* or a 完訳 *kan'yaku*. If a translator completes a translation, we might describe that instance of the act of translation with the verb 訳了する *yakuryō suru*. If her completed translation is an excerpt, it is a 抄訳 *shōyaku*. A first translation is a 初訳 *shoyaku*. A retranslation is a 改訳 *kaiyaku*, and the new translation is a 新訳 *shin'yaku* that replaces the old translation, or 旧訳 *kyūyaku*. A translation of a translation is a 重訳 *jūyaku*. A standard translation that seems unlikely to be replaced is a 定訳 *teiyaku*; equally unlikely to be replaced is a 名訳 *meiyaku*, or "celebrated translation." When a celebrated translator speaks of her own work, she may disparage it as 拙訳 *setsuyaku*, "clumsy translation," i.e. "my own translation," which is not to be confused with a genuinely bad translation, disparaged as a 駄訳 *dayaku* or an 悪訳 *akuyaku*. A cotranslation is a 共訳 *kyōyaku* or 合訳 *gōyaku*; a draft translation, or 下訳 *shitayaku*, may be polished through a process of "supervising translation," or 監訳 *kan'yaku*, without it becoming a *kyōyaku* or *gōyaku*. Translations are given different names depending on the approach they take to the original: they can be 直訳 *chokuyaku* (literally "direct translation"), 逐語訳 *chikugoyaku* ("word for word translation"), 意訳 *iyaku* ("sense translation"), 対訳 *taiyaku* ("translation presented with the original text on facing pages"), or in the case of translations of works by Sidney Sheldon, Danielle Steel, John Grisham, and other popular American writers, 超訳 *chōyaku* ("translations that are even better than the originals," an invention and registered trademark of the Academy Press). When what has been translated is a word, the translation is a 訳語 *yakugo*; a translation of a poem is a 訳詩 *yakushi*; if it is a lyric it is a 訳詞 *yakushi*; if you are discussing a translation as prose you say 訳文 *yakubun*; if the translation is a book it is a 訳書 *yakusho* or a 訳本 *yakuhon*, and the translated title is its 訳名 *yakumei*. When you translate as a mode of reading, you 訳読する *yakudoku suru*; when you translate in order to clarify the meaning of a text, you 訳解する *yakkai suru*; when you translate aloud, you 訳述する *yakujutsu suru*. A Braille translation is a 点訳 *ten'yaku*.

These examples should suffice to make my point. In order for "translation" to have any meaning at all, it must be translatable into other languages, but the moment it is translated, it is swept up in a system of differentiations different from the one in which it is enmeshed in English—indeed, it doesn't even have to be translated, because the word itself implies its own connectedness to these other systems of differentiation. Translation must be viewed as a node within which all the ideas of translation in all the languages there ever have been or could ever be might potentially congregate, intersect, mingle. Or we could say that the word "translation" is haunted by all the concepts it might translate, the words with which it may be translated. A word like "dog" can be understood, if only provisionally, in terms of its difference from an (indefinite) string of other terms in English; "translation" is made doubly provisional by its inevitable connection to other, non-English ideas of translation that could, at any moment, be brought to bear on the English word, just as the English word can be brought to bear, through a subtle process of productive mistranslation, on the Japanese word *hon'yaku*. "Translation" is, that is to say, always waiting to be redefined, not through its difference but through its similarity to other terms in other languages.

If this is not as obvious as it probably should be, it is because too frequently we consider translation from a perspective that has nothing to do with translation. We focus almost exclusively on translations. There are originals and translations, source texts and languages and target texts and languages, domestic and foreign, those who commission translations and those who consume them—everything but translators engaged in the act of translation. There are several reasons for this. The most important, perhaps, is that it is difficult to get a handle on what exactly a translator is doing when she translates. Consider this description of the process by Donald Philippi:

> Whatever happens after a translator sits down at the computer, it isn't anything material. What realm do we enter when we boot up our computer, attune our mental faculties to that odd wavelength of ours, and ascend into the ethereal realm of the translator's daily praxis? The translator's consciousness is not focused on any object, but is rather liberated from the world of material objects. The translator's realm is on a highly abstract plane, rather like that of a mathematician, grammarian or logician. The material objects are distanced. The domain of consciousness in which the translator operates is detached from the whole natural world. Abstracted from reality, the translator operates outside the spatio-temporal system in the world of pure consciousness. As Edmund Husserl would say: "Between the meanings of consciousness and reality yawns a veritable abyss. (Husserl, *Ideas*, p. 138.) [. . .] The translator's world is a world of incorporeal experiences based on contact with nonmaterial relationships and concepts. The habit of dealing with these incorporeal substances gives translators a good ability to attain high degrees of abstraction and to intuitively perceive relationships which are not obvious on the surface. Ghostly relationships are moving around almost imperceptibly in the ether; it is our task to identify and catch them, pin them down, then radically demolish them and reassemble them into an equivalent in the target language.[1]

This is a brilliant description of the experience of translating between "typologically diverse languages," but it is also alien to the everyday life of anyone but an experienced translator, or perhaps even to the everyday life of the translator, as the opening words of the passage suggest. Translation as an act is itself so foreign, you might say, that we feel compelled to domesticate it. We accomplish this through metaphors, by anchoring translation firmly in the "world of material objects," "the spatio-temporal system" outside of which the translator operates at the moment she is translating, speaking about translation as something that takes place between two languages, two cultures, two nations.

Translation comes from the Latin word *translatus*, the past participle of *transferre*, which might be translated as "carried across." We speak of translating *from* one language *into* another language, and translation is often described as a "bridge" between languages, cultures, nations. Both the notion of translation as something that takes place in an "in-between" place and the particular metaphor of the bridge are so common, and cleave so well both to the etymology of the word "translation" itself and to the spatial metaphors implicit in the language we use when we speak of translation (again: we translate *from* one language *into* another), that at times it seems almost impossible to think of translation in any other way. And this mode of thinking about translation is, indeed, ubiquitous: it figures in translators' discussions of translation, in the pleasantly optimistic advertisements of translation agencies, and in theoretically sophisticated treatments of translation of the sort one might read for a course on translation studies. I'll give you a few examples of what I mean, from writers who are using the metaphor to very good effect in very different ways.

> Translation is not the transfer of a detachable "meaning" from one language to another. It is a dialogue between two languages. It takes place in a space between two languages. And most often also between two historical moments. Much of the real value of translation as an art comes from that unique situation. It is not exclusively the language of arrival or the time of the translator and reader that should be privileged. We all know, in the case of *War and Peace*, that we are reading a nineteenth-century Russian novel: it should not read as if it was written yesterday in English.[2]

> By the very nature of things translation is a bridge between two languages, and if we speak of the problem of translation with regard to the literature of one particular language we appear to be dealing solely with either a beginning or an end, rather than with an entire process.[3]

> Translation is a bridge between cultures.[4]

All these quotations, and their invocation of spatial metaphors—the idea of the translator's or the translation's in-betweenness, the suggestion that translators and translations serve as bridges—dovetail neatly with the metaphors we use when we talk about language and "communication" (which itself contains a spatial metaphor): "Did you get my meaning?" "Did you catch what she said?" "Am I getting through to you?" "I hope I'm conveying myself." Translation is represented, then, in the quotations I just listed, as a version of communication that takes place between two languages, cultures, and nations, rather than between two people. But there is no analogy whatsoever. When a translator sits down at her computer to translate, she is alone. There is no communication happening. Indeed, there is no transfer of a message *from* one language *into* another, because from the perspective of the translator at the precise moment she is translating, she is not between languages, and her languages are not separate. We might say, rather, that she is saturated with two languages—that she is a node for two languages. Both languages are living inside her, in the same place, at the same time, in constantly shifting concentrations and configurations. She is not a bridge; she is something like a ghost.

And this is the antidote I would like to suggest to our habitual, perhaps unintended but nonetheless inappropriate metaphorical representation of translation as another version of communication: not a move away from metaphor, an attempt to clarify what happens when a translator translates, but a shift from the metaphor of the bridge to that of the ghost. Rather than imagine the translator as someone who stands between languages, cultures, and nations, we would do better to cultivate an image of him as a ghost who haunts languages, cultures, and nations, existing in two worlds at once but belonging fully to neither. The translator, as a ghost, is neither wholly domestic nor wholly foreign, because he is simultaneously both foreign and domestic; she is neither entirely visible nor entirely invisible to those who stand in one world or the other, even in the finished form of her product, because she is in their world but not of it. The translator, as a ghost, sees languages not as discrete, autonomous, unproblematically present unities but as—what else?—ghostly signs or echoes of each other. I began by noting that the word "translation" is always haunted by other words in other languages that could be used to translate it, or for which it might itself be used as a translation, but of course those "other words" are most clearly visible, clustering around, merging and separating, to the translator, for whom the "other languages" are never really "other," or fully "mine," just as English is never really "mine" or fully "other," and just as English and those "other" languages are never fully "other" to each other.

Conceiving of translation as a ghostly activity, rather than as a bridge—taking as a fresh point of departure the haunted, haunting experience of being simultaneously within two languages, cultures, and nations but belonging fully to neither—does not mean cutting translation off from the world, from economics, from global or domestic politics. It means reconsidering the relationship of translation to the world, economics, global and domestic politics, and so on from the perspective of a practice that cannot readily be assimilated to dreary nationalist narratives. From the point of view of the translator, translation should never have been conceptualized as something that takes place between two languages, cultures, and nations, because that is just the opposite of what it is: translation *doesn't* "take place," it is something translators do, and it isn't done between languages and cultures, it is done in languages, by people in whom languages and cultures merge. When translators translate, moreover, we work with and within two or more particular languages. If translation can be conceived of as a node, a ghostly act performed at a point of linguistic and cultural intersection, then the nature of the node is inevitably defined by the merging of *particular* languages and cultures.

Considering "translation" from the vantage of an individual translator, seeing it caught up in a flurry of different versions of itself, each one trailing its own history, allows one to settle on one's own working definition of the word, recognizing that no definition will ever be more than provisional. One might formulate a definition specific to the particular languages a translator engages with, emphasizing problems and issues that another translator who deals with different languages might never confront, or even imagine. One might define the word in a manner relevant to a given genre—translating a novel from one language to another is not the same, after all, as translating a cookbook or subtitling a movie. Or one might acknowledge that the notion of translation as an act performed only at the confluence of different languages is itself somewhat limited, and focus instead, for instance, on forms. Translating a script for performance may well require a different approach from translating a script for publication in a literary magazine. Translating a printed book into Braille is not the same as translating a poem from Punjabi into Swedish. Translating Dante Gabriel Rossetti's complete writings and pictures into the form of a hypermedia archive is not the same as translating 138 penciled note cards into a facsimile codex edition of Vladimir

Nabokov's *The Original of Laura*. And yet each of these different acts is, or could be considered, an instance of translation.

I myself define translation, very simply, as any change wrought upon a piece of writing intended to make it accessible to a new audience with particular needs or preferences. This is an extremely broad definition. But from my perspective as a scholar-translator who works with Japanese books, it seems an appropriate one. Or rather, I suspect that for all its malleability, this definition feels right to me precisely because I am a scholar-translator who works with Japanese books. The particular nature of its breadth, the direction its openness takes, betray the influence of my experiences with the languages I know, above all the two languages I translate from: Japanese and classical Japanese. Not everyone will agree that *The Original of Laura* or the Rossetti Archive can or should be considered translations; my engagement with Japanese literature, especially literature in classical Japanese, is a large part of the reason I do.

The Japanese language has a long history. For most of that history, writing of the sort we would now describe as "literature" circulated exclusively in handwritten copies. Woodblock printing found its way into Japan as early as the eighth century, but until the seventeenth century its use was reserved for texts deemed more valuable than mere fiction. *The Tale of Genji*, for instance, which was completed in the early eleventh century, survived for its first six hundred years only because members of the elite and their scribes kept transcribing it, each in their own calligraphic style. Then, at the start of the seventeenth century, fictional works, including *The Tale of Genji*, began to be printed and sold in woodblock editions. These new printed books could be mass produced, unlike the old labor-intensive transcriptions, but because the blocks were handcarved from manuscripts, essentially they were facsimiles of handwritten, calligraphic copies. If a person wanted to read a printed edition of *The Tale of Genji* or any other work, she still had to be able to read calligraphy.

This situation changed dramatically in the final decades of the nineteenth century, when moveable type rapidly supplanted woodblock printing. People soon grew accustomed to reading typeset text, and schoolchildren no longer learned to read the calligraphic forms of earlier ages, whether written by hand with a brush or printed from woodblocks. And so it became necessary to reprint early works of literature in the new form of the typeset book. In 1890, the first typeset editions of *The Tale of Genji* were published in Japan, and new ones have been appearing ever since. These days, apart from a tiny group of specialists, hardly anyone would ever try to read *The Tale of Genji* in a calligraphic form, whether handwritten or printed, for the simple reason that they couldn't. That old, calligraphic Japanese is utterly illegible to the vast majority of modern readers, even those rare souls who have a good knowledge of classical Japanese grammar and vocabulary. In order for modern readers to read *The Tale of Genji*, they need to have it transcribed into a recognizable form: the familiar, typeset Japanese of novels, signs, and menus. They need, in short, to have it translated—even when they can understand the language of the original.

But just what does that mean? What are we referring to when we speak of "the language of the original"? If someone were to read a sentence from a calligraphic copy of *The Tale of Genji* aloud, then read the same sentence from a typeset transcription, the two readings would sound the same. And yet most readers of classical Japanese would find the calligraphic copy illegible, and have no problem whatsoever reading the transcription. The two texts are the same, then—they are written in the same language—precisely to the extent that we ignore the visual form of the writing. They can be said to be the same, and to be written in the same language, only if we agree to ignore a difference so significant as to make one text legible and the other illegible.

The tendency to conceive of language phonocentrically and in terms of grammar and syntax, independent from its material forms, has deep roots and a long history, and it is hard to shake. My experiences with modern and classical Japanese, however, have impressed upon me just how much writing *matters*. I find it hard to ignore not only the visual element of writing, the marks on the page, but also its broader spatial dimensions: the physicality of paper itself, and of the book. Translation, as I understand it—as I define it for myself—is not simply an act of engagement with language as grammar and syntax, as mere recorded speech; when I translate, the original to which I address myself is not a specimen of Japanese language heard in my inner ear, but a piece of Japanese writing, a collection of pages, a Japanese publication.

In 2005, I published a translation of a novel by Akasaka Mari called *Vibrator*. About halfway through the book, the narrator, a woman with various psychological troubles who is riding from Tokyo up to northern

Japan in the cab of a truck driver she barely knows, finds herself gazing out the window into the night:

> Once more I looked at the map. Route 353 went around the southern side of the mountain. The shrine must be up at the peak, and that gateway we went under earlier must have been the outermost, the one that marks the entrance. The air down at sea level had been dry, but now that we were at a higher altitude I noticed tiny crystals drifting through the air, here and there, glittering. I kept gazing out at these crystals, and then after a while little white things started appearing, mixed in among the crystals. The white things soared through the air, weaving between the crystals as they dropped. And as I moved through these white flakes, it came to seem as if I were in a tube or a tunnel or something, cut off from the me I had been previously—here I was, moving within this space. Something before me leapt into action. The wipers had come on. It felt as if the meaning of the movement had seeped out from somewhere, that was how I understood it, and then gradually, ever so gradually, I began to remember my body.
> . . . . it's snow.
> The words appeared inside my mouth as if they had come bobbing up from an ancient layer of memory. I said them again: spoke the words clearly now, aloud. "It's snow." But then, as I continued staring out into the snow, the word "snow" started breaking apart—it disintegrated into s n o and w and the force that had hung there between the four letters, the force that had held them all together, was gone now, and there was no way to retrieve it. I no longer understood why s n o and w had been linked in that way, or why this was the name for that white stuff falling in front of me. Oh, OK, I get it. It's because the things linking them have disintegrated, that's why they're so dry and swishy and flaky, that's why they tumble down over everything—maybe.[5]

This passage is fascinating, in part, precisely because it deals with the materiality of language. The word "snow" has a physical dimension, and it can be broken down into its constituent parts. The disintegration of the word "snow" into the letters "s n o and w" is bound up, moreover, with the narrator's mental state—she is falling apart *like* the word, *together* with the word.

Japanese is not written with the Roman alphabet. When the English word "snow" falls apart, disintegrating "into s n o and w," it falls apart differently from the Japanese word for snow. Japanese makes use of two syllabaries called *hiragana* and *katakana* and a large number of ideographs known as *kanji*. In Japanese, words can generally be written in any of these three forms. The word "snow," for instance, which is pronounced "yuki," is most often written with the *kanji* 雪, but it can also be written in *hiragana* as ゆき or in *katakana* as ユキ. The *kanji* 雪, being an ideograph, inevitably calls up the particular meaning "snow." Since the *hiragana* and *katakana* forms represent only the sound "yuki," they are not tied to a fixed meaning. In the Japanese original of *Vibrator*, when the narrator first notices that "it's snow," her thought is expressed, not in *kanji*, but in *hiragana*: ゆきだ. In English, she goes on to explain that "the word 'snow' started breaking apart—it disintegrated into s n o and w." A bilingual translation of this same phrase in the original might look like this: "the word '雪' started breaking apart—it disintegrated into ゆ and き." Here the *kanji*, expressing both meaning and sound, is not itself broken down; it is first transformed into units of sound that do not in themselves have any meaning, and the narrator then loses her sense of "force that had hung there between the *two syllables*." In English, a word that has both sound and meaning is itself broken down into letters that have neither sound nor meaning. The relationship between sound, writing, and meaning is different in the Japanese and the English. Language hangs together, and falls apart, differently in the two languages. And the narrator, who falls apart with her language, falls apart differently in the original and the translation. In re-creating this passage in English, then, I had to translate one system of relationships between sound, writing, and meaning into another. In order for this passage to make sense, I had to deal, not just with the words, but with the words on the page—the very *thingness* of language itself.

As it happens, this same passage plays directly on the material, visual form of the words on the page. Novels in Japanese are usually read from right to left, and the text is printed vertically. English, needless to say, is printed horizontally and is read from left to right. Translation from English and various Western European languages has been so important in Japan that the act of translation is often described synecdochically with the phrase "from horizontal to vertical" or, in the case of Japanese–English translation, "from vertical to horizontal." My translation of *Vibrator* is an instance of the spatial, linguistic shift "from vertical to horizontal." This is especially apparent in the passage I have been discussing. The sentence that I translated as:

. . . . it's snow.

looks like this in Japanese:

゜
゜
゜
゜
゜
゜
゜
゜
゜
゜
゜
゜
゜
゜
゜
゜
゜
゜
ゆ
き
だ

In both Japanese and English, the printed sentence itself suggests not only the time that passes as the narrator, gradually beginning "to remember my body," remembers too what the white flakes drifting through the air around the truck are—but also, visually, materially, the snowflakes themselves. In Japanese, the snow is falling. In English, the snowflakes are whipping past the window as the truck tunnels through the darkness. It occurs to me that here, in the overlapping of these two sentences, translation and original, we might discover a visual representation of the act of translation. A depiction of translation not as a crossing over—not as something that takes place in an in-between state—but as an activity that a ghostly, disembodied translator does in the unstable, shifting confluence of the languages she lives within. In a place with no dimensions, a point of intersection, fleeting as a snowflake, falling through time, through history, mysterious and unique.

Part I: The Translator in the World

. . . . it's snow.

ゆきだ

Notes

1. Donald Philippi, "Translating Between Typologically Diverse Languages," *Meta* 34, no. 4 (1989): 680–681.

2. Richard Pevear, quoted in "Trials of the translator," a letter to the editor in the *Times Literary Supplement,* February 8, 2008.

3. Paul F. Guenther, "Faithful Ugliness or Faithless Beauty: The Translator's Problem," *The German Quarterly* 35, no. 4 (1962): 504.

4. This is the motto of GB Language Consulting in New York. See http://gblanguage.com/aboutus.aspx.

5. Mari Akasaka, *Vibrator*, trans. Michael Emmerich (London: Faber & Faber, 2005), 72–73.

FIVE

Translation as Scholarship

CATHERINE PORTER

In 2007, an MLA report on foreign languages and higher education rec-
ommended that departments develop programs in translation and interpretation, and explained why: "There is a great unmet demand for educated translators and interpreters, and translation is an ideal context
for developing translingual and transcultural abilities as an organizing
principle of the language curriculum."[1] This recommendation takes on
particular weight when viewed in light of a 2006 MLA report on evaluating scholarship for tenure and promotion which concluded that "[t]he
profession as a whole should develop a more capacious conception of
scholarship by rethinking the dominance of the monograph, promoting
the scholarly essay, establishing multiple pathways to tenure, and using
scholarly portfolios."[2] Taken together, these two reports suggest that the
profession has much to gain from encouraging institutional support for
translation as scholarship. If we agree that our institutions should help
meet the demand for educated translators and interpreters, we must make
room for translation studies in our curricula and develop a more capacious understanding of translation as a scholarly pursuit. It is my belief
that scholarly and literary translations should be accepted and evaluated
on the same basis as scholarly monographs in decisions about hiring,
promotion, and tenure.

The task doesn't promise to be easy: translators tend to have rather bad
press. In May 2009, a *Newsweek* article describing Douglas Hofstadter's
new translation of a book by Françoise Sagan observed that "[i]n the

literary world, translators are low in the pecking order."[3] Brief and super-ficial though it is, the *Newsweek* piece highlights the double bind in which translators regularly find themselves. If they hew closely to the source text and produce a seemingly transparent reproduction, their work is taken for granted, written off as mechanical, derivative, something any-one could do. If they become "co-generators" of the target-language text, if they "take liberties" and allow their own interpretations to become per-ceptible in that text (as Hofstadter chose to do), their work is declared untrue to the original author's "intent," condemned as unfaithful, dis-missed as a pastiche. On this bipolar view of the options, translators are obliged to choose between servitude—which will mean their work is perceived as transparent, while they themselves remain invisible—and collaboration—which will bring them criticism for asserting their role in shaping a new text. To my mind this is a false dichotomy, a facile and hopelessly oversimplified representation of the alternatives available to a translator. Serving the text and collaborating with its author are only two among the many, sometimes conflicting, responsibilities that a translator has to weigh and juggle.

Let me offer a little more anecdotal evidence of negative notice and of a situation that translators encounter even more frequently, that is, no notice whatsoever. Some years ago, a professor of German at Columbia University who had already published his translation of an important collection of poems under his own name, chose to publish his translation of Thomas Bernhard's *The Loser* under a pseudonym. When asked why he had done this, he explained that he was untenured at the time and had been advised by senior colleagues that too many translations on his CV would compromise his chances in the tenure review process.[4]

At an MLA convention a couple of years ago, when I queried a repre-sentative of Duke University Press about the presentation of a particu-lar book, he explained that the translator's name did not appear on the dust cover or in the catalog copy because translations don't sell as well as original works.

In late February 2009, a *New York Times* article featured Europa Edi-tions, a five-year-old publishing house in New York that has been suc-cessfully marketing foreign literature in translation.[5] Five authors and titles were cited in the article, but not one translator was mentioned; in-deed, the word "translator" never appeared at all.

The bias that *Newsweek* attributes to the literary world holds sway all too often in academia as well, with some paradoxical variants. In the academy, translators of literary works may be low on the pecking order in part because of a belief among literary scholars that language of a certain density or poeticity is ultimately untranslatable, so that any translation of a recognized work of literature is by definition an inadequate, impoverished, or degraded replica of the original. At the same time, translators of scholarly works are held in little esteem because of a corollary assumption that expository prose is necessarily straightforward and unproblematic, its referential content easily transferred intact from one language to another.

Dismissive or negative assumptions about translation indeed seem to permeate our culture. We've all heard the clichés. To translate is to betray: *traduttore traditore*. Translators should be invisible. Translation is impossible. Theorists and historians of translation have speculated widely about reasons for the low status of translators and their work. Tradition has it that, in the third century B.C.E., some seventy scholars were charged with translating the Torah from Hebrew into Greek. Working independently, they produced identical texts, the version known as the Septuagint. This familiar story lends itself to at least two incompatible readings. First, since translation is a strictly mechanical activity, any number of people in possession of the same two languages can translate from one to the other with exactly the same results. Second, accurate translation is impossible without divine intervention and guidance; the individual translator is merely a passive vessel through which sacred texts can be conveyed, and the convergence of seventy-odd versions is proof of a miracle.

In either case, the Septuagint story supports the view that every text has a single, true, original meaning. This meaning itself takes on a sacred aspect: in a successful translation, it must be grasped and transferred intact at all costs. Thus translation can be perceived as a treacherous act: it may corrupt the meaning of the original, it may endanger the recipients in some way, or it may betray secrets or misrepresent knowledge belonging to the community of origin. Perhaps to forestall the danger of corruption, some religious traditions—including both Judaism and Islam—transmit the ability to read the sacred texts in the original language from one generation to the next. Douglas Robinson alludes to the second danger, a threat to the recipient, in his book *Translation and Taboo* when he evokes George Steiner's exploration, in *After Babel*, of "the ban on translation in the ancient mystery religions," and hypothesizes that "a person in antiquity who was *able* to translate a sacred text into another language would have been *afraid* to do so without various ritual or ceremonial precautions and without careful control over target readers' access to the finished product."[6] As for the third danger, the betrayal or misrepresentation of privileged information, Robinson relates an encounter with a contemporary Native American group that explicitly opposes translation of certain of its texts.[7]

Another factor that may help account for the translator's peculiar status can be found in our own Anglophone cultural history. In his book *The Translator's Invisibility*, Lawrence Venuti traces the development of an ideology of fluency and transparency in the Anglo-American tradition of literary translation from the seventeenth century through the present day. He shows that this tendency is paralleled by an individualistic conception of authorship in which writing is understood to produce "an original and transparent self-representation, unmediated by transindividual determinants (linguistic, cultural, social) that might complicate authorial originality."[8] In this view, every translation is doubly inauthentic: it may not lay claim to originality, and it must not manifest any self-representation on the part of the translator. Servitude becomes the rule; any sign of translatorial collaboration with the author is to be repressed or condemned.

Interestingly, institutions of higher education, which are expressly devoted to the creation and transmission of knowledge, have in fact built into their organization and prevailing discourse assumptions about the value of translation and translators that belie some of these negative biases. Literary scholars acknowledge at least implicitly that translation is a defining condition of our field, a crucial form of rewriting that links our own work and the works we study to a vast array of other works, no matter how remote in space or time. Theorists in several disciplines have problematized the concept of authorial originality and dislodged the notion that every text has a single, sacred, original meaning. In departments of comparative literature and others, literary works are routinely taught in translation (though the fact of translation too often goes unmentioned or unexamined). In all fields, the need for translation of primary literature and important scholarly work is understood to be crucial for scholarly interchange and the global development of bodies of knowledge. University presses make studied decisions about which books to publish in translation. A peer-review process typically comes into play at three different points: in the selection of the book, in the selection of the translator, and in the prepublication assessment of the completed translation. In recent decades, increasing attention to translation theory in academia has provided telling insights into the problematics of translation, its practice as a form of scholarly understanding, its function as an indispensable instrument in transnational research and scholarship, and its contributions as lens and mirror in the study of culture. In response to growing student interest, translation courses and programs have been introduced into the undergraduate curriculum at an increasing number of institutions. Yet the practice of translation itself is still rarely acknowledged as a legitimate form of scholarly activity. Is the exclusion of translation a defensible practice, or, rather, the effect of a lingering bias that can be overcome?

Consider what translators actually do, once they have identified a text they deem worthy of translation—and this is a complex process in itself that demands knowledge, experience, and discernment. To begin with, a translator has to make a whole array of judgments. Literary and scholarly translation alike entail not just a transfer of meaning but a thoroughgoing recontextualization. In what contexts—literary, rhetorical, social, historical, political, economic, religious, cultural—was the source text embedded, and what adjustments will have to be made to transmit those contexts or produce comparable ones in the translation? Where does the source text fall on a continuum that might be characterized in shorthand terms as running between a poem and a laundry list? Does it belong to an identifiable genre or tradition, and is there a corresponding genre or tradition in the target literature? To what extent and in what ways is the source text innovative or deviant in its own cultural context, and how can these innovative or deviant aspects be represented in the target text? What aims and effects can be attributed to the original, and what aims and effects is the translation intended to serve, what effects to produce? What was the nature of the original audience, and how can the anticipated new audience be characterized? What range of voices, registers, and subject positions can be identified in the source text, and what adaptations will be required to render these in the target language? Once these initial determinations are made—subject to revision and refinement as the translation progresses—the translator can begin to engage with the text itself: word by word, phrase by phrase, sentence by sentence.

Each of the questions I've just raised could lend itself, of course, to extensive development and illustration; I offer here only a few glimpses into the process based on my own experience as a translator of scholarly works in the humanities and social sciences, starting with some broad issues of contextualization.

Over the years, I've become acutely aware of a set of cultural features specific to the publishing process in France. Where scholarly books are concerned, the pace of production tends to be far more rapid than in the United States. A professor of philosophy, for example, may pull together the previous year's lecture notes and transcribe them for submission as a book. If the author is well known, an editor may accept the manuscript without outside evaluation. Many publishing houses do not use copyeditors, so the book is likely to go into production pretty much unchanged. The cumulative effect of this culturally specific situation poses several types of challenges for the Anglophone translator. I give three examples:

First, a scholarly book based on lecture notes often bears marks of its origins in oral discourse: most notably, in the French context, a tendency toward repetition. On the basis of my assessment of the particular writer's attention to language and of my sense of the expectations of the target audience, I must decide whether to keep repetitions of this sort in the translation, modify them (by varying the vocabulary and phrasing, for example), or eliminate them altogether.

Second, the speed of publication and the centralization of French intellectual life in Paris combine to allow a kind of ongoing dialogue to take place in book form, much the way scientific dialogue takes place in article form. Members of the cultivated public and its disciplinary subgroups in France tend to read the same books (or book reviews), see the same talking heads on television, follow the fortunes of public intellectuals as schools of thought wax and wane. This participation can lead to highly allusive discourse that is essentially unintelligible to outsiders unfamiliar with the key players, and it can also lead to startling shifts in register between abstract argument and personal attack or diatribe. The translator must first of all be well enough versed in the intellectual milieu in question to read between the lines and then must figure out how to bring the new audience into the conversation.

Third, in the absence of a copyeditor to enforce styling conventions and ask authors to supply missing information, it falls to the translator to fill in the gaps. One of my recent translations, Maurice Sartre's *The Middle East Under Rome*, has 2,852 endnotes and a bibliography 87 pages long. The library research alone took about six months.

Another cultural difference, on a horizon that some would label political correctness, turned out to be critical in my translation of Patrick

Weil's *Qu'est-ce qu'un Français?* (*How to Be French*). The book traces the history of French nationality legislation from the Revolution forward. During much of this period, women and men were treated differently under the law: for instance, between 1804 and 1927, a French woman automatically lost French nationality if she married a foreigner; a French man did not. Now, in French, the masculine plural pronoun *ils* is still used indiscriminately to refer either to two or more male figures or to a group including both sexes. So I repeatedly had to ask the author whether women were included or not in a given statement, and adjust the translation accordingly.

Turning finally to the sort of challenge that the translation of a single lexical item can present, I draw upon my unpublished translation of a book called *Éloge de la trahison* ("In Praise of Betrayal").[9] In this set of reflections based on personal experience, Sylvie Durastanti exposes some of the critical moments and fundamental dilemmas that arise in the process of transposing a literary work from one language and cultural context to another. As I worked through this book, I set out to analyze my own translation process, devoting four pages to the opening eight-word sentence alone. Here I'll narrow the focus to the final word:

> *Traduire, c'est éprouver que les mots manquent.*
> To translate is to find that words are wanting.

The verb *manquer* can mean "to be lacking, absent, missing," "to be missed," and "to lack, to fall short, to be deficient." "Missing" is not a perfect match; it might suggest that words that were once present have somehow disappeared, have been lost, mislaid, confiscated. "Lacking" preserves at least two of the source term's meanings: (1) some words, some of the words a translator needs, are missing, unavailable, nonexistent; and (2) some words, or even words in general, in the target language lack certain features that would make them perfect equivalents for words in the source language. "Wanting" does the same work; the online *American Heritage Dictionary* defines the adjective succinctly as (1) "absent, lacking," and (2) "not measuring up to standards or expectations." Its use in conjunction with the verb "find" reinforces the second meaning by evoking an expression with biblical overtones, "found wanting." Understood in this sense, "wanting" introduces into the English text the idea of testing and some of the associated affect (suffering from disappointment, a sense of failure) that is conveyed by the French *éprouver* but lost in the choice of "find." There is also a possible reading in which words take on agency, have wants or desires of their own. A phonological factor, finally, is the clincher. "Wanting" has a decided aesthetic advantage over "lacking," in that its alliteration with "word" parallels the repetition of the initial *m* in French. For while Durastanti's book unquestionably belongs to a broad class of texts that can be categorized as expository prose, it is more specifically a lyric essay.[10] Its prose is carefully wrought, highly self-conscious in its cadenced phrasings and extensive use of metaphor. Durastanti's writing commands attention not only for its rhetorical structures and cognitive content but also for its poetic features.

The close reading that I've excerpted here illustrates the aspect of the translator's invisible work that requires both an intuitive and an analytic command of the interlocking features and structures of two language systems. The passage chosen also helps, I hope, to blur the distinction between literary and nonliterary texts. One cannot posit a simple dichotomy between works that privilege artistic form and those that privilege the communicative function, if one is to do justice to a text like Durastanti's, or, indeed, to a great many texts in the humanities and social sciences.

Once a literary or scholarly text has been deemed worthy of translation, the skilled scholar-translator is bound to become its most intimate reader, an exemplary interpreter who brings to bear prior knowledge of the field, thoroughgoing mastery of at least two languages and cultures, plus highly developed research skills and a healthy measure of critical acumen.

Our academic lives are structured by personnel policies and procedures that reinforce a tendency to view our work in terms of another overly simplistic dichotomy: we see scholarship as the creation of new knowledge, teaching as the transmission of knowledge to students. If we look closely, however, at what has actually counted as scholarship over time, we find that scholars can also be recognized when they create, make accessible, and/or transmit knowledge by way of textual criticism, scholarly editions, annotated bibliographies, edited anthologies, and so on. Like these latter endeavors, translation pulls scholarship in an outward direction, with less emphasis on knowledge creation for its own sake, more emphasis on identifying, interpreting, and conveying valuable works of literature or scholarship to a community of peers and to the public at large. Scholars have always depended on, and built on, the work of others. Unless we believe that the only literature worth reading and the only scholarship of value are produced in English and perhaps in the handful of other languages that we happen to know, we need to acknowledge that reliable translations produced by accomplished scholar-translators are crucial to the continuing development of our fields. Once we have done that, we should be ready to rewrite our personnel policies so as to recognize these scholar-translators as full-fledged colleagues and evaluate their work accordingly.

Notes

1. MLA Ad Hoc Committee on Foreign Languages, "Foreign Languages and Higher Education: New Structures for a Changed World" (May 23, 2007), http://www.mla.org/flreport.

2. MLA Task Force on Evaluating Scholarship for Tenure and Promotion, "Report of the MLA Task Force on Evaluating Scholarship for Tenure and Promotion," in *Profession 2007* (New York: MLA, 2007), 9–17.

3. Tony Dokoupil, "Pardon My French: You Suck at This," *Newsweek* (May 11/May 18, 2009), 10.

4. The professor of German I allude to here, Mark Anderson, has publicly acknowledged these facts. See Jennifer Howard, "Translators Struggle to Prove Their Academic Bona Fides," *The Chronicle of Higher Education*, January 17, 2010.

5. Motoko Rich, "Europa Editions Finds Success Translating Literary Novels," *New York Times*, Feb. 25, 2009, http://www.nytimes.com/2009/02/26/books/26europa.html.

6. Douglas Robinson, *Translation and Taboo* (DeKalb: Northern Illinois University Press, 1986), 48.

7. Robinson, *Translation and Taboo*, 171–75.

8. Lawrence Venuti, *The Translator's Invisibility* (London: Routledge, 1995), 6.

9. Sylvie Durastanti, *Éloge de la trahison* (Paris: Le Passage, 2002).

10. For a definition, see Deborah Tall, Editor and John D'Agata, Associate Editor for Lyric Essays, *Seneca Review*, http://www.hws.edu/academics/community/senecareview/lyricessay.asp.

Six

Translation

The Biography of an Artform

ALICE KAPLAN

For a long time, I've thought about writing a book on translation. What interests me is the possibility of accounting for the lived experience of translators—those silent agents of literary history. I'm equally intrigued by the complex relationship between writers and translators. And while there are many theories of translation, very little has been written about the everyday psychology of translating.

The possibilities for both real and imaginary relations between translator and author are endless: they may become lovers, enemies, rivals, or traitors to each other's cause. When everyone gets along, when translator and author negotiate smoothly, when the editor serves as a guarantor of rights on both sides, translation can be an extremely satisfying undertaking for both author and translator, in which each feels fulfilled and grateful to the other. But when something goes wrong, a translation conflict can be exceedingly complex and difficult to resolve.

The kind of conflict I am alluding to is often merely a hypothetical drama on our minds as we, the translators, go about our workaday business. The dilemma takes place within ourselves, and we resolve it by the time the work of translation is finished. But what happens when the conflict is not merely theoretical, a working principle, but breaks out into an actual fight between two or more of the parties involved? I enjoyed an article I read several years ago by an excellent translator called "The Only Good Author Is a Dead Author," explaining the headaches she had working with a difficult and demanding author. And I've recently heard about the troubles of a translator whose author—a Japanese essayist of great renown—insisted on continually revising his work. Just as the translator would finish a draft of an essay, the author would send an entirely new version of the text, demanding a retranslation. The translator was Sisyphus, except that the boulder changed shape each time he had to lug it up the hill.

There are many stories of prominent writers who insist on challenging the translations of their work into languages they barely know. Writers want to control language—this is their job—and they're only too ready to believe that their talent for words extends across all linguistic boundaries. Vladimir Nabokov was famous for his vigilance concerning every word of his translations—and when this polyglot spotted an error, he could be unreasonable. His wife Véra, as vigilant as he, pored over the Swedish translations of his *Pnin* with the help of a dictionary and determined that entire passages were missing, and that the anticommunist slant of the original had been muted. She ordered the entire Swedish stock of both *Pnin* and *Lolita* destroyed. In July 1959, the Nabokovs' lawyer served as witness to an enormous book burning on the outskirts of Stockholm.[1] It's a rare event in literary history when a writer burns his own books.

The problems that translators have with living authors are well known, and we can understand what it means to want to work on a writer whose life's work is complete, and who is no longer around to pass judgment on a translation. Fortunately, there are many dead authors who have yet to be translated. And unfortunately, the opposite can never be true: a dead author can have a living translator, but no living author can ever work with a dead translator. Some would like to!

A Translation Fiasco

The following story about a very living translator is a rather personal one, and, in retrospect, it's amusing to recount. But it is also instructive, and I believe it can shed light on the problems I've outlined above.

I'll call my translator, in the interests of privacy, "Mr. X." Mr. X was hired by a French publisher to translate my book, *French Lessons*, an autobiographical essay about an American who falls in love with the French language. As in all such stories, the path of my love for French was not always a smooth one. Nor, as it turned out, was the path of translation. I should preface this story by explaining that Mr. X had an excellent reputation as a translator of social science—history in particular—and that he was an exacting, detail-oriented translator who was used to working closely with his authors. Translation was his only source of income, and he had an ongoing relationship with a powerful editor at this particular publishing house; this editor had imposed him on the more junior editor who had acquired my book.

There was an implicit difficulty in translating my book into French which any translator would have to have faced. In the original English, it presented the French language as an object of desire, a coveted and foreign language world that resisted being conquered. The French language, you might say, is a character in the book—or, to use another metaphor, the book's landscape. French words and sounds occur within the text, in their otherness. About a first trip, to boarding school in Switzerland, the young adolescent narrator writes:

> The driver came in a Mercedes van. He looked like a soccer player. He said to me in French: "Don't try to speak to me in English because I don't understand." He was testing me. He said, "Where are your bags?" The word came up from my throat. "Là-bas," I said, pointing. (45)

or

> The French have a verb for the kind of work I did at the Swiss school: bosser, which comes from a word meaning "hunched" and means hunkering down to work, bending down over some precious matter and observing it. (56)

The translator who would have to render this otherness in French itself—where the French words would no longer stand out from the rest of the words in the book—was facing a challenge. It wasn't clear that the "mirror" would work: i.e., would French readers be interested in the experience of an American learning their language? Or was the book only readable to an American reader who could identify with the difficulties of an American trying to learn a foreign language? There are ways to handle this—putting words in quotation marks or all caps to make them stand out from the text, using phonetic or at least nonstandard spelling to indicate an American accent in French, or perhaps even adding some American words to the French text to represent the two language worlds.

Mr. X's first response to the book was wild enthusiasm. He was excited to be doing his first literary translation. He fantasized an enormous commercial success for my book, and media stardom for me—thanks to him—complete with an appearance on Bernard Pivot's literary talk show, with his expert coaching to prepare me. From these ambitious and enthusiastic beginnings, things went quickly downhill. In order for my book to achieve this status, Mr. X was convinced it needed serious adaptation. It would not work, as it was, for a French public. He therefore set out to rewrite it, according to his idea of the image a French reader would want to have of an American learning French.

At the time I felt at a disadvantage: I had an immediate instinct that this was the wrong approach, but I did not have the scholarly ammunition to bolster my argument against my determined translator. I had not read much of the theoretical literature on translation. I needed a theorist to explain X's attitude, and to give me grounds on which to oppose him. I later found this theorist in Antoine Berman, author of *L'épreuve de l'étranger*, and *La traduction et la lettre ou l'auberge du lointain*.[2] He had a view of the relationship between author and translator that was respectful and nuanced and that felt right to me. Berman writes:

> J'appelle mauvaise traduction la traduction qui, généralement sous couvert de transmissibilité, opère une négation systématique de l'étrangeté de l'oeuvre étrangère.
>
> I call bad translation any translation which, using the pretext of transmissibility/communication, works towards a systematic negation of the foreignness of the foreign work.

Even though I don't always agree with Berman when it comes to his evaluation of specific translations—I think his defense of foreignness is exaggerated and often untenable—I relish this argument that makes Mr. X into the epitome of the ethically bad translator.

Not only was X an ethnocentric translator, he was an egocentric translator: the combination of nationalism and a certain psychology were fatal. "If I don't change the text as I'm translating it, I feel castrated," he explained. A sensitive fellow! Change the text he did. . . . He changed the order of sentences in a paragraph if he felt my construction wasn't French enough. He cut sentences he didn't agree with. He especially resented a sentence in the beginning of my book—which explained the minimalist style in which the book was written:

> My mother still corrects my English grammar, in speech and in writing: "to whom," not "to who"; "effective," not "affective," "he did well," but not "he is good." She corrects the number of times I use "very." She is against waste in language. Her sentences are short and blunt, yet ripe with innuendo and the promise that more is being said than meets the ear. Now I write in the staccato midwestern style she taught me. (7)

This "argument de style" he complained, was going to hamper *his* style. . . . He hadn't spent all those years at the rue d'Ulm honing an extremely sophisticated prose style, nourished by the best that had been written in French, from Chateaubriand to Proust, only to be forced to write like a monosyllabic halfwit. Yet my book actually talked about its own style: I, the author, was committed to straightforward, simple writing. I intended that my language sound more like an elementary French lesson than *Mémoires d'outre tombe*. . . . If Mr. X disobeyed the metacommentary on style within my book, his own prose would be wrong. This annoyed him greatly.

For all his resistance to my foreignness, Mr. X would occasionally surprise me with a plunge into American consciousness. There were two characters in *French Lessons*, my brother and sister, whom I did not mention by name. This was in part to protect their privacy, in part to give the early childhood section of the book the feeling of a fairy tale or myth, one step removed from documentary or history. My translator—obviously not a reader of Marguerite Duras!—explained to me that it was very ugly in French to refer to any characters as "il" and "elle"—indeed, this wasn't possible. Therefore he proposed to give them names, averting what he considered an embarrassing French mistake. He chose the names "Betsy" and "Joey" for my siblings. Why? He explained that his favorite American television show was *Friends* (on cable TV), and he wanted to use names from that show. There is a character named Joey on *Friends*, but no Betsy, as far as I know. Perhaps he was thinking of Betsy Ross, who sewed the first American flag—a figure every American schoolchild learns about. The ways of Mr. X were mysterious, but this, in any case, was his bow to representing American culture in my very American text.

He pointed out what he claimed were constant French mistakes in my discussions of my attempt to master the French language. "Trust me for the French," he kept saying. And "I will make you into a real French girl." The problem was, *French Lessons* is about the experience of someone who lives between languages—who wants to escape into French but never quite makes it. Transforming me into "a real French girl" was tantamount to being unfaithful to the book's essence and spirit. For the translation to be viable, the character I had created needed to be slightly foreign, between worlds: my translator resisted this foreignness, believing that it was his duty to naturalize me and render my book in authentic French.

If I wanted to give an affectionate account of this translator's mistake, I'd put it this way: I had created a character who wanted more than anything to be French. But instead of representing her desires, my translator was "solving" the character's problem, trying to fulfill her desires.

And so the process devolved: the more I fought his changes, the more critical he became of my own text. Finally, all communication between us ceased. He sent an erudite 14-page single-spaced critique of the book to my editor. I later learned that, as a social science translator, he had a track record of contentious relationships with authors, and the file drawers of my publisher contained several brilliant letters arguing against the books he was working on. But at the time I had no knowledge of his propensity for the attack.

What a long road he had taken, from being wildly enthusiastic about making my book his own to maligning it utterly. He refused to sign his own name to his translation and chose a pseudonym. And finally, I refused his translation. The press refused to commission a new translator, and the contract has since expired. What relief I felt! Mr. X had cured me of my desire to be translated.

Although my translator's reactions were extreme, caricatural, still I could recognize in his reactions experiences and feelings that I too have had as a translator.

I recognized, first of all, the intense critical response one can have to a book one is in the process of translating: we translators can love, but we can also see every flaw, every mistaken fact, every awkward transition in the work we are translating. I also recognized in him, again in exaggerated form, something we might call the "dépit amoureux" of the translator: the desire to get into the skin of a book, the desire to become its author—to create, not just translate. We translators ought to defend ourselves by claiming rights that are akin to rights of authorship: the right to innovate, the right to create, the right to be considered a writer, rather than merely a clerk. But translation is also, by definition, a crossing of boundaries—a stranger entering into a literary space and claiming it for himself. Here is where intangible emotions—love, envy, generosity, competition, and combat—come into play for the translator. X approached my text as a conqueror, and he violated my boundaries. And that experience, for this author, was something I can only describe as "creepy." . . .

When Translations Go to Court: The Case of France

In the course of my experience with X, I often asked myself, "What are my rights as an author?" and "What are his rights as a translator?" According to French law, my moral right as an author had precedence over his moral right as a translator. I had the last word and was able to say, "No, I refuse this translation." Still, his translation belongs to him, and I cannot use it as a basis for another translation of my book. If the book is ever to be translated, the translator will have to start from zero, and will not be able even to consult Mr. X's manuscript. On the other hand, Mr. X is unable, by law, to publish the manuscript of his work—it is his, but not his, because it is a translation.

The type of conflict I had with Mr. X can, and did, go far. In our case, it resulted in the cancellation of the contract. The intensity of our conflict made me curious about other cases of conflict between translator and author—and more generally, about the relationship that authors and translators have had, especially in this century with its sharply defined intellectual property rights.

Translation cases only rarely go to court, and when they do, the judgment is often usually financial, rather than literary. In combing French journals of intellectual property rights, I've found a very few cases where a court of law makes an aesthetic judgment for or against a translator. I'll outline two of these briefly:

In 1950, the employees of the Gibert Jeune Bookstore used the title *Les Hauts du Hurle-Vent* on a poster they hung over a table covered with sale copies of a translation of *Wuthering Heights*, a work which, for mysterious reasons, has been translated and retranslated countless times into French, with just as many attempts to translate the title alone: *Les Hauts des Quatre-Vents* (1935); *Le Domaine des Tempêtes* (1959); *Les Hautes des*

Tempêtes (1950) *Haute Plainte* (1937); *Les Hauteurs battues des vents* (1950); *Les Hauteurs tourmentées* (1949); *Heurtebise* (1947); *La Maison des vents* (1942); *La Maison maudite* (1948); *Les orages du coeur* (1950); *Le Château des Tempêtes* (1951). A number of French translators have simply used the original title, *Wuthering Heights*: Louise Servicen in 1947; Henri Picard in 1948; Albert Glorget in 1949; Gaston Bacarra in 1950 (about whom more below); Jean Talva in 1955; Geneviève Mecker in 1959; Henriette Guex-Rolle in 1968; Catherine and Georges Vertut in 1969.

The problem in the case that went to court was that the translation Gibert Jeune was selling was not Frédéric Delebecque's 1925 *Les Hauts du Hurle-Vent*: it was Gaston Bacarra's 1950 translation, which used the original English language title, *Wuthering Heights*. The bookstore was exploiting the fact that most French people had come to identify the Emily Brontë novel by the title *Les Hauts du Hurle-Vent*. With all the titles that existed in France for Emily Brontë's novel, *Les Hauts du Hurle-Vent* had stuck.

In deciding against the bookstore, and for the publisher of Frédéric Delebecque's translation, the Editions Payot, who held the copyright on the title *Les Hauts du Hurle-Vent*, the courts extended the protection of a translation to its very title. They recognized the fact that there is creativity in the translation of a single phrase, or a title—as well as in the translation of a whole work:

> Given that the title *Les Hauts de Hurlevent* constitutes an original invention and not a literal translation of the English title, the word *Wuthering* having no direct equivalent in the French language, and besides, only being used locally in English-speaking countries—[we conclude that] this is not a case of a translation, but rather of a new interpretation on the part of Delebecque, which can be valued as a personal work and which, as such, has claims to literary property, granted exclusively by him to his publisher, the Editions Payot.[3]

Today, the section of the French penal code on literary and artistic property refers to this landmark case:

> For an emphasis on the investigation of merit, see, re the title "Les Hauts du Hurlevent," nonliteral translation of Emily Brontë's novel "Wuthering Heights," the decision that the title was an original discovery, rendering the harrowing nature of the original title in an intimate, musical, and disturbing fashion.[4]

Part I: The Translator in the World

This case is unusually satisfying from a translator's point of view, for here the law is acknowledging, with admirable specificity, the difficulty and challenge of a single act of translation. The court's judgment is a form of literary criticism—the evaluation of the leap of imagination involved in finding a French word for "Wuthering." The court recognizes in Delebecque, the translator, much the same power that Virginia Woolf recognizes in Brontë herself in her famous assessment of *Wuthering Heights*: "She could . . . by speaking of the moor make the wind blow and the thunder roar."[5]

A second case stands out in the judicial literature on literary translation for very different reasons. This time it's a case of retranslation, or rather, a wish to revise and correct a dated translation, and of the ensuing conflict between an editor and a translator's heirs. The case concerns the collection of Kafka texts gathered together for a Gallimard Pléiade edition of Kafka's complete works. All these works were originally translated for Gallimard by the eminent Kafka specialist Alexandre Vialatte, who began translating Kafka in the 1930s. He had died just as the Pléiade complete works were taking shape. The editor of the Kafka Pléiade, Claude David, wanted to make a whole series of corrections of what he considered errors in Vialatte's translations. Vialatte's son took Gallimard to court, arguing that his father's moral right over his translation was being violated in the new corrected edition. The court decided in favor of the Vialatte estate.[6] You can see the result of their decision in the Pléiade edition of Kafka we use today. A prefatory page summarizes the decision by the 1974 Paris court and explains that Vialatte's translation has been reprinted and appears unchanged from the previous edition; only text that was previously missing has been added in brackets. The editors also indicate that they've inserted "a certain number of rectifications in the form of a series of notes indicated by capital letters which one can find in the critical apparatus at the back of the volume" [«...des notes appelées par des majuscules et qu'on trouvera dans l'appareil critique à la fin du volume, un certain nombre de rectifications.»].[7]

If Gallimard had wanted to pay for an entirely new translation of Kafka, they would have been legally entitled to supersede Vialatte's original translation. But they didn't decide to start from scratch with a retranslation— out of respect for tradition, according to them, but also surely because an entirely new translation would have been a mammoth undertaking, both financially, intellectually, and in terms of time. So, without the permission of Vialatte's heirs to correct his work, they were legally obligated to respect the copyright governing the translation they did use. The Pléiade Kafka text is replete with tiny letters that direct the reader to a thick collection of notes in back of the book. Each note leads the reader to a suggestion for a correction of the translation: Alexandre Vialatte's "On avait sûrement calomnié Joseph K"—the first clause in the first sentence of the *Trial*—ought to have been rendered, according to Claude David's notes, as: "Quelqu'un avait dû calomnier Joseph K."[8] Vialatte's translation has been improved, but because the improvements are isolated in the critical apparatus, they are unable to affect our reading experience. There is something tragic (dare I say Kafkaesque?) in this visible but, at the same time, distracting revision of the French Kafka.

The Vialatte story points to a larger issue: translations that are, in and of themselves, historically significant. It is often acknowledged, for example, that Jean Giono's 1941 translation of Melville's *Moby-Dick* (with Lucien Jacques and Joan Smith) contains just as much Giono as Melville. One might say the same of Baudelaire's translations of Poe or De Quincey. Or Gérard de Nerval's fanciful *Faust* (1828), which Goethe is said to have preferred to many more accurate translations. Who would dare to retranslate these texts which, despite their mistakes or *contresens*, exist as dialogues between two great writers, masterpieces in and of themselves? When the translator is considered a great artist, he or she is often granted the right to err. Or, we might say, the errors of an artist are considered interesting, innovative interpretations rather than clumsy mistakes. The Vialatte estate lawsuit claimed something like this historical and artistic privilege for Vialatte's Kafka.

Although intellectual property is a burgeoning branch of the law in the age of the Internet, cases concerning literary translation are relatively uncommon in the law books, in both France and the United States. And they have rather little to tell us about the actual working relationship between writer and translator. That relationship rarely emerges in detail in legal suits: it takes place almost entirely behind the scenes. The law is schematic, often purely commercial, in its view of translation.

By comparison, there is surely more to learn from what goes on in publishing houses, in the negotiations between author, translator, and editor, than there is in the courts. When translator and author don't live in the same place, as is usually the case, negotiations often take place through correspondence, and these exchanges are potentially very interesting. Understandably, publishers are not eager to open contentious or even harmonious private correspondence to a literary historian. It may be that interviews with working translators and their authors, and, in the absence of these primary sources, literary histories and writers' biographies, offer a surer path to the heart of the question.

Complicity

The history of modern French literature is full of stories of friendships between authors and translators: Grace Frick, an American, became the lifelong companion of Marguerite Yourcenar, and because of Grace Frick, France's first female Académicienne spent most of her later years on an island in Maine. Yourcenar's love for her translator led to her exile and certainly influenced the classical beauty of her prose, which stands outside her own time and place. Until Frick died, Yourcenar refused to let anyone else translate her into English. . . . In the tradition of Yourcenar and Frick are a number of translator–author marriages: Marie Chaix met her husband, Harry Mathews—the only American member of OuLiPo—because he translated her autobiographical novel, *Les Lauriers du Lac de Constance*. She then became his translator.[9] The Guadeloupian francophone writer Maryse Condé, who lives in New York, is married to her translator, the Englishman Richard Philcox. It is a partnership made especially meaningful by their American residency and her growing celebrity on the U.S. literary scene: he makes her work accessible to the public in the place where she lives and works.[10]

There is a less romantic moral to the story of Louis-Ferdinand Céline's friendship with his first English-language translator, John Marks. Céline visited Marks several times in London, and helped him with the translation of *Voyage au bout de la nuit* and *Mort à crédit* in the early 1930s. In turn, Marks took him out onto the streets of London and arranged some pretty wild parties for him with English girls. The problem, it turned out, was that Céline was completely indifferent—if not intellectually opposed—to the idea of translation. For him seeing his books come out in English was primarily a commercial venture; his correspondence with his American publishers, Little Brown, shows that he was interested in sales figures to the detriment of content.[11]

In the absence of any objections by Céline, and with the encouragement of his English and American publishers, John Marks substituted polite words for Céline's gynecological and sexual vocabulary: for example, he changes the word "abortion" to "miscarriage" in *Voyage*. Moreover, Marks regularly corrected Céline's syntax, erasing the famous three dots and restoring Céline's sentences to something resembling normal polite English prose. What is shocking is not that Marks misunderstood Céline's revolution in prose—that was common among many of his contemporaries—but that Céline himself went along with Marks. He was more interested in having a good night on the town in London than in confronting his translator with the specificity of his language.[12] In an article on Céline's hostility toward translation, Philippe Roussin untangles the linguistic nationalism at the root of Céline's attitude.[13] In *Bagatelles pour un massacre*, the anti-Semitic diatribe from 1937, Céline declares war on a "robotic" style that he blames on the invasion of bad translations and the erosion of real French into what he considers a standardized, robotic, "Jewified" language. The paradox is that he was uninterested in defending the linguistic specificity of his own language with Marks, and aided and abetted a "standardized" version of his own work. It wasn't until the 1960s, with the retranslations by Ralph Manheim, that Céline found an English-language translator sensitive to his quirks and innovations.[14] So we see that while hostility between translator and author can lead to disaster, complicity can also create problems. In translation relationships—as in so many other human encounters—tact, sympathy, intimacy, and distance are all necessary ingredients.

The Gift of Translation

My own work as a translator began with one author. I discovered Roger Grenier in 1995 through *Le Rôle d'accusé*, in which he described covering a number of purge trials in postwar France. I was taken with his irony, his sense of psychology, and his lucidity in explaining the workings of a French courtroom. Although the book was an essay—his first, dated 1948—it had a great deal of narrative and stylistic power, qualities I discovered were borne out in his fiction.

In March 1996 I took ill with bronchitis, lost my voice, and was confined to bed. During that month, I read most of Grenier's fiction. In one novel in particular, *Le Pierrot noir*, the story of a group of young people during the Nazi occupation of France, I had what I can only call in retrospect a sense of recognition as I was reading. It had to do—and here I am certainly guilty of what Berman calls severe ethnocentrism—with the feeling that I was reading an American novel set in the southwest of

France. This was not merely a hallucination brought about by fever, since the feeling continued long after my recovery. What I was sensing was triggered by the fact that Grenier himself has been deeply influenced in his own writing by the American modernism of the early twentieth century: by his readings of Jack London, Hemingway, Henry James, and Melville (the short stories in particular), and especially by F. Scott Fitzgerald, to whom he's devoted a book of criticism. Any American reader, or reader of American fiction, inevitably feels this influence on Grenier's writing. Someone once called Roger Grenier "the most French of American authors." The joke goes a long way in explaining what drew me to translate him. I was, quite simply, drawn to his American side, which contributed to my sense that translating him into English would be, in a sense, "bringing him home."

As far as Grenier's celebrated "Americanness" goes, what I discovered when I actually began the sentence-level work of translating him was that the American feel of his fiction, its very simplicity, was based on an extremely classical and Latinate syntax and prose style that is foreign to English. His simple and limpid French becomes contorted if you try to render it word for word.

My work on this most French of American writers has made me think more generally about the relative translatability of modern American writers into French. Why did Faulkner, with his extremely difficult, local, and often wild prose, find his match right away in Coindreau, while the much more limpid Fitzgerald has been so much more of a challenge for French translators?[15] Like a simple melody on the piano, a simple prose style in the original exposes the translator. It can be much harder to play.

As for our working relationship, I have been lucky to find in Roger Grenier an author who is knowledgeable about English. Our best collaborative effort, I believe, has been on a novel called *Partita*, where I had the luxury of reading each chapter out loud to him in draft. He heard mistakes in vocabulary or idiom; I could hear the music of the American English taking shape. He suggested a title for the U.S. version, and *Partita* became *Piano Music for Four Hands*, a title I now think of as a metaphor for translating—when it goes well.

Every act of translation is an act of attentiveness. As a translator, I notice aspects of style and language that would have escaped the part of me who is simply a reader, and even a literary critic. I retain this attentiveness in my own writing—and this is one of the great gifts translation has offered me. In the act of translating, we come closer to the literary object than anyone else except the writer who has created it; and in so doing, we learn something about ourselves as writers. Writing is an open field for invention, while translation offers a limited space in which to observe and practice the rules of writing. It should come as no surprise that so many writers become translators at some point in their careers. There is no better writer's workshop.[16]

Notes

This essay began as a talk for Peter Burian's seminar on translation in the Program in Literature at Duke University, April, 2001; a subsequent version, translated by Sophie Queuniet, was presented in Fabienne Durand-Bogaert's seminar on translation at the Ecole des Hautes Etudes en Sciences Sociales, Paris, in May 2001. A version was first published in English in the bilingual online journal, *Mots pluriels*. I am grateful to Brice Amor and Geraldine Freed, Editions Gallimard, for their generous assistance with legal sources.

1. Stacy Schiff, *Véra (Mrs. Vladimir Nabokov)* (New York: Modern Library, 2000), 241.

2. Antoine Berman, *The Experience of the Foreign: Culture and Translation in Romantic Germany*, trans. S. Heyvaert (Albany: SUNY Press, 1992); *La Traduction et la lettre ou l'auberge du lointain* (Paris: Le Seuil, 1999). On Berman, see also Fabienne Durand-Bogaert, "Pour oublier la langue: sur *La Traduction et la lettre ou l'Auberge du lointain* de Antoine Berman et sur *Poétique du traduire* de Henri Meschonnic," *Critique* 643 (December 2000): 1059–1069.

3. Tribunal commercial de la Seine, 26 June 1951, "Editions Payot c. Librairie Gibert jeune, affaire *Les Hauts de Hurlevent*, inédit," quoted by Henri Desbois, "Chroniques de Législation et de jurisprudence française," in *Revue trimestrielle de droit commercial*, vol. IV, 1951, 763.

4. *Code pénal de propriété littéraire et artistique*, Article L. 112–4; Protection par le droit d'auteur: originalité. Receuil Dalloz et Sirey, 41.

5. Virginia Woolf, "*Jane Eyre* and *Wuthering Heights*," in *The Common Reader: First Series*, ed. and introduced by Andrew McNeillie (New York: Harcourt Brace, 1994), 161.

6. Tribunal de Grande Instance de Paris (3e chambre), 25 September 1974, Editions Gallimard c. Pierre Vialatte, cited in *Revue Internationale du Droit d'Auteur*, vol. LXXXIII, January 1975, 135–138.

7. Franz Kafka, *Oeuvres complètes*, edition de Claude David, traduit de l'allemand par Alexandre Vialatte, tome 1 (Paris: Gallimard, Bibliothèque de la Pléiade, 1976).

8. "Jemand musste Josef K. verleumdet haben . . ." Breon Mitchell's new English translation from 1998 reads, much as Claude David suggests, "Someone must have slandered Josef K. . . ."

9. Harry Mathews' translations of Marie Chaix include *The Laurels of Lake Constance* (New York: Viking, 1977) and *Silences, or a Woman's Life* (New York: Dalkey, 2013). Marie Chaix's translations of Harry Mathews include *Plaisirs singuliers* (Paris: P.O.L., 1983), *Cigarettes* (Paris: P.O.L., 1988), and *20 Lignes par jour* (Paris: P.O.L., 1994).

10. Philcox is not Condé's only translator, but he has translated her best-known novels: *The Last of the African Kings, Heremakhonon; Crossing the Mangrove; A Season in Rihata*; and *I, Tituba, Black Witch of Salem*.

11. Alice Kaplan, ed., "Selling Céline: The Céline-Little Brown Correspondence" (1934–1938), in *Céline, USA*, ed. Alice Kaplan and Philippe Roussin (Durham: Duke University Press, 1994), 373–420.

12. See Alice Kaplan and Philip Watts, "Les vicissitudes de la traduction anglaise de *Voyage au bout de la nuit* et de *Mort à crédit*," tr. Sophie Queuniet, in *L'Année Céline 1996* (Tusson: du Lérot/IMEC, 1997), 303–24.

13. Philippe Roussin, "La traduction et l'identité de l'oeuvre littéraire selon Céline," in *Violence et Traduction: Actes du Colloque de Melnik, Bulgarie* (7–10 May, 1993), ed. Fabienne Durand-Bogaert (Paris and Sofia: EHESS/Université de Sofia, éditions Sofia, 1995), 159–77.

14. See Kaplan and Watts, "Les vicissitudes de la traduction anglaise de *Voyage au bout de la nuit* et de *Mort à crédit*."

15. Coindreau's affinity for Faulkner has been attributed to his Vendéen sensibility. See Maurice-Edgar Coindreau, *Mémoires d'un traducteur: entretiens avec Christian Guidicelli* (Paris: Gallimard, 1974).

SEVEN

The Will to Translate

Four Episodes in a Local History of Global Cultural Exchange

ESTHER ALLEN

"Translation is inevitable!" a distinguished fiction writer exclaimed during a panel on the subject circa 2006. It's a thrilling and romantic notion. Literary masterpieces are penned; their worth is recognized; the endless task of translating and retranslating them into all the languages of the world is launched. Such contingencies as the language the masterwork happens to be written in, the place of origin of its author, the motivation and artistic skill of a given translator, and the language and political context into which that translator introduces the work are irrelevant. Literary greatness alone is the guarantor of translation. Or, to paraphrase the idea in other terms, the invisible hand of the cultural marketplace will always ensure that literary value will be perpetuated equitably across language barriers.

While both the romantic and capitalist formulations of this sentiment may strike many who are reading this as suspect, the idea that the translation of literary works of genuine significance is inevitable—and hence that those works not translated must inevitably be of lesser significance— is a commonplace of book review sections and international book fairs, not to say university classrooms. Yet it's clear that the translation of a given text often depends largely or perhaps wholly on contextual factors that have less to do with the work's intrinsic value (whatever that might be and however you might measure it) than with encounters between individuals and the shifting cultural and political contexts within which those encounters take place.

In what follows, I briefly describe the work of four translators of Latin American literary prose into English in and around New York City across the nineteenth and twentieth centuries and into the twenty-first. The translation of Latin American poetry follows a somewhat divergent pattern that begins earlier and has a different set of milestones and cast of characters; for the present I leave that story to others.[1] I've chosen New York City for its long-standing and vibrant Latin American community and its equally long-standing position as a center of the U.S. publishing industry. Each of the translators I evoke inhabits a unique moment in the history of cultural contact between the United States and Latin America, and in the evolution of ideas of translation and of the role of the translator in the United States. In this history, little is inevitable.

I. Mary Tyler Peabody Mann

In 1868 the New York publishing house of Hurd and Houghton brought out *Life in the Argentine Republic in the Days of the Tyrants; or, Civilization and Barbarism*, taken, the title page states, "from the Spanish of Domingo F. Sarmiento, LL.D., Minister Plenipotentiary from the Argentine Republic to the United States," and including a "biographical sketch of the author" by "Mrs. Horace Mann" (also the person who extracted the work from the Spanish). The absence from this page of the title of the original work—the resoundingly Hispanic surname *Facundo*, the title by which Latin American readers commonly refer to this inflammatory 1845 biography of the provincial Argentine *caudillo* Juan Facundo Quiroga—and the anxious bolstering of the work's status via its author's academic credentials and diplomatic post and the prominent placement, in type as large as that used for the name of the author himself, of the resonant name of the late Horace Mann, renowned education reformer, abolitionist U.S. congressman, college president, and brother-in-law of Nathaniel Hawthorne, can be accounted for by one crucial feature of its context: this is the *only* book-length work of literary prose by a Latin American author translated from Spanish to English and published in the United States prior to 1890.

Several clarifications are now in order. First: this is not to say that *Life in the Argentine Republic* was the only literary work by a Latin American author to have been published in New York City or in the United States before 1890. Nothing could be farther from the truth. To take the Cuban community alone, high points on the list of classic texts first published in New York City—*in Spanish*—include the *Lecciones de filosofía* (G. F. Bunce, 1832) by exiled activist priest Felix Varela; novelist Cirilo Villaverde's canonical *Cecilia Valdés* (El Espejo, 1882), often described as one of the greatest Latin American novels of the nineteenth century; and virtually the entire poetical *obra* of Cuban poet, journalist, and revolutionary José Martí, most notably the *Versos Sencillos* (Louis Weiss & Co, 1891), as well as the bulk of his journalistic and political work.[2]

This is not to say, either, that there were no translations from or into the Spanish language published in New York during the nineteenth century. Washington Irving's 1829 *Tales of the Alhambra* crystallized an interest in classic Spanish literature that gave rise to multiple translations of masterworks of the Spanish Golden Age, accounts of Spain's conquest of Latin America, and the works of Catholic spiritual figures such as Santa Teresa de Avila. Nor was interest confined to texts hallowed by centuries of prestige: contemporary Spanish novelists such as Benito Perez Galdós, Juan Valera, and Emilia Pardo Bazan were translated, as well, particularly during the second half of the century.

Why did it make such a difference whether a work originated in Spain or Latin America? The question is particularly pertinent in light of the fact that throughout the nineteenth century, as now, the Spanish-speaking population of New York City was of predominantly Latin American origin. Census figures for 1870, 1880, and 1890 show that natives of Spain generally made up only 18 to 23 percent of the city's total Hispanic population, which grew from 3,605 in 1870 to 5,994 in 1890. But for the Anglophone New Yorkers of the time, the distinction between the Spanish speakers who hailed from Europe and those from elsewhere in the Western Hemisphere was crucial. Spain, land of Cervantes and Quevedo, had precisely the literary capital the United States was acutely aware of lacking during its first century of nationhood—and that it viewed the Latin American countries as lacking, too. Pascal Casanova puts it this way: "The classics are the privilege of the oldest literary nations, which, in elevating their foundational texts to the status of timeless works of art, have defined their literary capital as non-national and a-historical—a definition that corresponds exactly to the definition that they have given of literature itself."[3] Spain, from this perspective, possessed a cultural history that belonged to the exalted category of "literature"; works by its writers, past and present, were thus of foundational interest to a newly postcolonial nation wishing to gain a universal literature of its own. Latin America, newly postcolonial itself, or still colonized, could offer no such cultural capital.

Finally, this is not to say that the nineteenth-century United States was in no way engaged in any kind of translation that involved Latin American Spanish. On the contrary, New York City in particular was very busy indeed with a thriving industry centered on Latin America that made translations *into* Spanish, which New York publishing houses sent south in such quantity that by the mid-1860s, the celebrated house of D. Appleton alone was shipping out nearly fifty such translations a year. This was cultural capital of a different order. This thriving industry provided income and employment to quite a number of Latin American exiles who lived in the city, including the Puerto Rican educator and philosopher Eugenio María de Hostos, and José Martí, whose several translations for D. Appleton & Co. are included in the various editions of his *Obras completas*.

In 1887, at his own expense, Martí translated into Spanish, published, and distributed across Mexico Helen Hunt Jackson's *Ramona* (1884), a hugely popular novel about racial tensions in California following annexation by the United States in 1850. He wanted to alert Mexicans to the dangers of U.S. expansionism, but was also motivated, as his preface states, by admiration of the work's literary qualities. He believed these, along with its subject matter, gave it a rightful place in Latin American literature. In *Ramona*, Martí writes by way of introduction to his translation, "Helen Hunt Jackson . . . has perhaps . . . written *our* novel"—"*nuestra* novela" (emphasis mine).[4]

The imbalance is clear. In his preface to "the first Mexican historical production to be deemed worthy of translation into the English language"—*The Other Side; or Notes for the History of the War between Mexico and the United States* (New York: Wiley, 1850), a compilation of accounts by various Mexican military and political figures—the book's editor, Albert C. Ramsey, a colonel with the 11th infantry during the U.S. invasion of Mexico in 1846, had noted that, "The [Mexican people] are far better informed on subjects pertaining to the United States than are the American people informed on subjects pertaining to Mexico."

Nueva York is consubstantial with New York; it walks down the same streets, endures the same blizzards, hunches over tables in the same libraries, stares out of windows at the same rivers, is blinded by the same hard, glittering light. The city's streets echo with English, Spanish, and many other languages. But even after decades of *convivencia*, the Latin American writers who inhabited Nueva York and composed and published their books here—and who read the work of their Anglophone counter-parts with keen interest, as Martí's impassioned essays on Whitman, Emerson, and a host of other North American luminaries attest—had no hope of seeing their work gain access to the Anglophone literary sphere. A novel that has reposed on the shelves of the New York Public Library since it was founded, and that graced the shelves of the Astor Library (now New York's Public Theater) before that, evokes this divide. Titled *Los dramas de Nueva York* (Mexico City: J. Rivera, Hijo y Comp., 1869), it was ceremoniously presented by its author, José Rivera y Rio, to Colonel Albert S. Evans in 1869. Evans describes their encounter in a handwritten inscription that appears on the book's flyleaf:

Regents of Astor Library

Gentlemen

While in Mexico with Mr. Seward I made the acquaintance of the au-thor of these volumes who desired me to say to you that he was taken prisoner by the French in Puebla and sent to France from whence he escaped to the United States. Here he remained some time in exile and while here, spent many hours in the Astor Library. He demonstrates his appreciation of the library as a noble public institution by present-ing these volumes and requesting that they be placed on its shelves.

With much respect,

Colonel Albert S. Evans
Liberty House, New York, Feb. 2, 1870

Rivera y Rio does not envisage that anyone might read the book he bequeaths—a novel of manners set among Latin Americans in New York City—and certainly not that anyone might translate it; he asks merely that it be placed on the library's shelves, simply to be present in the physi-cal space of the city it describes, as its author once was.

Los dramas de Nueva York was not the only volume on the Astor Library's shelves to result from Evans's journey to Mexico. Evans himself pro-duced a lengthy account of his travels,[5] adding one more title to the ever-expanding library of books about Latin America by visitors from the United States. (In an unpublished work, I documented almost 200 such accounts by U.S. travelers in Latin America produced over the course of the nineteenth century.[6]) These travel accounts attest to the fact that the inhabitants of the United States were not incurious about Latin America. But there is a difference between the work of the travel writer and that of the translator. Certainly, Mary Mann's recasting of *Facundo* without the title *Facundo* can attest that a translation is not necessarily any more pure, transparent, apolitical, or fully accurate in its reflection of what it represents than a travel account. But to have travel accounts without translations—the bookstores and classrooms of the nation's English-speaking majority continually restocked with descriptions of Latin American by U.S. travelers who generally spent a few weeks or months there, and often barely spoke Spanish, while remaining almost devoid of any work written by a Latin American—was clearly to ignore Latin America in a profound way: to busily produce books *about* Latin America while granting little or no voice to Latin Americans themselves.

As for the translator of that first Latin American literary book, Mary Tyler Peabody Mann had befriended the young Sarmiento—"dear Mr. Sarmy," as she liked to call him—when he arrived in the United States in 1847, bearing a letter of introduction to her distinguished husband. Like the Manns, Sarmiento was an educational reformer, and much of his later interaction with Mrs. Mann would be focused on the reforms he sought to achieve in Argentina. During that first visit, Sarmiento spoke no English and communicated with the Manns in French. When he returned to the United States in 1865, as Argentina's ambassador, he renewed his friendship with Horace Mann's widow. Only then did he learn that as a result of two years spent as a governess in Cuba during her youth, Mary Peabody Mann spoke Spanish. "The Lord has appointed you my guardian angel and it is your duty to submit with Christian resignation," he wrote her in tones of delight that would later give rise to groundless rumors of a love affair between them, and she duly embarked on several decades of tireless assistance to his literary, political, and educational projects.[7] During the earlier visit, the Manns had introduced Sarmiento to Henry Wadsworth Longfellow (so taken with the young Argentine that he briefly toyed with the idea of an *Evangeline*-like romance based on *Facundo*). It was to Longfellow, whose first published book had been a translation of the fifteenth-century Spanish poet Jorge Manrique's *Coplas por la muerte de su padre*, that Mary Mann turned when she encountered difficulties with Sarmiento's Spanish. The established cultural mode of translation from the classic literature of Spain thus lent a hand to the groundbreaking translation of the new literature of Latin America.

Among Mary Mann's other works is a three-volume *Life and Works of Horace Mann* (1865–68), in which, famously, she alludes to her own presence in Horace Mann's life in only one sentence. She was also reluctant to be viewed as an active presence and participant in the cultural exchange she was energetically effecting via translation. "I had rather it not seem to come through my agency," she wrote in an 1868 letter to a fellow reformer, asking for assistance in placing her translation of a letter from Sarmiento in a Washington, D.C. newspaper.[8] When not ignored, Sarmiento's translator has sometimes been chastised for cutting portions of the original text, for her neglect of Sarmiento's use of metaphor, and for being more concerned with his political than his literary ambitions (as, perhaps, was he).[9] Mann's translation has rarely been acknowledged as the landmark of U.S.–Latin American cultural exchange that it was—*Life in the Argentine Republic* would be reprinted for over a century—or seen in the context of her lifelong personal concern with giving voice to those in the Americas who were excluded from U.S. political and cultural discourse.

To give but one additional instance of that concern, Mary Mann would use the political and cultural clout of her husband's name on behalf of yet another marginalized writer in 1883. While the title page of the novel of her own that she published very late in life bore the name "Mary Mann,"[10] "Mrs. Horace Mann" was again credited as editor of *Life Among the Piutes: Their Wrongs and Claims* (New York: G. P. Putnam's Sons), a book by Sarah Winnemucca Hopkins, a Paiute woman born in 1844 in what is now Nevada who had risen to prominence as a Native American activist and educator. Mann met Winnemucca during the latter's lecture tour of the Northeast and immediately offered to help rework her lecture materials into a book and secure publication for it. This would appear to be a departure from Mann's work with Sarmiento, who, in *Facundo*, had developed the notion that Argentina's native peoples were resistant to the sort of modern educational reforms he enlisted her help in pursuing, and who believed that Argentina needed to follow the U.S. model by suppressing its natives and promoting immigration from Europe—an ideology he would implement during his six years as Argentina's president. For Mary Mann, however, the translation of Sarmiento and the editing of Winnemucca were quite consistent. In her "Editor's Preface" to Winnemucca's book, she explains that she devoted her energies to it because: "At this moment, when the United States seem waking up to their duty to the original possessors of our immense territory, it is of the first importance to hear what *only an Indian and an Indian woman* can tell" (my emphasis). In much the same way, her translation of Sarmiento had brought the U.S. reading public, for the first time, one of the stories a Latin American and only a Latin American could tell.

II. Rollo Ogden

Twenty-two years later, it happened again. In 1890, Harper and Bros. published an English translation of *María*, a novel by the Columbian writer and politician Jorge Isaacs. By then an acknowledged classic of Latin American Romanticism, *María*, the story of a wealthy family's decline and its scion's doomed love for his mortally ill adopted sister, was originally published in Colombia in 1867. Its 1890 publication in New York makes it the first Latin American novel to be published in English translation in the United States.[11] That the date of this publication happened to coincide with the First International Conference of American States—or "Pan-American Congress," as it was known—is no coincidence whatsoever. The Congress, which took place in Washington, D.C. from January to April, was the first official gathering of all the nations of the Western Hemisphere. In addition to creating a new receptivity to all things Latin American, which presumably opened the way for the book's translation, the Congress was of direct assistance to the work of *María's* translator, Rollo Ogden, who, in his introductory note, thanks "Señor Cárlos Martinez Silva, LL.D., delegate from the republic of Colombia to the Pan-American Congress, for valuable aid kindly rendered the translator."

Son of a Presbyterian minister, Rollo Ogden had at first followed his father into the ministry. In 1881, at the age of twenty-five, he was sent to Mexico City, where he and his wife were missionaries for two years and where he became fluent in Spanish. Four years after his return, he underwent a spiritual crisis and left the ministry to pursue a literary career in which the translation of *María* was one of the early steps. He also began writing for magazines, including *The Nation*, to which he contributed a number of editorials that marked him as one of the Anti-Imperialists—a group that included Henry and William James, William Dean Howells, and Mark Twain. Translation was, for Ogden, a response to U.S. imperialism, which he well understood to be cultural as well as political. In an

1895 editorial for *The Nation* on the apparent decline of interest in missionary work in the United States, his stance is clearly derived from his experience in the mission fields and his work as a translator: "In the face of [our] better knowledge of many of the people whom we have been wont promiscuously to call heathen, it has been getting more and more impossible to be so sure that they have everything to learn from us, and we nothing from them."[12]

By then, Ogden was on the staff of the *New York Evening Post,* of which, in 1903, he would become chief editor—a position previously held, from 1828 to 1878, by William Cullen Bryant, sometime translator of the Cuban poet José María Heredia. Ogden's continued interest in Latin America is evinced by his 1904 biography of the historian and Hispanist William H. Prescott, eminent chronicler of Spain's conquest of America.[13] In 1920, he left the *Post* to join the staff of *The New York Times,* becoming its editor-in-chief within two years; he remained in that position until his death, twenty-five years later. When Ogden passed away on February 23, 1937, his obituary appeared on the front page of the *Times,* outlined in a black box.

Fifteen years after Ogden's death, Saul Bellow published his landmark novel *The Adventures of Augie March.* In an early section of the novel, as he contemplates his humble Chicago origins and future prospects, its eponymous picaresque hero comments, "But when there is no shepherd-Sicily . . . but deep city vexation instead, and you are forced early into deep city aims, not sent in your ephod before Eli to start service in the temple, nor set on a horse by your weeping sisters to go and study Greek in Bogotá, but land in a poolroom—what can that lead to of the highest?"[14] In this string of rapid-fire allusion—"shepherd-Sicily" may refer to the Greek pastoral poet Theocritus (third century B.C.), who hailed from Sicily, while it was certainly the Old Testament prophet Samuel who wore his ephod to serve Eli as a child (1 Samuel 2:18)—the one set on a horse by his sisters to go and study Greek in Bogotá is the narrator of Jorge Isaacs' *María.* Ogden's version of *María*—then and now the only published translation of the book into English—thus makes a cameo appearance in one of the canonical U.S. novels of the twentieth century; Augie March both claims and rejects it as an antecedent, a model of some literary ideal, unavailable to him, that he calls "the highest." Few readers of Bellow's novel can have caught the reference; *María* remains a rather obscure work among English speakers.[15] But there it is: the prose fiction of Latin America and that of the United States catching each other's eye in a fictional character's fleeting dismissal of the models for living proposed by the universe of world literature—a universe that, here at last, includes Latin America.

III. Harriet de Onís

Though Latin American writers who lived and wrote in Spanish in nineteenth-century New York were beyond the margins of Anglophone literary culture, they were strongly rooted within their own language community; theirs was not a tragedy of neglect. As exiles or immigrants, their lives were divided and they faced prejudice, but they did not feel torn between two languages. Martí had a gigantic literary reputation that extended across the hemisphere, and even a writer like Rivera y Rio returned home to an established, if minor, place in Mexican literature.[16] Whether or not they dreamed of one day influencing U.S. literature in the same way it had influenced them, the possibility of translation was so remote that its unavailability was simply part of the order of things and does not seem to have been particularly destabilizing. It isn't until the first half of the twentieth century that the language politics of Nueva York produced writers who endured what Pascal Casanova calls the "tragedy of translated men,"[17] writers caught in a double bind between two languages, at home in neither, and deeply suspicious of translation. The fullest exploration to date of these writers and their dilemma is offered by Gustavo Pérez Firmat in a study eloquently titled *Tongue Ties*.[18]

Calvert Casey (1924–1969), for example, was born in Baltimore but raised largely in Havana; he began his writing career in English and then switched to Spanish, but returned to English to write an unfinished novel titled *Gianni* that he then attempted to destroy. Casey died by his own hand in Rome, at the age of forty-five. Felipe Alfau (1902–1999) was the child of Spanish parents who immigrated to New York when he was fourteen. He made the decision to write his novel, *Locos: A Comedy of Gestures*, in English because, a note on the author explains, "he felt he could not reach a Spanish audience."[19] The main character of *Locos* is named Fulano—or "So-and-So"—and is described thus: "It seems that about Fulano's personality, if we are to grant him a personality, hung a cloud of inattention which withstood his almost heroic assaults to break through it."

In an interview with Ilan Stavans in 1993, the elderly Alfau, whom Stavans had tracked down in a retirement facility, exhibits supreme indifference to writing, literature, publication, and translation.[20] He declares himself a radical outsider to every language he speaks, a writer who claims to write for no one and to care not at all whether anyone reads him. "Better to be all alone," he tells Stavans. "Alone and silent." Alfau's second novel, *Chromos*, not published until forty years after it was written,[21] is set in New York among Spanish-speaking immigrants, a fact its first paragraph reflects upon:

> The moment one learns English, complications set in. Try as one may, one cannot elude this conclusion, one inevitably comes back to it. This applies to all persons, including those born to the language, and, at times, even more so to Latins, including Spaniards.

Chilean Maria Luisa Bombal, whose childhood was divided between Latin America and Paris, emigrated to the United States in 1940, at the age of 30, leaving behind a growing literary reputation. She would spend the next three decades reworking two of her early tales into English and loading them with so much additional material, in what seems to have been an attempt to make them palatable to a U.S. audience, that she ended up destroying much of their original interest. Her 1935 surrealist novella *La última niebla,* for example, metastasized over a 12-year period into a 243-page English novel called *House of Mist.*[22] Agreement on the superiority of the earlier work is unanimous, and "The Final Mist" was later published in an English translation by Richard and Lucia Cunningham as part of a collection of short stories.[23]

During the same period, the figure of the translator was coming more fully into view. Unless they were canonical writers like Longfellow or Bryant, or were married to famous men, nineteenth-century American translators, of Spanish and other languages, were often anonymous or no more than a cryptic name (sometimes female or of indeterminate gender) about which virtually nothing was known. For Anglophone women, in the nineteenth and well into the twentieth century, a prevailing view of the translator's task as one of accurate reproduction devoid of all intentionality meant that translation was a safe way to channel intellectual and creative impulses. "Translation . . . might be a sign of conformity with traditional values. Its ancillary nature allowed those who so desired to shy away from public recognition."[24] One of the earliest translators of prose to consolidate a presence in the twentieth-century New York publishing scene both fits into and breaks this mold. Like Mary Mann, she was married to an influential man and was diffident about self-promotion. Unlike Mann, she specifically made a name for herself as a translator of Latin American literature and thus helped to establish that possibility for translators of Latin American and other literatures who came after her.

Harriet Wishnieff was the daughter of immigrants from Russia, born on New York's Lower East Side, and raised on a farm in Illinois. After returning to New York for a bachelor's degree in English from Barnard College in 1916, she spent what must have been a rather exciting period as secretary to the modern dance legend Isadora Duncan. She then set her sights on Spanish. "After the First World War, the importance of the Hispanic world became clear," she would later tell the Buenos Aires magazine *El Hogar*.[25] Well before 1933, when FDR announced that the United States would henceforth pursue "the policy of the good neighbor" with regard to the nations of Latin America, awareness was on the rise. In 1918, James Alexander Robinson founded the *Hispanic American Historical Review*, the first U.S. academic journal devoted entirely to Latin America. By 1920, Harriet Wishnieff was spending her days working for a Spanish book importer and taking night classes in Spanish at Columbia University, where she met Federico de Onís, a Spaniard who emigrated in 1916 when he was invited to found Columbia's Spanish department. When they wed, she became Harriet de Onís, and under that name published more than forty works of translation from the Spanish and Portuguese over the next several decades. (Here let me take the opportunity to note that the use of a spouse's famous or culturally resonant name for the benefit of the work one translates is not limited to female translators: in 1942, Doubleday brought out a translation "by Katherine Anne Porter" of the work often cited as the first Mexican novel, José Joaquín Lizardi's 1816 *El Periquillo sarniento*. In fact, the translation was done by Porter's then-husband, Eugene Pressly, and the work has later been reissued as "translated by Eugene Pressly and edited by Katherine Anne Porter."[26])

Harriet de Onís's translation career began in the late 1920s when her husband encouraged her to translate *El águila y la serpiente*, by Mexican novelist Martín Luis Guzmán. By coincidence, a few days later a friend who had landed a job at the prestigious publishing house of Alfred A. Knopf happened to call and ask her to translate it, as well. The context that produced such consensus on the need for a translation was strikingly similar to the one that resulted in Mary Mann's translation of Sarmiento, sixty-two years earlier. After playing a role in the Mexican Revolution, Guzmán had arrived in the United States in 1916 and stayed on until 1920, living primarily in New York City. In 1923, he returned, this time—like

Sarmiento before him—as an official envoy of his nation's government.[27] Like Sarmiento, Guzmán had written a sprawling work about the overthrow of a tyrant in Latin America; Guzmán's novel was likewise published in abridged form in its English translation. De Onís approached the work of translating it very seriously, engaging Guzmán in lengthy correspondence, an approach she would maintain with many of the other writers she translated. Puzzled by the word "Mitigüeson," which came up several times, she included it in one of her lists of queries. Guzmán replied that this was how the soldiers in the Mexican Revolution spoke of their guns, "Mitigüeson" being a phonetic rendering of the Mexican pronunciation of "Smith and Wesson."[28]

The Eagle and the Serpent came out in 1930 and de Onís's career was launched. She soon became not only a colleague but also a friend to Blanche and Alfred Knopf. Backed by her husband's prestigious academic position and with access to the ear of one of U.S. publishing's most influential couples, she took on a curatorial as well as a performative role, acting as a strong advocate for works she felt should be translated. "She exercised a great deal of power over the field for many years," a recent study by Deborah Cohn suggests. While she's been accused of sometimes doing inferior work, particularly when translating from the Portuguese, many of her translations were highly praised, by Dame Edith Sitwell and others. Cohn suggests that de Onís staved off recognition of the experimental modernism that would dominate Latin American fiction in the 1950s and 1960s by her personal preference for regional and folkloric works, which shaped the Knopf list.[29] This charge is belied by her documented effort, from the late 1940s through 1952, to try to convince her editor at Knopf, Herbert Weinstock, to publish the work of a certain Argentine writer she was entranced with. The effort failed. "I cannot urge the book on Alfred and Blanche in view of the uniformly bad sale of Latin American literature here," Weinstock—not the last editor to invoke the marketplace in rejecting a work of translation—informed her. Jorge Luis Borges would have to wait until 1962 for his first publication in English.

She did play a part in the first English translation of the prose work of José Martí, *The America of José Martí*, published by the Noonday Press in 1954, almost sixty years after Martí's death. It was a family project: the book was edited and introduced by Federico de Onís, and credit for the translation is given to Harriet and Federico's son, Juan. It was the only translation produced by Juan de Onís, who would go on to a career as a journalist, and the skill with which he rendered Martí's difficult prose into English has led some to suspect that a maternal hand played a role in his work.

Jorge Luis Borges read the page proofs of Harriet de Onís's 1935 translation of Ricardo Güiraldes's classic novel of the Pampas, *Don Segundo Sombra*, and hailed the novel's new incarnation in English. Borges understood translation as few others have before or since,[30] and on re-reading the Argentine classic in its new language, he rediscovered it: "As I went through the English version of *Don Segundo*, I was continually aware of the gravitational pull and accent of the other essential book of our America: Mark Twain's *Huckleberry Finn*."[31] Borges had not grasped that de Onís was the work's translator (he thought it was Waldo Frank), but he did understand that the translation was furthering inter-American literary connections, and that may have mattered more to de Onís herself, whose forty books very rarely bore her name on their covers.[32]

In a recent study of style and ideology in de Onís's work, Jeremy Munday subjects eight of her translations to computer-assisted analysis.[33] This methodology limits him to a focus on individual word choice, as opposed to the more crucial and elusive quality of voice, which defines the success or failure of a translation but defies computer analysis. Munday's study attributes variation between original and translation to bias on the part of the translator, which ignores the Anglophone norm wherein books are worked over intensively during the process of publication. As Maureen Freely's account of her translation of Orhan Pamuk in this volume attests, an individual word choice in any given translation may have been made by the book's editor, its copyeditor, or some other party, including its author; few writers and fewer translators who publish in English can claim to have full and final control over every word in a text. Indeed, Munday himself reports that Waldo Frank boasted of having rewritten de Onís's translation of *Don Segundo Sombra* to repair what Frank viewed as its stylistic deficiencies. Nevertheless, when Munday identifies a supposed Christian religious veneer imposed on *Don Segundo Sombra* by the translation of "un perdidito" as "a limb of Satan," this is described an instance of "aggressive . . . ideological intervention" by de Onís.

The most damning such "intervention" Munday identifies occurs in a sentence from the translation of Cuban ethnomusicologist Fernando Ortíz's fundamental *Cuban Counterpoint: Tobacco and Sugar* (Knopf, 1947):

[Los negros] . . . se traspasaron de una cultura a otra más potente, como los indios.

[The Negroes] . . . were transferred from their own to another more advanced culture, like that of the Indians.[34]

In order to charge de Onís with the translation crime of "domestication," Munday fixes on the translation of the word *potente* (potent or powerful) as "advanced," which, to him, "reveals an attitude of superiority from the translator." He does not note that the translation has seriously garbled the grammar of the original sentence, which could accurately be translated, in the idiom of de Onís's era, as "The Negroes, like the Indians, were transferred out of one culture into another that was more powerful." In Spanish, the final clause *como los indios* links the Africans' experience to the Indians' earlier one. By erroneously inserting a relative pronoun and possessive preposition not present in the Spanish, the clause "like that of the Indians," makes the culture of the Indians equivalent to the"more advanced culture" described in the clause that immediately precedes it. This contradicts the original text, but also the attitude of superiority de Onís is accused of. The failure here (and I don't claim to know whose failure it was) is less one of ideological bias than of syntax and voice. De Onís devoted most of her life to translating works like Ortiz's which overtly challenged prevailing values to promote greater appreciation of African and indigenous cultures. It should not dismay us overmuch if individual words in texts that bear her name sometimes fail to conform to the standards of politically correct speech in our own time.

The work of de Onís and other translators who introduced Latin American literature to the United States under the aegis of the Good Neighbor policy is widely acknowledged for establishing the context that allowed the extraordinary surge of the 1960s to take place. While the quality of her work may have varied, there is no doubt of her devotion to José Martí's project of bringing Latin American culture into the United States to counteract the prevailing ignorance. Her role as translator and curator created a foundation on which others would build. "She had a good eye for books that should have been translated." Gregory Rabassa said of her.[35]

IV. Gregory Rabassa

Much of the next section of this fast-forwarded history remains too well known to require telling, and in any case Rabassa himself has told his story in an award-winning memoir.[36] In an extraordinary reversal of the nineteenth-century cultural dynamic against which Mary Mann and Rollo Ogden had worked, the generation of translators that followed Harriet de Onís—whose husband was still chair of Columbia University's Spanish department when Rabassa earned his Ph.D. there in the late 1940s after he returned from serving as an OSS cryptographer in World War II—went on to achieve a stature previously undreamed of, and achieved it for their translations of Latin American literature. In addition to Rabassa, this group includes Helen Lane, Alistair Reid, Margaret Sayers Peden, Alfred MacAdam, Edith Grossman, Suzanne Jill Levine, and several others. Most of them have, like Rabassa, done the inestimable service of writing about their lives and work as translators, perhaps because the mid-century period of fervent translation of Latin American literature in the United States known as the Boom coincides precisely with a period of increased professionalization for U.S. literary translators, with the formation of organizations such as the PEN Translation Committee (founded in 1959, just prior to the Boom) and the American Literary Translators Association (founded in 1978, as the Boom was winding down).

The work of this group of translators was supported by a new Center for Inter-American Relations; the importance of that work was acknowledged by a National Book Award in Translation, which Rabassa was the first person to win, in 1966, for his brilliant translation of Julio Cortázar's *Hopscotch*, the first book-length work he ever translated. Rabassa's work on *Hopscotch* was so extraordinary that Cortázar advised Gabriel García Márquez to delay the publication of his book in English until Rabassa could do the translation. Rabassa's best-selling 1970 translation of García Márquez's *One Hundred Years of Solitude* is said by U.S. President Bill Clinton to be his favorite book. In 2006, in a ceremony at the White House, President George W. Bush awarded Rabassa the National Medal of Arts, the nation's highest honor for artistic excellence.

This transformation in the cultural status of Latin American literature and its translators may in retrospect seem to have been inevitable. At the time, it was carefully nurtured by well-placed funding from the Rockefeller Foundation, which founded the Center for Inter-American Relations, three years after the Cuban Revolution of 1959, in order to "develop the goodwill and respect of leading Latin Americans as the sensitive interpreter in the United States of their desires for understanding and recognition." Mary Mann's role as Sarmiento's "guardian angel" had been taken on by a vast private fortune, closely allied to the U.S.

government. Members of the Inter-American Committee, the name under which the CIAR began to function, "drew on their connections to get public officials such as Richard Goodwin, Deputy Assistant Secretary of State for Inter-American Affairs, and Arthur Schlesinger, historian and special assistant to President Kennedy, to attend the IAC's symposia, and participants also met with President Kennedy, Robert Kennedy, Hubert Humphrey, and numerous other White House and State Department officials." The Center's literature department not only provided grants to translators (assisting Rabassa's translation of *One Hundred Years*), but also became "a nexus for networking and support of all aspects of the translation, publication and promotion of Latin American literature."[37] This Cold War–motivated support for translation went hand in hand with a cultural moment during which, as Eliot Weinberger notes in his essay included here, translated literature was also embraced as an alternative by those in active rebellion against the U.S. government and American social norms.

Perhaps because conventional wisdom both disparages them for being mere copyists and mistrusts them for not being mere copyists, translators often evince an odd relationship to their own powers of agency. In his memoir, Rabassa suggests that his career results from no more than a fortuitous series of coincidences and that he translated all his books without reading them through beforehand because he was "just too lazy to read the book twice."[38] Rabassa himself does not go so far as to wonder what might have become of works of Latin American fiction now widely regarded in the United States as iconic had they been entrusted to a less brilliant translator. However, we can compare the fate in English translation of other towering classics of twentieth-century Latin American literature such as Alejo Carpentier's 1962 *Siglo de las luces* (translated into English by John Sturrock from a French translation and retitled *Explosion in a Cathedral*) or João Guimarães Rosa's 1956 *Grande Sertão: Veredas* (partially translated by Harriet de Onis while she was in very ill health, completed by James L. Taylor, and published under the title *The Devil to Pay in the Backlands*)[39] and ask the question ourselves. Given the powerful political forces at work during the period, it may well have been quite inevitable that novels like *One Hundred Years of Solitude* and *Hopscotch* would be translated (unlike the vast majority of Latin American novels that preceded them). The fact that their English translations have achieved classic canonical status strikes me as less inevitable.

My interest here is not in the Boom itself or the fascinating dynamic that led powerful entities in the United States to oppose the spread of

Communism in Latin America by supporting the translation of works by writers who were often of avowedly Communist inclinations or connections. The fact is that as a result of the Boom, not only was the cultural capital of Latin American literature immeasurably and permanently enhanced worldwide, but generations of writers within the United States were no longer faced with the dilemma that had confronted Casey, Alfau, and Bombal. A Latino literature emerged that explored its direct lineage to Latin American literature, addressed and made use of the interplay between English and Spanish, consolidated literary traditions that stretched back centuries, and gave literary voice to what would become the country's largest minority. This, in turn, seems to have led to a decline in the publication of translations. When translator Magda Bogin queried publishers about this decline in 1998, she was told, "We've discovered we don't have to go abroad for the kinds of qualities we were seeming to find in Latin American literature." To which Bogin herself added, "It's about time that Latino writers in the United States got the apparatus and wherewithal to be heard . . . but it shouldn't knock out the rest of the continent."[40] U.S. Latino writers themselves have been increasingly aware of this issue, and a number of them—Francisco Goldman, Daniel Alarcón, and Mónica de la Torre, to name but three—have done a great deal to address it, as both translators and advocates for translation.

For, of course, literary translation itself was by no means permanently bolstered by the Boom's successes. Even at its height, a "Translator's Manifesto" by Robert Payne, published by the PEN Translation Committee in 1969, opens with this marvelously flowery complaint: "For too long [translators] have been the lost children in the enchanted forest of literature." The National Book Award in Translation lasted a decade or so and then petered out.[41] The vogue for discovering new Latin American writers passed, and while the writers whose work had been introduced by the Boom continued to be translated, the generations that immediately succeeded them found it increasingly difficult to break into English—as, indeed, did writers everywhere. In the past ten years, the issue of translation into English, the global vehicular language, has been vociferously raised by writers, translators, and publishers around the world, but actual numbers have not risen all that much, and have no doubt fallen as a percentage of all books published. A total of 299 works of prose fiction in translation were published in the United States in 1999, and 341 appeared in 2010—a year when the U.S. publishing industry turned out well over 200,000 books.[42]

Nor has appreciation of the nature of a translator's work notably increased in the media. On March 9, 2010, a *New York Times* article by Miguel Helft headlined "Google's Computing Power Refines Translation Tool" reported that Google's translation service has set itself apart from other online translation tools by adopting a statistical approach. Rather than seeking to translate on its own, Google Translate is a search engine that scans "thousands or millions of passages and their human-generated translations in order to make accurate guesses about how to translate new texts." The *Times* decided to put Google Translate to the test by feeding it and several other digital translation services the first lines of some famous novels and comparing the results in a chart.[43] The other digital translators produced odd, awkward phrases, but Google Translate's version of the first line of García Márquez's *Cien años de soledad* differed from that of the "human translator" by only a single word. Which, given that Google Translate is a search engine and the translation of *One Hundred Years* one of the most famous texts of our time, widely available across the Internet, should not seem any tremendous feat (indeed, that very slight difference might be deemed a carefully planned denial of plagiarism). As David Bellos pointed out later in response, "All you need to do is get the old paperback from your basement."[44]

Gregory Rabassa's name was absent both from the chart and the article, which cited Franz Ochs, a brilliant linguist and the head of Google's translation program, to the effect that "This technology can make the language barrier go away." It's a familiar scenario. Translation will be not only inevitable but also unnecessary for humans to bother with: the spaceship arrives at the unknown planet and the computer instantly makes full communication with its alien inhabitants possible. Bellos warns of a closely related misconception that the *Times*'s chart tends to confirm: the idea that there is a single "correct" translation of any given phrase or literary passage, and that if the human just thinks hard enough, or the machine crunches enough data, both will arrive at that unique and identical formulation. I would append a footnote to this warning: if we deem language to be information and nothing more, and translation no more than the transfer of that information, this misconception may become our truth.

The curious notion that translation is inevitable must have enormous appeal, for it recurs persistently in different guises, embraced by wild-eyed literary romantics and computer geeks alike. Its charm may lie in the way it liberates us from the random, serendipitous, and fallible figure of the translator, reassuring us that literary value is concrete and universal and linguistic meaning certain. I've sketched this thumbnail history in an attempt to show that any given act of literary translation is a product of unique political, linguistic, cultural, technological, historical, and human contexts. Translators, like authors, are the product of social structures and circumstances; translators, like authors, play a role in bolstering or challenging those structures and continually altering the linguistic and narrative tools brought to bear on them, as well as the attitudes and norms that produce them. What I want to underscore, in conclusion, and what I hope these four episodes have shown, is that the *political gesture* enacted by a translator is entirely separate from that enacted by the writer of the work translated. Translators have their own motives and their own artistry. The translator's political gesture may be aligned with the writer's or may contradict it, but it is, in all cases, apart from it, distinct, and unique. Translation is not inevitable. The will to translate is a key component of any translation, and it must exist at many levels, both societywide and individual, in order for a given work of literary translation to come into existence and take on cultural relevance within its language.

Notes

1. Two excellent sources for a corresponding history of the translation of Latin American poetry would be Kirsten Silvz Gruesz, "Tasks of the Translator: Imitative Literature, the Catholic South, and the Invasion of Mexico," in *Ambassadors of Culture: The Transamerican Origins of Latino Writing* (Princeton: Princeton University Press, 2002), and Jonathan Cohen's recent work on William Carlos Williams as translator: *By Word of Mouth: Poems from the Spanish, 1916–1959* (New York: New Directions, 2011). Eliot Weinberger's translations of Octavio Paz and others constitute another significant thread in this history; see his essay, "Anonymous Sources," in the present volume.

2. Another work often mentioned in this context is *El Laúd del desterrado* (*The Exile's Lyre*), a collection of poems by exiled Cuban poets published in New York in 1858 that has been reissued in a critical edition by Matías Montes-Huidobro (Houston: Arte Público Press, 1995).

3. From "Principles of a 'World History of Literature'" in *The World Republic of Letters*, trans. M. B. DeBevoise (Cambridge, Mass.: Harvard University Press, 2004), 15.

4. For a valuable discussion of Martí and translation, see Laura Lomas, "Thinking Across, Infiltration, and Transculturation: José Martí's Theory and Practice of

Post-colonial Translation in New York," ed. Carmen Boullosa and Regina Galasso, *Translation Review 81*:12–33.

5. *Our sister republic: a gala trip through tropical Mexico in 1869–70. Adventure and sight-seeing in the land of the Aztecs with picturesque descriptions of the country and the people and reminiscences of the empire and its downfall* (Hartford, Conn: Columbian Book Company. / W. E. Bliss, Toledo, Ohio. / A. L. Bancroft & Company, San Francisco:1870).

6. Esther Allen, "This Is Not America: Nineteenth-Century Accounts of Travel Between the Americas" (Ph.D. diss., New York University, 1991).

7. Cited by Alice Houston Luiggi, "Some Letters of Sarmiento and Mary Mann, 1865–1876, Part I," *The Hispanic American Historical Review* 32, no. 2 (May 1952): 188. For more on Sarmiento and Mary Mann, see Deshae E. Lott, "Like One Happy Family: Mary Peabody Mann's Method for Influencing Reform," in *Reinventing the Peabody Sisters*, ed. Monika Maria Elbert, Julie Elizabeth Hall, and Katherine Rodier (Iowa City: University of Iowa Press, 2006), 91–107; and *My Dear Sir: Mary Mann's Letters to Sarmiento (1865–1881)*, ed. Barry L. Velleman (Buenos Aires: ICANA, 2001).

8. Letter from Mary Mann to Henry Barnard, February 7, 1888. Cited in Luiggi, "Some Letters," 208.

9. See, for example, Doris Somers's critique of the way Mary Mann's translation suppressed Sarmiento's use of metaphor in *Foundational Fictions: The National Romances of Latin America* (Berkeley: University of California Press, 1991), 344, n. 17. See also *Facundo: Civilization and Barbarism: The First Complete English Translation*, trans. Kathleen Ross (Berkeley: University of California Press, 2003). In her introduction, Ross describes Mary Peabody Mann only as the "wife of the famous United States senator Horace Mann" and makes no mention of her other works.

10. *Juanita: A Romance of Real Life in Cuba Fifty Years Ago* (1887; reprint, Charlottesville: University of Virginia Press, 2000), ed. and with an introduction by Patricia M. Ard.

11. My claim about the unique status of these two book-length translations of Latin American literature into English—Mann's *Facundo* and Ogden's *María*—is based on a number of bibliographical sources compiled during the first half of the twentieth century, clearly in response to the dawning perception of the dearth of Latin American material available in English. These bibliographies include Remigio U. Pane, "Two Hundred Latin American Books in English Translation: A Bibliography," *The Modern Language Journal* 27, no. 8 (Dec. 1943): 593–604; William H. Fletcher, *A Guide to Spanish and Spanish-American Literature in Translation* (Los Angeles Junior College, 1936); Sturgis E. Leavitt, *Hispano-American Literature in the United States: A Bibliography of Translations and Criticism* (Cambridge, Mass.: Harvard University Press, 1932). I'm very grateful to Fernando Acosta-Rodriguez, the Librarian for Latin American Studies at Princeton University's Firestone Library, for helping me locate some of these resources.

12. "Embarrassed Foreign Missions" (Editorial), *The Nation* 60, no. 1559 (May 16, 1995): 376. *The Nation's* editorials were published anonymously at the time; the information attributing this piece to Ogden comes from David Anderson Thomas's rather adversarial M.A. thesis about Ogden, "Rollo Ogden: An Ideologue of Op-

position to United States Imperialism at the Beginning of the Twentieth Century" (Georgia State University, 1972). The phrase I cite here, particularly in its rejection of the word "heathen," hearkens back strongly to Roger Williams's haunting 1643 *Key into the Language of America*.

13. Rollo Ogden, *William Hickling Prescott* (Boston and New York: Houghton Mifflin and Company, 1904).

14. Bellow, *Adventures of Augie March* (1953; reprint, New York: Penguin, 1999), 90–91.

15. I owe the Isaacs–Bellow connection to Professor Edward Mendelson, who provided the reference in a letter to the editor of the *New York Review of Books* (April 28, 2011), in belated response to perplexity expressed in a 2004 review of *Augie March* by J. M. Coetzee.

16. Rivera y Río belonged to a group of mid-nineteenth-century novelists known for their "social novels" written under the strong influence of French novelist Eugène Sue. See Adriana Sandoval Lara, "'Las novelas sociales' del siglo XIX. Un primer acercamiento a José Rivera y Río," in *La república de las letras: asomos a la cultra escrita del México decimonónico*, vol. 1, ed. Belem Clark de Lara and Elisa Speckman Guerra (Mexico City: Universidad Nacional Autónoma de México, 2005).

17. See "The Tragedy of Translated Men," in Casanovas, *The World Republic of Letters*, 254.

18. Gustavo Pérez Firmat, *Tongue Ties: Logo-Eroticism in Anglo-Hispanic Literature* (London: Palgrave Macmillan, 2003).

19. Felipe Alfau, *Locos: A Comedy of Gestures* (1936; reprint, Champaign, Ill.: Dalkey Archive Press, 1988).

20. Ilan Stavans, "An Interview with Felipe Alfau," *Review of Contemporary Fiction* 13, no. 1 (Spring 1993).

21. Felipe Alfau, *Chromos* (Champaign, Ill.: Dalkey Archive Press, 1999).

22. Maria Luisa Bombal, *House of Mist* (New York: Farrar, Straus & Giroux, 1947).

23. Maria Luisa Bombal, *New Islands and Other Stories by María Luisa Bombal*, trans. Richard and Lucia Cunningham (New York: Farrar, Straus & Giroux, 1982), 3–50.

24. Susanne Stark, "Women." In *The Oxford History of Literary Translation in English, Vol. 4: 1790–1900*, ed. Peter France and Kenneth Haynes (Oxford: Oxford University Press, 2006), 126.

25. Cited in Trudy Balch, "Pioneer on the Bridge of Language" in *Américas* 50, no. 5 (November/December 1998), 46–51.

26. See Nancy Vogeley, "Introduction," in Fernández de Lizardi, *The Mangy Parrot, Abridged*, trans. and ed. David Frye (Indianapolis: Hackett Publishing, 2005), ix–xviii.

27. "De la Huerta Envoy Arrives on Mission; Deputy Guzmán Going Today to Washington to Open Revolution's Agency," *New York Times*, December 15, 1923.

28. See Balch, "Pioneer."

The Will to Translate

29. Deborah Cohn, "A Tale of Two Translation Programs: Politics, the Market, and Rockefeller Funding for Latin American Literature in the United States During the 1960s and 1970s," *Latin American Research Review* 41, no. 2 (2006): 139–164.

30. See Efraín Kristal, *Invisible Work: Borges and Translation* (Nashville: Vanderbilt University Press, 2002).

31. "Don Segundo Sombra en Inglés," published in *Revista Multicolor* 53 (August 11, 1934). From *Borges en Revista Multicolor*, ed. Irma Zangara (Buenos Aires: Editorial Atlántida, 1995), 203.

32. See Elizabeth Lowe and Ezra Fitz, *Translation and the Rise of Inter-American Literature* (Gainesville: University Press of Florida, 2007).

33. Jeremy Munday, "The Relations of Style and Ideology in Translation: A Case Study of Harriet de Onís," in *Actas del III Congreso Internacional de la Asociación Ibérica de Estudios de Traducción e Interpretación. La traducción del futuro: mediación lingüística y cultural en el siglo XXI*, ed. L. Pegenaute, J. DeCesaris, M. Tricas, and E. Bernal (Barcelona: PPU, 2008), 1:1, 57–68. See also Jeremy Munday, *Style and Ideology in Translation: Latin American Writing in English* (New York: Routledge, 2008).

34. Cited in Munday, "The Relations of Style and Ideology in Translation," 64.

35. Cited Balch, "Pioneer," 47.

36. Rabassa's *If This Be Treason: Translation and Its Dyscontents* (New York: New Directions, 2005) was awarded the PEN/Martha Albrand Award for the Art of the Memoir in 2006.

37. Cohn, "Translation Programs," 146–148.

38. Rabassa, *If This Be Treason*, 27–28.

39. For a compelling account of the publication of Guimaraes Rosa's masterpiece in the United States, see Piers Armstrong, *Third World Literary Fortunes: Brazilian Culture and its International Reception* (Plainsboro, N.J.: Associated University Presses, 1999), 110–127.

40. Cited by Balch, "Pioneer," 51.

41. In 2007, a Best Translated Book Award, given by the University of Rochester-based weblog Three Percent with support from Amazon.com, was launched.

42. The 1999 figure was established by a study done by the National Endowment for the Arts. The "2010 Translation Database" is downloadable from Three Percent: http://www.rochester.edu/College/translation/threepercent/index.php?id=2420 (accessed December 3, 2011).

43. "Putting Google Translate to the Test," *New York Times*, March 9, 2010.

44. David Bellos, "I Translator," *New York Times*, March 20, 2010.

PART II
The Translator at Work

⌘EIGHT

The Great Leap

César and the Caesura

FORREST GANDER

In 1972, Robert Bly published an issue of his *Seventies Press* journal that interspersed several short essays on what he called "leaping poetry" with translations of Lorca, Vallejo, Takahashi, de Otero, and other poets, including Rilke. In a final section, Bly included "Home Grown Poems" that he felt continued or extended the quick-associative, "leaping" spirit of his international exemplars. In some ways, the essays served to critique what Charles Bernstein would later come to call Official Verse Culture. Bly's main prescription for change was a good dose of Latin American surrealism. The translations he showcased were lively, and the effect of anthologizing a small, handpicked group of terrific poets from Latin America, Spain, Germany, Sweden, Japan, and China was exhilarating and popular. The whole shebang, retitled *Leaping Poetry: An Idea with Poems and Translations*, was reprinted as a hardback three years later.

Heap on thirty-plus years and here we are, in time to revisit *Leaping Poetry* to see how Bly's "idea with poems and translations" resonates in the current milieu. Might Marjorie Perloff's characterization of poetic indeterminacy or Stephen Burt's notion of "elliptical poetry" or Kamau Brathwaite's "sycorax typography" be developments of "leaping poetry"? Are translations of Spanish and Latin American poets still leading the way for us? And what exactly *was* leaping poetry, anyway?

Whatever else it was, Bly's leaping poetry was a guy thing. The single woman represented in his anthology, Marguerite Young, was once Bly's professor. The poems in English (by Jerome Rothenberg, Bill Knott, Allen Ginsberg, John Wieners, and others) and the translations are still great to read . . . if only they weren't contextualized by Bly's preposterous prose.

To be fair to the time, it's true that in the 1970s, Ezra Pound's proclamations ("Go in fear of abstraction," etc.) were still swooping through the air like Valkyries, and (mostly male) writers were looking to jack their reputations by packing together pseudo-authoritative pronouncements on all of human history, art, and literature and lobbing them into the cloud of a "new idea" that would inevitably happen to validate each writer's own personal style. In fact, what Bly's "leaping poetry" boils down to—"leaping is the ability to associate fast"—is a diffusion of Ezra Pound's translation of Aristotle: "Swift perception of relations, hallmark of genius." So there was some precedence for Bly's presumption that he could single-handedly explain the excitement in "'modern poetry' in all European countries" or sweepingly declare that due to the leap-blocking efforts of Christianity, there were "eighteen hundred years of no-leaping" poetry prior to William Blake. There was precedence too for the wacky language Bly uses to make his case. His references to "blocked love-energy," "Great Mother mysteries," and to a spark that can rocket (evidently like a pachinko ball) from one side of the brain to the other and then down through three layers of brain—"When the new brain is receiving energy from the other brains, then leaping poetry is possible"—are cartoonish. And how do you respond to someone who claims that "Poems of steady light always imply a unity in the brain that is not there" if the term "Poems of steady light," like "hopping poems" or "tame association," drifts off like a vitreous floater every time you try to focus on it?

But Bly at least was reading international poetry, translating it, and championing it to others. *Leaping Poetry* was enormously influential; many young poets in the seventies who had not been reading work in translation began to do so. The poets introduced in Bly's anthology were soon retranslated by others. *Leaping Poetry* helped ignite a Lorca craze, every poet in the '70s was longing for *duende*, and Spanish and Latin American surrealism, adopted and converted, may have helped resuscitate North American poetry for a while.

And what about now? Are translations and international literature central to North American poetry? Was surrealism curative? My own perspective is not exactly disinterested. It seems to me that translation is more than ever a part of American literary life, but that poets are not necessarily looking to the same countries or for the same kind of leap that Bly celebrated.

Look at all the new Mexican poetry that has carried across the border. Besides anthologies such as *Reversible Monuments: Contemporary Mexican Poets*; *Connecting Lines: New Poetry from Mexico*; and *Sin Puertas Visibles*, books by important individual poets like Gloria Gervitz, Laura Solorzano, and Coral Bracho are now available in English. And this translated work has already been striking sparks of response from U.S. poets, among them poets who don't read Spanish, like Stephen Burt, C. D. Wright, and Michael Palmer.

I would guess that translations of contemporary French poetry have had the greatest impact on U.S. poetry in the last twenty years, and books by younger poets like Lisa Lubasch (*Twenty-One After Days*), Marcella Durand (*Western Capital Rhapsodies*), and Laura Mullen (*Subject*), among others (Michael Palmer, Rosmarie Waldrop, Cole Swensen), make that case. But the spectrum of influence is much wider. John Ashbery lifts a Finnish form for his own "Finnish Rhapsody." Serial poems by Charles Bernstein take their cue from Louis Zukofsky's homophonic translations of Catullus. Slovenian poet Tomaz Salamun's translated work is the catalyst for John Bradley's book of poetry and invented correspondence, *War on Words*. Prageeta Sharma's new work reveals an infatuation with translations of Kim Hyesoon, and Brenda Hillman's "water" poems were nourished, in part, by Hans Favery, a Surinam-born poet who wrote in Dutch. We can see that Guy Davenport's Greek translations inspired Kent Johnson to write *The Miseries of Poetry: Traductions from the Greek*, and that Sappho translations affected the form and tone of Mei-mei Berssenbrugge's early poems. In his book *O Wheel*, Peter Sacks acknowledges the influence of translations of medieval Hebrew poet Shmuel HaNagid. Juliana Spahr's *This Connection of Everyone with Lungs* is strongly marked by her reading of *Alphabet,* the English translation of a seminal book by Danish writer Inger Christensen. Both Paul Hoover's recent *Poems in Spanish* and George Kalamaras's *Even the Java Sparrows Call Your Hair* are inspired by translations of Spanish-language poetry. And Gerald Stern is one of several poets to record his encounter with translations of poems by Taha Muhammad Ali, a Palestinian poet. Arabic, Spanish, Danish, Hebrew, Greek, Slovenian, Korean, Danish, Latin, Finnish,

French . . . I could continue, but I think the point is clear: contemporary American poets are being influenced by translations from all over the world.

Several years ago, before I was hired as the Briggs-Copeland poet at Harvard, I was interviewed by Helen Vendler, who asked me, after looking at examples of my projected syllabi, how I could teach books of translation to students who were not even thoroughly familiar with their own (by which she meant British and North American) literary tradition. It was, probably, an appropriate question to pose to someone about to be hired into something called the Department of English and American Literature and Language. And yet the notion that literary tradition might be pruned between geographic lines seems to me a constructed and unhealthy convenience, and one that runs the danger of advocating a kind of academic feudalism. I don't believe that writers care where their influences come from. They're alert for images, rhythms, forms, anything at all that will feed the burning tree. I think readers are the same. Chaucer had his ear tuned to French poetry before he shifted the rhythm of his own lines from tetrameter to pentameter. Shakespeare cribbed more than once from Arthur Golding's translation of Ovid. For George Herbert and Henry Vaughan, the translation of the Bible they read was a matter of the utmost seriousness. Keats penned an ecstatic poem to honor a translation of Homer. And Hopkins, when he wrote "Wreck of the Deutschland," had Pindar in mind.

There are, of course, political ramifications to crossing linguistic borders. Each language is a modality of life. We might go so far as to say that one form of totalitarianism is the stuffing of expression into a single, standardized language that marches the reader toward some presumptively shared goal. If our country's self-assurance, its reliance on a grammar of linearity and commerce, its obsessive valuation of measurement and scientific objectivity brackets off realms of perception, of possibility and difference, then translation offers refreshment. It shifts our perspective and realigns our relation to the world, bringing us into proximity with other modalitites. With others. It can draw us across that most guarded border, the one we build around ourselves.

The big question for me, then, is: To what degree do host languages and host cultures attest to constructions of the world that are incommensurable with my own?

Part II: The Translator at Work

For instance, I wonder at the implications of the metonymic location of agency in Spanish—*I* don't hurt my hand, but *me duele la mano,* me it hurts the hand—and what seems (from my linguistic perspective) to be a separation or objectification of body parts. An English reader wonders how anyone can think of their own hand as "the hand," as if it were an independent entity. (In English, we only speak of the body in this way when the body is a cadaver.)

The zinging run-on sentence that launches the marvelous César Aira's *Diario de Hepatitis,* deployed with serial prepositions, past and present participles, conditional and future tenses, mentions a number of such body parts. Here's my English translation:

If I'm found undone by disgrace, destroyed, impotent, in extreme physical or mental anguish, or both together, isolated, for example, and condemned on a steep mountain, drowned in snow, frozen to the core, after a fall of hundreds of meters, bounced from the edges of ice and rock, with both legs severed, or my ribs smashed and cracked and all their points perforating my lungs; or at the bottom of a ditch or the end of an alley, after a shootout, bleeding into a sinister dawn which, for me, would be the last; or in the ward for incurables at the hospital, losing hour to hour my last functions in between paroxysms of atrocious pain; or abandoned to the avatars of mendacity and alcoholism in the street; or with gangrene shooting up my leg; or in the phantasmal progression of a glottal spasm; or purely insane, going about my business in a straitjacket, imbecilic, opprobrious, lost . . . it's probable that, even having a little pencil and a notebook at hand, I wouldn't write. Nothing, not a line, not a word. I absolutely wouldn't write. Not because I couldn't, not on account of the circumstances, but for the same reason I don't write now: because I don't feel like it, because I'm tired, bored, fed up; because I can't see it serves any purpose.

In Spanish, it's:

Con las dos piernas arrancadas
Colloquially: with both my legs severed
Literally: with *the* two legs severed

   O las costillas aplastadas y rotas y todas sus puntas perforándome los pulmones

The Great Leap: César and the Caesura

111

Colloquially: Or my ribs smashed and cracked and all their points perforating my lungs
Literally: Or the ribs smashed and broken and all their points perforating me the lungs

O con la gangrena subiéndome por una pierna—
Colloquially: Or with gangrene shooting up my leg—
Literally: Or with the gangrene climbing me by a leg—

If we want to translate the lines so that they have an equivalent *impact* on the English-language reader, we're going to choose the colloquial translation, because in Spanish, the syntax doesn't incite the Spanish-language reader to think twice about agency or the relation of a self to its constituent parts.

But if we translate it colloquially, are we simply undermining one of the most interesting differences in the ways that the two languages negotiate experience?

And then, again, if we draw attention to differences by foregrounding the literal—"Or with the gangrene climbing me by a leg"—aren't we merely exoticizing a distinction imposed by our foreignness, by our own point of view, one that isn't discerned by the readers of the host language—as Pound and Fennellosa did in their ascription of ideograms to Chinese? (Chinese readers, it must be acknowledged, simply don't see in their characters "the horse" or "the sun in the trees" that the Americans were delightedly deciphering.)

These are the sorts of questions that interest me.

The language of the South American Aymara also interests me, and in particular because I've cotranslated two books by the Bolivian poet Jaime Saenz, whose work is notably influenced by Aymara language and culture. In Aymara, it is impossible to say something like "Joan of Arc burned at the stake in May 1431" since that statement is unqualified by anyone's experience and because every sentence must express whether an action or event was personally witnessed or not. According to Rafael Nuñez, a cognitive scientist at the University of California, San Diego, Aymara is the only studied culture for which the past is linguistically and conceptually in front of the people while the future lies behind them.

To speak of the future, he notes, elderly Aymara thumb or wave backward over their shoulder. To reference the past, they make forward sweeping motions with their hands and arms. "The main word for 'eye,' 'front,' and 'sight' in Aymara means the past, while the basic word for 'back' or 'behind' also means the future."

It has been suggested that in a culture that places a premium on stipulating degrees of evidential investment—distinguishing the observed from the unobserved, the known from the unknown—it makes sense to metaphorically position the past in your field of vision while the future—always speculative—remains invisible behind you.

In this case, and others (like the widely publicized research by Daniel Everett on the "Cultural Constraints on Grammar and Cognition in Pirahã"), there seems to be a close relation between the particularities of language and the perceptions and conceptions of the speakers of that language.

Here's the Bolivian poet Jaime Saenz channeling an Aymara spiritual regard for the harmony of opposites into a philosophical grammar:

What is the night?—you ask now and forever.
The night, a revelation still veiled.
Perhaps a deathform, tenacious and flexed,
perhaps a body lost to the night itself.
Truly a chasm, a space unimaginable.
A subtle, lightless realm not unlike the body dwelling in you,
which hides, surely, many clues to the night.

. . .

One time I came close to my body;
and realizing I had never seen it, even though I bore it with me,
I asked it who it was;
and a voice, in the silence, said to me:
I am the body who inhabits you, and I am here in the darkness, and I
    suffer you, and I live you, and die you.
But I am not your body. I am the night.

That indelible tone—meditative, poised, haunting, mystical—and Saenz's use of the full phrase as a line penetrated me and strongly affected the development of poems I wrote after finishing the Saenz translation. My own poems at the time were particularly attentive to line breaks, percussive prosody, and polyrhythms.

Soon after translating Saenz's *La Noche*, I wrote a poem called "A Clearing" to accompany photographs by Raymond Meeks. I wasn't

The Great Leap: César and the Caesura

113

conscious of the Saenz effect until months after I had written the poem that begins:

> Where are you going? Ghosted with dust. From where have you come?
> Dull assertiveness of the rock heap, a barren monarchy.
> Wolfspider, size of a hand, encrusted with dirt at the rubble's edge.
>
> What crosses here goes fanged or spiked and draws its color from the ground.
> Xanthic shadow at the edges.
> Where are we going? Ghosted with dust. From where have we come?

This may be an obvious instance of a translation influencing my own writing. But I wasn't at all aware of it as I wrote; the influence had been absorbed and metabolized.

And it has happened the other way as well. In my last book of poems, *Eye Against Eye*, I worked a medial caesura, a wide blank space, into the lines of a number of poems. In addition to gapping pentameter rhythms, the caesura represented for me the call and response of Southern work songs and the experience of talking to my wife as we walked in ruts on either side of a hump in the dirt road where we spent a summer in Arkansas.

Last year, giving readings from *Firefly Under the Tongue*, a translation of the selected poems of Mexican poet Coral Bracho, I found my eyes sliding across the gutter of the en face edition—as though I were reading the inside margin as a caesura in one of my own poems—and plucking Spanish lines from the left page as I read the translations in English on the right. I developed a strategy for including Spanish lines as part of a performance that allows an audience to hear the original language in conversation with English. Surprisingly, rather than deforming the music of the poem, the technique seems to me to intensify and clarify the music.

Most recently, when I was translating poems from *Santa y Seña* (*Watchword* in my version), the Villarrutia Award-winning book by Mexican poet Pura López Colomé, I began to incorporate Spanish lines into the English translations "where I heard them," sometimes preceded or followed by their English translations. Occasionally, where I meant to stress an ineluctable music in Spanish or where I thought semantic meaning would be intuited in context, I didn't translate the Spanish at all.

Part II: The Translator at Work

Three horses came down the hill
and sumptuously entered
the river's transparency
a la diafanidad del río.
One
waded out next to me.
At times, it paused to drink.
A ratos se detenía a beber.
At times, it looked me in the eye.
A ratos me miraba fijamente.
And between us both,
y entre ambos,
an ancient murmur passed
on its sojourn.

I realize my method—which is derived first from my own poems and my development of a caesura to approximate the effect of call and response, and then from my performance of translations at public readings—complicates the translation in ways that don't represent the original. But I wonder if the goal of "representing" the original is the goal of translation at all, given that the work in translation is necessarily subjected to alteration, transformation, dislocation, and displacement. Maybe there are times when *not* "representing" the original is precisely what permits the creation of something less definitive but more ongoing, a form of translation that amplifies and renews (and even multiplies) the original poetry's meanings.

And if the point of translation, to begin with, is that one language is not enough, doesn't the interaction of two languages celebrate that apriorism by refusing to fully convert the foreign into a version of the familiar?

I'm influenced in my approach to translation both by Brechtian theater, its acknowledgment of artifice, and by Spanish philosopher José Ortega y Gasset's interpretation of translation as "another genre entire" from the original, but it is nevertheless my intention to create poems in English, poems with a comparable impact on the reader. Surprisingly, rather than disfiguring the poems or turning them into experiments in scholarship, occasional bilingualisms feathered into the translations can

The Great Leap: César and the Caesura

allow English to embrace Spanish (perhaps it's more like a cheek kiss) while encouraging both languages to harmonize at key moments so the poetry is less diminished, less often "lost in translation." From even such intermittent linguistic collaborations, a whole new realm of sonorous interaction and implication becomes possible, allowing me to create a more expansive and expressive prosody and inviting readers to venture a little further across the border.

NINE

Misreading Orhan Pamuk

MAUREEN FREELY

The Museum of Innocence is (among many other things) an ode to a particular form of Turkishness. Its characters belong to their time and place and no other; every significant object is meticulously named and catalogued. The hero, who is also the curator of the museum, is aware that foreigners and future generations might not "read" the objects (or indeed the story that connects them) as he does, so he pauses from time to time to offer naïve anthropological descriptions of strange and puzzling customs. Contemporary Turkish readers will have no trouble reading between the lines of these sweet but troubled asides, for they play on long-standing national anxieties about "how the world sees us," offering an elegant and understated riposte to the distorting Western gaze. They will also be well versed in the tradition that sits at the heart of the book: the transmission of meaning through gesture, expression, and the artful arrangement of symbolic objects. They will enjoy the way Pamuk evokes this silent code, even as he breaks its golden rule by putting it into words.

Most importantly, Turkish readers will understand in the most visceral way how and why the novel refuses the marginalizing labels accorded to their history and culture by most of the rest of the world, and most particularly in the West. *The Museum of Innocence* refuses to see itself through Western eyes. It claims its place at the center of its world: it aspires to permanence in a real space beyond the words and the story. It is a house full of objects that carry the past inside them. The objects are there not just to illustrate one man's story, but to invite reader-visitors to immerse themselves so deeply into his world that they dream the same dreams. As our naïve hero tells his respectful chronicler, the novelist Orhan Pamuk, he hopes that visitors to his museum will find their dreams "merging with ours." He takes issue with what the young boy says about foreign readers at the end of *Snow*—that they cannot "understand us from afar." This, Kemal, the curator, innocently suggests, is a problem you can solve by cutting out the distance. "Visitors to our museum and people who read our book will understand us," he says. It is never clear if his chronicler agrees with him or simply wishes it were so.

How many of these subtly layered meanings will fall by the wayside when the novel goes out into the world, to be translated into more than sixty languages? Should its translators ignore the competing meanings that Turkish and foreign readers will impose on it? Do they have a duty, once the book has been published, to provide some sort of context—or should they bow out graciously, reminding themselves that no translator and indeed no writer can control for meaning, let alone context?

My aim here is to cast some light on the political dilemmas of translation as Turkish letters enter the global age, and to describe how I have tried to address them since beginning to translate Orhan Pamuk eight years and five books ago. But let me first pause to explain that I am not a translator by profession. Before trying my hand at translation, I had worked for twenty-five years as a novelist, journalist, and university lecturer. However, I have a lifelong interest in Turkey, where I spent my childhood and where my family still lives. I have known Orhan Pamuk since the late 1960s, when he and I attended brother and sister lycées, though my friend in those days was his elder brother. Orhan and I rediscovered each other in the early 1990s, when his first books were published in English translation. When he wrote to me in 2002 to ask if I would consider translating *Snow*, my first response was terror. I could not help but remember how often I had lost the thread while navigating his longer sentences when reading the novel in Turkish, and how, each time, I had spared a kind thought for the poor soul who would have to translate it. But when I agreed, it was because I had an idea as to how I might negotiate the long and Escher-like landscape between Turkish and English.

Turkish is an agglutinative language with a great deal more flexibility than English: root nouns in ordinary sentences can carry strings of eight or more suffixes. There is, even in the colloquial, a pleasing sense of compression that we in English expect to find only in poetry. Turkish

is more precise in its tenses—offering, for example, a distinction between eyewitness reports and hearsay—though its fondness for the passive voice means that it is often difficult to know who did what when. It
has no need for a verb "to have" and no verb "to be," and its single word
for "he," "she," and "it" is expendable. It is fond of long clauses beginning
with verbal nouns, while the verb that decides how these clauses will be
linked comes at the end of the sentence, which is often so long that the
English translator, lacking the sentence's governing idea, can feel like
she's carrying a week's worth of groceries without the benefit of a bag.

Another layer of difficulty comes from the extreme degree of political
oversight and interference in the public use of the Turkish language. This
dates back to the early 1930s, when the founder of the Republic, Mustafa
Kemal Ataturk, launched the so-called Language Revolution, creating
new words to reflect the spirit of the new republic, and replacing old
words that threatened to tie it to the past. Over two generations, this
program of state intervention in the Turkish language has resulted in
the loss of 60 percent of its vocabulary. Most of the lost words are of
Arabic or Persian origin. Even today it is controversial to draw upon the
language's lost words: novelists and translators of my acquaintance who
have dared to do so have been accused of "political inconsistency" and
even "betraying the revolution." Meanwhile, even highly educated Turks
have difficulty reading a newspaper from the 1930s. As for Ataturk's own
Oration, which forms the basis of Turkey's official history—it has been
"translated" into "new Turkish" twice since it was first published in 1933.

It is, perhaps, because grammatical structures remained untouched
and uncontroversial during the language revolution that today novelists,
poets, and playwrights take such pride and pleasure in them. When playing with their possibilities, writers can practice their art, and develop an
aesthetic, without interference. And yet these structures are difficult and
sometimes impossible to translate into English. A series of verbal nouns
can turn a fluid and cascading sentence into an avalanche of pebbles.
The reliance on the passive voice can, if replicated in the English, give an
air of obfuscation to a sentence that was once light and clear. And because
words are repeated more often in today's ethnically cleansed Turkish
than we expect to see in literary English, translators will often have to
guess whether or not the author meant mind or intellect; happiness, bliss,
or mirth.

I knew all this when I agreed to translate *Snow*, just as I knew that
Orhan might be inclined to judge a translation a dismal failure unless it

replicated the Turkish grammatical structures. But I believed he would be better served by a translation that delved underneath the visible structures, capturing the thought at the heart of each Turkish sentence, reforming each into an English sentence that was true to the original but also fluid—and if not as compressed as the Turkish, then at least echoing its music.

Though I knew my decision not to replicate the grammar at any cost would cause shock and concern among some established translators, I did still think that any controversy would be a paper war, centering on questions of language. I even thought I had found a peaceful alternative to freelance journalism: now I would be able to work from home, and even see my family. All I needed to do was to find the right words and arrange them into sentences that evoked the same powerful narrative trance as Orhan had in Turkish. I did have a jolt several weeks into the translation, when a nationalist paper misquoted me on the subject of headscarves following an online interview to which I naïvely agreed; in the weeks that followed, I was harassed by an Islamist newspaper whose agents used almost the same words as the Islamist assassin I'd been translating in *Snow*. But I was still safe in my chair, immersed in Orhan's words and mine.

Orhan and I had agreed that we would go over my finished working draft together. I knew that I was taking liberties, and I thought it important to know (and respond to) his views. I had seen several poets collaborate in this manner, and felt that the discussions between drafts had enriched their translations enormously. I thought the same approach might work for us—because we were friends and both novelists, because English was his second language, and because we both knew that the English translation would form the basis for most translations into other languages (almost forty in number then, and now more than sixty). When I finished my working draft, I sent it off to him. He spent several weeks reviewing it with his often impatient and exasperated pen (Maureen! Your energies are bad today! And how could you make such a mistake?). When he had finished, we met for a week at his summer home on the Princes Islands outside Istanbul to argue our way through the draft, sentence by sentence. There were many days when I approached Orhan's desk with trepidation, wondering what was in store for me. But I now look back on those intense and volatile exchanges with great affection. Through the text on the desk, we would enter into a fictive world that I had been living inside for more than a year, and for a time, we would live there together.

Then we'd bump into the next sentence that didn't work. Our original agreement was that we would change whatever he took issue with. In practice, there were matters we never managed to settle. For example, I wanted to use the Turkish term for anything that an English speaker in Turkey (and there are a lot of us) would not think to translate. These included words like *börek*, *yalı*, and *meyhane*. Orhan (dismissing my proposal as "ethnic" and "folkloric") wanted me to translate these words as "cheese pie," "Bosporus waterside mansion" and "modest drinking establishment," even when they made multiple appearances in a single paragraph. If you look at the five books we have worked on together, you'll see that the battle lines kept changing. But there were other times when Orhan won important victories (as when I agreed never to start a sentence with "and"). And there were edicts I resisted (as when I successfully withstood a sudden and temporary ban on the semicolon). While I refused to make any compromise that resulted in a sentence that sounded foolish in English, I grew to respect Orhan's long, winding sentences as I came to better appreciate their cumulative effect.

Our greatest area of difficulty was the language of emotion, which tends to be expansive and even anatomical in Turkish. Sometimes—as when Orhan decided that the hero of *Snow* went into a panic too often— he decided to change his own text. This would lead to problems later, when conscientious translators working in minor or non-Western languages referred to both the English and the Turkish versions and found discrepancies. Many took the trouble to write to me for clarification. But scholars finding differences between the two versions have been less inclined to consult before charging me with Orientalism. There is now a small but vigorous literature examining the ways I have set out to make Orhan more palatable for Western readers.

But when we sent our final version of *Snow* out to the publishers, both Orhan and I thought we'd done an honest job. I also thought my job was more or less over. Having brought the book into an English translation that reflected his aesthetic as well as mine, I could fade into the woodwork to watch from a distance as the book spoke for itself.

Naturally I assumed that I would be consulted during each stage of the publication process, as I would be with a novel of my own. What a shock it was to discover that my publishers were shocked to hear this. It could not be, they said. There was no room in the schedule. After I pressed my point, they changed their schedules, but the budget on one side of the Atlantic was such that the copyeditor could not (or would not?) track his changes. This made for difficulties, because this copyeditor was unhappy with the time shifts and decided to insert every backward shift inside brackets. He also disapproved of the way the hero treated women, so he changed that too. He even took it upon himself to rewrite the final paragraph. He did all this in the name of "the reader"— meaning, of course, "the Western reader."

Although other editors and copyeditors I have worked with better understood the importance of respecting the integrity of the text, seeking guidance when they found certain passages confusing, they too inserted many innocent (and telling) mistakes. For example, toward the end of *Snow* a fireman tells a story to the sad strains of the *saz*. The editor changed the sentence so that this fireman sitting in the city of Kars in the southeast of Turkey told the story to the sad strains of the *sax*.

He being a fine editor in a fine publishing house that prides itself on tracking and reviewing all changes, the matter was discussed thoroughly, and the *x* was duly changed back into a *z*. Nevertheless, I was shocked to discover how little even the very best people in the industry knew about Turkey and its history, and how this ignorance shaped their understanding of the book itself. And I was mystified by this assumption that "the reader" could not fend for himself—that texts from outside "the reader's" home terrain had to be adjusted to his tastes—or else. I assumed that the "or else" referred to instant death in the marketplace. This was certainly not the fate of *Snow*. But over the past eight years, I have heard many thousands of innocent (and very telling) foreign readings of this and the books by Pamuk I went on to translate afterward. Lacking any grounding in Ottoman or Republic history, most Anglophone readers of *Snow* seem to have a hard time following the complex endgame in which the army, the intelligence service, and the police compete for dominance even as they use a three-day window of opportunity to cleanse the city of Kurdish separatists, new Islamists, and the old Left. In a sense, these readers don't need to understand this in the same way as a Turkish reader or a reader familiar with Turkey: the story is strong enough to pull them across this foreign terrain, and its elements are described so clearly that even if they don't understand them, they can see them. But what they see, they believe to be the truth—not just about Turkey, but about what they so disarmingly call "that part of the world." And what they see is not a struggling and marginalized republic, but a nation harking to the cries of Islam, a clash of East and West. To put it crudely, all they see are their fears.

When *Snow* went out into the world, I again revised my job description. A translator did not just need to find the right words, stay in close conversation with the author, and run interference for him as the book made its way through the publication process. She also had to do everything she could to contextualize the book for readers who were not familiar with Turkey—not inside the text but outside it, in journals and newspapers, and at conferences, symposia, literature festivals, and a long sequence of very frustrating dinner parties. As I made the rounds, I was at first encouraged by those who said to me, "I knew nothing about Turkey until I read *Snow*, you know, but now I can see it's a really fascinating country so I'd like to know more about it." I thought the most important thing was that they were interested. Only good could come of that, I thought.

I was wrong.

Because now it was 2005 and Orhan Pamuk had provoked an ultranationalist firestorm after making an off-the-record remark to a Swiss journalist about a million Armenians and 30,000 Kurds having been killed "in these lands." His life in danger for having broken the state-imposed taboo on discussion of the Armenian genocide, he fled the country, going briefly into hiding. Not long after returning, he was prosecuted for "insulting Turkishness." Though the coverage abroad was extensive, even excessive, and though every story mentioned his famous statement, most of his readers in the Anglophone world—at least, most of the hundreds and thousands of readers who shared their views with me—did not understand that he was being pursued by ultranationalists sponsored by a shadowy group inside the military known colloquially as the "deep state." Lacking any knowledge of the deep state and its workings, most readers outside Turkey assumed that Orhan was being prosecuted by Islamists on account of his Western ideas. Now, Turkish politics is hard enough to understand for those of us who've lived in Turkey. But it should, I thought, be possible to get across a few essential facts. I'd had twenty years' experience as a journalist. I knew how to communicate, to reach my readers and start from where they were. But though I did take every opportunity offered to me, it was like writing in the sand during a hurricane. The clash of civilizations may not exist, but it has a powerful grip on the collective imagination. Just as powerful is the romance of

Misreading Orhan Pamuk

the dissident writer—the lone star who dares to speak truths that his nation cannot stomach, who champions Western values in the East.

Running concurrently back in Turkey (but never properly noted or understood abroad) was the virulent media hate campaign, which was also sponsored by the abovementioned "deep state" networks, and which would lead to Orhan and about a dozen other writers and activists becoming death targets. Orhan's international success was used against him: he was cast as a traitor who had sold his country to Europe for his career. In 2006 the story gained another twist: he became a traitor who had been so successful in "selling his country to Europe" that he won the Nobel Prize. It was not just the newspaper-reading public in Turkey who thought that. During the scores of English, European, and American interviews I did after he won the prize, the first question was always: Did I think he had won the prize because of the work he had done for free expression?

By now I was not just translating his books, and putting them into context, and telling the story of his shameful prosecution and persecution—I was part of that story. I was attending trials, walking through funnels of riot police, and coming face to face with deep state thugs. Wherever I happened to be in the world, a day rarely went by without a very strange person crossing the room with a boxy smile to offer me a very strange calling card. I was myself treated to a tiny media disinformation campaign, which caused me no real harm but promoted a version of my friendship with Orhan that he cannot have failed to find insulting and denigrating. There was a time when hardly a week went by without some literary or public figure saying that he wrote his books for one person and one person only. That person was his English translator. Poor Orhan would write his books and bring them to me and I would tell him "what to do."

I would prefer to think that we are often a match for each other. Our arguments have only served to deepen my understanding of his work. There has never been a day when I've sat down to translate a page by Orhan in which I haven't been taken by surprise and learned something. But after I became a pawn in the hate campaigns against him, I was again obliged to expand my understanding of a translator's job. It was not enough to find the right words, and defend them, and work on the literary peripheries to provide some sort of context, and fight to protect the author as he was attacked on all sides in the name of 1,001 political agendas. I also had to fight for room to breathe—not just for the writers and translators of fiction, but for literature itself. When the President of the Swedish Academy introduced Orhan Pamuk's Nobel lecture, he quoted the previous year's winner, Elfriede Jelinek, who spoke about how important it was for writers to retain the right *not* to talk about politics. It seemed to me that many of Orhan Pamuk's well-wishers in the West were often, without knowing it, conspiring with his enemies in Turkey to take that right away from him.

In the end he came back fighting, with an artful, generous, and redemptive novel in which there is no clash of civilizations, and politics is a distant dark cloud, and the set is so well annotated that all its readers should—by the time they leave the book, and no matter how new they are to its world—blend its dreams with their own. In the Turkish, each and every sentence has been structured to work toward this end. Though airy and transparent on the surface, each is shaped in such a way as to link into a coat of armor, protecting the fictive world from outside influence. So in my English translation, I faced a starker version of the choice I'd first made with *Snow*. To have attempted a replication of its linguistic structures would, I felt, have created too thick a coat of armor. After much deliberation, not just with Orhan but with our excellent editor, I chose clarity over structural correctness. My guide in this was the narrator, Kemal with the transparent heart. If I could make his voice heard in English, he would, I hoped, have no trouble making his world visible, even when addressing readers coming to him from a great distance.

To Orhan's mind, a translation should be "perfect," by which I think he means it should follow the author's intentions so precisely that it exerts no influence over its readers whatsoever. But I have known since childhood that translation is never neutral. It is politically charged at every stage. Over the last eight years I have learned how much it costs to engage in literary experiment in this fraught terrain—though the cost to the translator is nothing like the cost to the author. I have come to understand what Turkish writers are up against as they enter the global age, how they are misrepresented both at home and abroad and their words misconstrued.

But there's more to it than that. My understanding of cultural exchange has been profoundly affected by what I've seen during my work as a translator. It has given me a chance to stand outside my own world, to be on the receiving end as its ivory towers decide who outside the West should be read, and how. If I have the confidence to assert that translators are best placed to make these practices visible, it is because I have yet again changed my understanding of what it means to be a translator. Our work might begin on the page, but it rarely lets us stay there. It sends us out into the world, to take words across borders only rarely breached. Along the way, we witness strange and ugly things that illuminate to us the grammar of politics. So that even when we are home again, sitting in our armchairs and wrestling with sentences, we are never just translators. We are witnesses, with tales to tell. We are writers, with our own voices. Whenever we see literary culture distorted for political advantage, it matters very much that we speak.

Part II: The Translator at Work

On Translating a Poem by Osip Mandelstam

JOSÉ MANUEL PRIETO

TRANSLATED BY ESTHER ALLEN

I

In 1996, the Mexican historian Jean Meyer asked me to translate a poem by the Russian poet Osip Mandelstam (born in Warsaw in 1891; died in the Vtoraya Rechka transit camp, near Vladivostok, in 1938). The poem was the celebrated "Epigram Against Stalin," which begins with the line *"My zhivem pod soboiu ne chuia strany"* ("We live without feeling the country beneath our feet"). In 1980, I'd moved from Havana, my birthplace, to Siberia to study engineering at the University of Novosibirsk, and like anyone else who lived in Russia through the end of the 1980s and beginning of the 1990s, I knew the poem well. I had often recited it aloud in admiration of its formal qualities, in particular that first line, whose words have almost magical force.

No version of the poem then existed in Spanish; the French translation that had just appeared in Vitaly Shentalinsky's *La parole ressuscitée* made so impoverished a contrast to the extraordinary beauty of the original that I immediately began translating a more satisfactory variant, trying to capture the poem's charm while preserving its severe gravity. I worked on it for several days and came up with a translation that Jean Meyer included in his history of Russia and its empires, and that I posted on the wall over my desk.

The poem had cost Mandelstam his life; writing it was an act of incredible recklessness, bravery, or artistic integrity. In the years since,

I've never stopped thinking about it, and one thought has never left me in peace: though I labored long and patiently over my translation, I wasn't at all satisfied with the results. The poem simply would not take; the translation felt like a pallid copy of the original Russian, which is as beautiful and powerful as if it had been carved in stone. Unlike the work of Joseph Brodsky, whom I've also translated extensively, Osip Mandelstam's poetry is amazingly concentrated and not particularly discursive. It was virtually impossible to translate its sonorities, or the richness of many images that don't come through or resonate in the target language—in my case, Spanish. As the poem moves from one language into another, the aura of meaning and allusion that is absolutely transparent to the Russian listeners the poem was addressed to is lost. It's as if the poem were a tree and we could only manage to transplant its trunk and thickest limbs, while leaving all its green and shimmering foliage in the territory of the other language.

In any case, my translation of Mandelstam's poem was well received. Years passed without my looking at the translation again until recently, when I had the idea of including it in a personal anthology of Russian poetry I'm working on. After an attentive rereading, I didn't think it was possible to change any of the solutions that in their moment I had hit upon, but I decided it would be fitting to add some commentary, as another way of transmitting that halo of meaning.

In Russia, the poem is known as the "Epigram Against Stalin," a title some consider inadequate and belittling. Others say the title resulted from a maneuver by Mandelstam's friends (among them Boris Pasternak) to make the poem seem nothing more than a kind of pithy, off-the-cuff quip meant to sting or satirize, in the genre that found its highest expression in Martial, the Latin poet of the first century A.D.

Described by one critic as the sixteen lines of a death sentence, this is perhaps the twentieth century's most important political poem, written by one of its greatest poets against the man who may well be said to have been the cruelest of its tyrants.

II

Мы живем, под собою не чуя страны,
Наши речи за десять шагов не слышны,
А где хватит на полразговорца,

Там припомнят кремлёвского горца.

Его толстые пальцы, как черви, жирны,

А слова, как пудовые гири, верны,

Тараканьи смеются усища,

И сияют его голенища.

А вокруг него сброд тонкошеих вождей,

Он играет услугами полулюдей.

Кто свистит, кто мяучит, кто хнычет,

Он один лишь бабачит и тычет,

Как подкову, кует за указом указ:

Кому в пах, кому в лоб, кому в бровь, кому в глаз.

Что ни казнь у него—то малина

И широкая грудь осетина.

EPIGRAMA CONTRA STALIN

Vivimos sin sentir el país a nuestros pies,

nuestras palabras no se escuchan a diez pasos.

La más breve de las pláticas

gravita, quejosa, al montañés del Kremlin.

Sus dedos gruesos como gusanos, grasientos,

y sus palabras como pesados martillos, certeras.

Sus bigotes de cucaracha parecen reír

y relumbran las cañas de sus botas.

Entre una chusma de caciques de cuello extrafino

él juega con los favores de estas cuasipersonas.

Uno silba, otro maúlla, aquel gime, el otro llora;

sólo él campea tonante y los tutea.

Como herraduras forja un decreto tras otro:

A uno al bajo vientre, al otro en la frente, al tercero en la ceja, al cuarto

en el ojo.

Toda ejecución es para él un festejo

que alegra su amplio pecho de oseta.

—translated into Spanish by José Manuel Prieto

On Translating a Poem by Osip Mandelstam

We live without feeling the country beneath our feet,
our words are inaudible from ten steps away.
Any conversation, however brief,
gravitates, gratingly, toward the Kremlin's mountain man.
His greasy fingers are thick as worms,
his words weighty hammers slamming their target.
His cockroach moustache seems to snicker,
the shafts of his high-topped boots gleam.

Amid a rabble of scrawny-necked chieftains
he toys with the favors of such homunculi.
One hisses, the other mewls, one groans, the other weeps;
he prowls thunderously among them, showering them with scorn.
Forging decree after decree, like horseshoes,
he pitches one to the belly, another to the forehead,
a third to the eyebrow, a fourth in the eye.

Every execution is a carnival
filling his broad Ossetian chest with delight.

     —translated from José Manuel Prieto's Spanish version

III

Commentary

We live without feeling the country beneath our feet,
Мы живем, под собою не чуя страны,

The first line seems to present no particular difficulty other than that of conveying with absolute clarity how hazardous the life of the citizens has become, the sharp danger everyone takes in with every breath. The image is amplified by the verb Mandelstam uses, which I translated into Spanish as *sentir* (to feel or to smell), but which in the original is *chuyat'*, a word whose first meaning, to sniff out or to scent, has a dimension of the hunt, the vague, peripheral perception of a wild beast detecting a predator. The entire line projects an image of a people adrift in apprehension, an existence that has lost every point of reference, even the ground beneath it; the words transmit a sensation of urgency and danger, of pursuit.

> our words are inaudible from ten steps away.
> Наши речи за десять шагов не слышны,

The citizens of Soviet Russia had acquired the habit of speaking in low voices for fear of being overheard; parents avoided talking about any delicate matter in front of their children; lovers feared the ear of every passing stranger. Informers like the one who told the authorities about the epigram were a standard feature of the time. It became habitual to simply go out into the street to talk about anything, even matters of little importance. When Isaiah Berlin visited Anna Akhmatova in postwar Leningrad, the poet pointed to the ceiling at the beginning of the interview to signal that someone might be listening. In *Against All Hope,* the memoirs of Nadezhda Mandelstam, Osip's widow, the poet speaks of returning from a trip to the countryside to discover that telephones all over Moscow had been smothered in pillows; a rumor had gone around that they were all bugged (which in fact would not have been possible with the technology of that era).

Another memoir, *Avec Staline dans le Kremlin,* by Stalin's former secretary, Boris Bazhanov, recounts that Stalin had a small personal switchboard installed in the Kremlin, which enabled him to listen in on the conversations of the other Communist leaders. One afternoon, Bazhanov, who had no prior inkling that such a thing existed, opened the wrong door and found Stalin in a small room with a pair of earphones on his head, deeply absorbed in eavesdropping on a conversation among the elite Party leaders who enjoyed the privilege of living in the Kremlin. That one glimpse was enough to precipitate Bazhanov's escape across the Iranian border, in 1929, on foot.

> Any conversation, however brief,
> А где хватит на полразговорца,

In the original, literally: "when there's enough for half a conversation" or "when we work up a short conversation" (*razgoborets*). The "there's enough" (*khvatit*), which could be translated as "we work up," alludes as much to the constant rush, the lack of time, as to the fear that is garroting everyone.

In 1934, on a visit to Pasternak's home, Mandelstam could not keep himself from reciting the epigram. It was an act of total insanity, for several of those present would hurry to inform the authorities. Emma Gerstein, who was very close to both Pasternak and Mandelstam, speaks in her *Memoirs* of yet another recitation, attended by Nikolay Gumilyov's son Lev, who would also spend many years in the gulag. This patently suicidal conduct on Mandelstam's part had an additional explanation: he would compose his poems in his head, and only when they were ready, after a lengthy process of intense internal labor, would he put them down on paper. Mandelstam knew that the epigram would never be published and was trying to leave it imprinted on as many minds as possible, to keep it from disappearing with his death.

gravitates, gratingly . . .
Там припомнят . . .

In Russian, literally, they "mention" Stalin (*pripomniat*). Did Stalin actually enjoy the blind admiration of his people that many still credit him with in those years before the Great Terror and the Moscow show trials? The verb used here, *pripomniat,* carries with it a trace of annoyance. You say to someone: "I'll remind you of this" (*ya tebie pripomniu!*), in the sense of "you'll pay me for this" or "I'll get you back for this." It isn't merely that the dictator perpetually comes to mind, but that the thought of him is irritating.

During an earlier visit to Moscow that winter, Mandelstam had recited the poem in private to Pasternak, always the more cautious and astute of the two (Pasternak would die in his bed, in the privileged writers' villa of Peredelkino). His response was:

What you have just recited to me bears no relationship whatsoever to literature or to poetry. This is not a literary achievement but a suicidal action of which I do not approve and which I do not wish to have any part in. You have not recited anything to me and I did not hear anything and I beg you not to recite this to anyone else ever.

Nevertheless, the poet did so, and on more than one occasion. One memoirist accuses him of having acted out of a terrible hatred for Stalin.

Part II: The Translator at Work

. . . toward the Kremlin's mountain man.

. . . кремлёвского горца.

For an intellectual of the old school like Mandelstam (a graduate of the same elite Tenishev School attended as a boy by Vova—diminutive of Vladimir—Nabokov), the image of a Georgian, a "mountain man" (*gorets*), in the Kremlin symbolized something absolutely alien, a descent into savagery. Those who occupied the highest government positions in Soviet Russia were little more than coarse peasants. In 1921, when friends interceded for the life of the poet Nikolay Gumilyov (Anna Akhmatova's first husband, falsely accused of participating in a royalist conspiracy and executed by firing squad), they were surprised to discover that the presiding judge—the commissar of the Cheka, to use the revolutionary terminology—looked and acted like a dry goods merchant of the tsarist era. As the judge was confessing that there was nothing he could do to save the poet's life, he moved his hands with the slow, smooth gesture of "one measuring out or assessing the quality of some fabric." But what he had in his hands was the life of Nikolay Gumilyov.

His greasy fingers are thick as worms,

Его толстые пальцы, как черви, жирны,

The era's "greatest" poet, the artist most exalted by official propaganda, was neither Vladimir Mayakovsky nor any of the other three titans of the Russian twentieth century: Marina Tsvetaeva, Boris Pasternak, or Anna Akhmatova. The proletariat's great bard went by the name of Demian Biedny—Demian "the Poor"—and was an immensely popular versifier of Party-inspired couplets. His position within the Soviet hierarchy was such that he had an apartment in the Kremlin. He was said to be an incorrigible gambler, and would pay the debts thus incurred with slugs of gold that he cut off with pliers and weighed on a small scale placed atop the card table's green baize. He was, accordingly, one of Joseph Stalin's neighbors, and the dictator would sometimes borrow books from this false poet of the working classes, books he later returned, Demian had noted in his diary, "with the marks of his greasy fingers all over the pages." Mandelstam appears to have been acquainted with the anecdote and therefore metamorphosed Stalin's fingers into "greasy worms."

On Translating a Poem by Osip Mandelstam

his words weighty hammers slamming their target.

А слова, как пудовые гири, верны,

In the original, literally: "And his words like one-pood weights, on target." Throughout his life, Stalin, who was educated for a time in an orthodox seminary in Tiflis (the current Tbilisi), retained a strong Georgian accent. He chose his words slowly when speaking Russian, a language he came to use with some facility but which never ceased to be foreign to him. Among the accents a Russian can readily distinguish, the Georgian particularly stands out for its heaviness. Innumerable jokes are based on Georgian pronunciation, which tends to be spittingly hard and entirely insensible to the gamut of Russian phonemes.

The one-pood weights evoke another memory: during my early years as a student in Russia, I used to do my morning exercises with one of them (a pood being an antique Russian unit equivalent to 16 kilos or about 35 pounds). Made of cast iron in a design that goes back to the nineteenth-century craze for Swiss gymnastics, the weights are essentially cannon-balls with a handle attached by which you lift the thing with one hand, then the other, right, left, right, left, taking fearful care not to let it fall on your foot. Nowadays the old one-pood weights are no longer sold; they've been replaced by chrome-plated Western barbells with interchangeable disks.

His cockroach moustache seems to snicker,

Тараканьи смеются усища,

In the original, literally: "His cockroach moustache laughs." A childish image that echoes a beloved children's poem by Korney Chukovsky in which a "huge and moustachioed cockroach" (*usatii tarakanishe*) terrorizes a forest's animals until a "brave sparrow" faces him down and gobbles him up with a single peck of its beak.

In her invaluable memoirs, Yevgenia Ginzburg relates that one day she began to read Chukovsky's poem to the children of the kindergarten where she was working, in the distant province of Magadan. On hearing Chukovsky's phrase "the terrible huge and moustachioed cockroach," a colleague understood in horror what one reading of that passage might be and was on the verge of denouncing her for having read *that* poem aloud to the children. Since children all over Russia memorize Chukovsky's poem even today, the Russian understanding of the Mandelstam line passes, invariably, through that locus of memory, an image at once comic and terrifying.

> the shafts of his high-topped boots gleam.
> И сияют его голенища.

Lenin's attire—the Swiss burgher's vest he hitches his thumb into as he harangues the crowd in front of the Finland Station on April 3, 1917—is visibly that of a man of peace, a civilian. It was Leon Trotsky who, in 1918, at the height of the war between Whites and Reds, had himself photographed in a get-up of leather and straps that scandalized Moses Nappelbaum, portraitist of the Nevsky Perspective. To Nappelbaum, whose photos of the St. Petersburg elite, among them Anna Akhmatova herself, were famous, the militaristic garb looked like some absurd chauffeur's uniform, inappropriate to a leader of the World Revolution. The style caught on nevertheless, and became the distinctive uniform of the Cheka's commissars and, in slightly altered form—high-topped boots, canvas army jacket—of the entire Bolshevik leadership.

> Amid a rabble of scrawny-necked chieftains
> А вокруг него сброд тонкошеих вождей,

Mandelstam uses the word *sbrod*, which I translated into Spanish as the pejorative *chusma* or rabble. According to the Russian critic Benedict Sarnov, this line almost certainly prolonged Osip Mandelstam's life. The epigram's first, terrified audience thought Mandelstam's arrest and execution must be imminent. Instead, Stalin ordered a measure that, within the Soviet arsenal of punishments, was fairly light: "administrative exile" to the city of Cherdin, where Mandelstam's wife was allowed to accompany him. Later, the punishment would be softened even further when, in 1935, the two were permitted to move to Voronezh, a small provincial city in the south with a more temperate climate.

According to Sarnov, Stalin wanted Mandelstam to write a poem dedicated to him. "Stalin knew perfectly well that the opinion future generations would have of him depended to a large degree on what the poets wrote about him." And especially Mandelstam, so perceptive a writer that he had understood precisely the type of individual—the "scrawny-necked chieftains"—who surrounded the dictator, as well as the way he toyed with and dominated them. Such penetration, such subtle understanding

On Translating a Poem by Osip Mandelstam

of the leader's life, seems to have impressed Stalin. This may explain the insistence with which Stalin, in a famous conversation, would ask Pasternak whether Mandelstam could be considered a "true master." His question was, "But is he or is he not a master?"

Indeed, Stalin proved to be a psychologist no less keen-eyed and penetrating than the poet (which shouldn't surprise us). For in the city of Voronezh in January 1937, Mandelstam did write a sad "Ode to Stalin" which includes this line: "I would like to call you not Stalin but Dzhugashvili." That is to say, not by the official Party pseudonym, but by the more human name that the man was born with, thereby approaching him from his softest, most redeemable side. A similar "commission" was given to Mikhail Bulgakov, who would also spend almost a year at the end of his life, already mortally ill, writing a play called *Batum* about the heroic youth of the young Dzhugashvili in prerevolutionary Batumi.

Pasternak, always more subtle, sent Stalin, during the period of mourning for his wife Nadezhda Alliluyeva, a telegram, subsequently published in the *Literary Gazette*, which some believe saved him from the gulag: "I join in the sentiments of my comrades. I spent yesterday evening lost in long, deep thoughts about Stalin, as an artist, for the first time." It was a veiled promise to someday use his talent to leave a "human" or literary image of the dictator.

Many years later, when I was studying at the largest technical university in Siberia, in the deep hinterlands of the Soviet Union, I spent half an hour in one of its lecture halls conversing with the son of Lev Kamenev, one of the "chieftains" executed in 1936. The son had lived all those years under the false name of Glebov and had not yet emerged from his relative anonymity. I realize now, looking back at the memory, that he didn't have the scrawny neck Mandelstam alludes to, though he did have the hairless wattles of a *gospodin professor*. Short and stout, he smoked incessantly in an auditorium where smoking was strictly prohibited. He was a brilliant philosophy professor, and I well remember our discussion of Aristotle's *Aesthetics*. At the end of the 1980s he reclaimed his true surname, and I have since seen him interviewed about his father and himself on television, cigarette permanently in hand.

He toys with the favors of such homunculi.
Он играет услугами полулюдей.

The USSR of the 1930s saw the blossoming and expansion of a complicated system of patronage between the Party high command and the intellectual elite, described by Sheila Fitzpatrick in *Everyday Stalinism* (1999). It was common for writers and poets to attend the "salons" of the new governing class, and it was that sort of friendship which united Nikolai Bukharin, "the Party favorite," and the Mandelstams. Bukharin was among those who, when the affair of the epigram exploded, first tried to intervene and then recoiled from the situation in terror.

To write to Stalin, to turn to him directly and ask him to straighten out a matter of political persecution or imprisonment, had become a habit among Soviet writers who were in trouble with the state. In 1931, Yevgeny Zamyatin, author of the celebrated dystopia *We* (1921)—precursor to Aldous Huxley's *Brave New World* and George Orwell's *1984*—had written to Stalin asking for permission to emigrate, which was granted. Mikhail Bulgakov would also write with the same request, but his petition was rejected.

Curiously, in Mandelstam's case, it was Josef Stalin himself who decided to call Pasternak, with the clear intention of interceding on the poet's behalf, and even throwing in Pasternak's face the fact that he and his colleagues had done nothing to save Mandelstam. What took place then was the famous conversation in which the dictator, above and beyond all else, wanted to know the opinion that Pasternak and his fellow writers had of Mandelstam's skill as a poet. The conversation took place at 2:00 a.m. Pasternak was in his dacha. The phone rang.

Stalin: Mandelstam's case is being analyzed. Everything will be worked out. Why haven't the writers' organizations come to me? If I were a poet and my friend had fallen into disgrace, I would do the impossible (*I would scale walls*) to help him.

Pasternak: Since 1927, the writers' organizations have no longer dealt with such matters. If I hadn't taken steps, it's unlikely you would ever have learned of the situation.

Stalin: But is he or is he not a master?

Pasternak: That is not the issue!

Stalin: What is the issue then?

Pasternak: I would like to meet with you . . . and for us to talk.

Stalin: About what?

Pasternak: About life and death . . .

On Translating a Poem by Osip Mandelstam

At which point Stalin hung up.

One hisses, the other mewls, one moans, the other weeps;
Кто свистит, кто мяучит, кто хнычет,

The Russia of 1933 had yet to witness the Moscow show trials, which began in 1936 and continued through 1939, during which the majority of the "scrawny-necked chieftains" would find themselves in the defendant's box. Nor was the nation yet acquainted with the spectacle of self-incrimination by former Bolshevik leaders accused of every imaginable crime. Mandelstam's description foresaw the trials with prodigious exactitude: more than one of the defendants wept on hearing his sentence and fell to his knees to beg forgiveness from Stalin and the Party.

When Mandelstam was taken prisoner on the night of May 13, 1934, the NKVD did not yet have a definitive version of the poem. The presiding judge asked the poet to write out an authorized version of the poem for him, and the poet obligingly did so.

He wrote out the poem with the same pen the judge used to write the sentence that would seal his fate.

he prowls thunderously among them,
Он один лишь бабачит . . .

I translated the Russian *babachit*—a neologism—as "*campea tonante*" or "prowls thunderously." Though previously nonexistent, the verb presents no difficulty to the Russian speaker because it is an onomatopoeia: to say *ba-ba-chit*, in other words, is to say "blah, blah, blah" in thunderous tones, to talk nonsense in the authoritative voice of the boss.

. . . showering them with scorn.
. . . и тычет,

Here, both the Spanish and the Russian reflect Stalin's use of the familiar second-person pronoun, the Spanish *tú*, the Russian *ty*. A primary meaning of *tykat* (the verb meaning "to address someone as *ty*") is to point with a finger, to force something onto someone, to treat someone in an insolent and inconsiderate manner, and the word's meaning moves between those two usages. In Russia, it's unusual for

Автограф стихотворения
«Мы живем, под собою не чуя страны...»,
записанный на допросе в тюрьме (ЦГАЛИ)

Manuscript of the "Epigram Against Stalin" written out while Mandelstam was in prison, and discovered long afterward by Vitaly Shentalinsky in the KGB archives.

two strangers to use the familiar voice with each other; proper etiquette demands the most rigorous use of *vy*, the formal form of address, equivalent to the Spanish *usted*. The familiar voice is the prerogative of street sweepers and top bosses. During a sidewalk altercation, the use of "*ty*" is immediately perceived as a violent act of aggression. Mandelstam uses it here as an example of the abuse to which Stalin subjected his subordinates.

On Translating a Poem by Osip Mandelstam

Forging decree after decree, like horseshoes,
Как подкову, кует за указом указ:

The word for decree here is *ukase*, widely used in the West, as well, to refer to an order that takes effect immediately and is without appeal. The image of decrees forged like horseshoes echoes a more quotidian Russian phrase, "to do something as if making blinis or blintzes," in other words, rapidly and without thought, which amply conveys the banalization of the act of governing.

In 1929, Stalin believed that the moment had arrived to strip Russia of the useless appendix of capitalism. Yevgeni Preobrazhensky, the celebrated economist, theorized about how to use the wealth the peasantry had undoubtedly accumulated during its years of greater freedom as a platform to launch the nation's industrialization. But forced collectivization met with generalized rejection, the peasantry fiercely resisted, and Stalin launched a terror campaign. At least six million Ukrainian peasants died of hunger. The cities filled with fugitives who spoke of the horror in hushed voices. By 1934, it was clear that the country was living under the tyranny of a police state, compared to which the rule of the tsars seemed benign and magnanimous.

he pitches one to the belly, another to the forehead,
a third to the eyebrow, a fourth in the eye.
Кому в пах, кому в лоб, кому в бровь, кому в глаз.

However shoddy a dime-store emperor he might have been, his decrees had fatal consequences: the banalization of government had become a banalization of death. The zoom-in with which the poet shows the parts of the body struck by the horseshoe/*ukase* resembles the close-ups in Eisenstein's *Battleship Potemkin*, where an enormous pupil looms behind the lens of a pair of pince-nez, a mouth opens in a scream, the rictus of a face fills the whole screen.

Mandelstam, a poet of deep lyrical inspiration, would never have written poetry exalting the Revolution, unlike other poets of his time who passionately saluted the advent of October. Alexander Blok published a poem called "The Twelve" which celebrates the revolutionary triumph in images replete with evangelical symbolism. Vladimir Mayakovsky believed the Revolution was the apotheosis of the futurist aesthetic that had given rise to the "loudmouthed bossman" persona he adopted in his elegy "At the Top of My Lungs." It wouldn't be long before Mayakovsky realized that in Stalin's Russia there could be only one "thundering voice." By the time destiny placed him on a collision course with Stalin, Mandelstam had published a number of books, but not one of them was in a political register. They were books of such poetic value that all Russia—or at least that one percent which reads poetry—viewed him as a Master, with a capital M.

> Every execution . . .
> Что ни казнь у него . . .

In the mid-1970s, Lev Razgon, a gulag survivor and author of the implacable memoir *Nepridumannoye* ("Not made up," translated into English as *True Stories*), was hospitalized in a Moscow clinic for a heart problem. A neighboring bed was occupied by a former Party official who was kind to the other patients and, in particular, to the writer, whom he cared for solicitously. Gradually he and Razgón came to be friends, and the man ended up telling him about something he had never before confessed to anyone: his work as a member of one of the thousands of brigades of executioners that operated in the USSR during the 1930s. Razgon listened: the 100 grams of vodka the executioners drank at the beginning of each night, the trucks loaded with prisoners driven to outlying forests, the women sobbing at the edge of the pit, the cheers for the Party some of the men gave, the shot to the back of the neck, the swift kick that sent the victim into the pit at the precise moment the trigger was pulled because the executioners' wives were tired of laundering military jackets splashed with blood. . . .

> . . . is a carnival
> —то малина

Literally: "is for him a raspberry," a word with deep connotations of the criminal underworld. In Russian slang, *malina* (raspberry) refers to a criminal organization and the hideout from which crime lords carry out their schemes. Here, Mandelstam underscores the singular symbiosis between criminals and Bolsheviks, the impulse of vengeance and score-settling typical of the *lumpen* world the Bolsheviks allied themselves with. Every memoirist of the gulag mentions how the camps used common criminals against those incarcerated on the basis of Article

On Translating a Poem by Osip Mandelstam

58—the "politicals," accused of betraying the country. The common criminals did not participate in the original sin of being "class enemies" and therefore could be "reeducated"; they were assigned the easier service tasks as cooks, kitchen supervisors, or bathhouse workers—in Siberia, where heat, in and of itself, is a privilege.

> filling his broad chest . . .
> И широкая грудь . . .

In the original, the line begins, "And his broad chest. . . ." Skinny, only 168 centimeters or five and half feet tall, his face marked by smallpox, one arm half-paralyzed by polio, Stalin was a disappointment to people who had been expecting to meet with the colossus suggested by the supposed doppelgangers in granite and stone erected across the USSR. For Mandelstam, the broad chest that rejoices here is not a human chest but one made of iron. Inside, as if in the interior of a Minoan bronze bull, the millions of victims rage.

> filling his broad Ossetian chest with delight.
> . . . осетина.

Was Iosef Dzhugashvili a Georgian or was he from Ossetia, the small Caucasian republic next door? Ossetians are deemed less refined and more violent; therefore Stalin was officially considered a Georgian. Curiously, the poem's two final lines did not convince Mandelstam at all. It is astonishing that a fact as remote from politics as the verbal perfection of these final lines could occupy his mind during the suicidal sessions when he recited the poem aloud, but people remember him saying: "I should get rid of those lines, they're no good. They sound like Tsvetaeva to me." But there was no time for that, and the lines remained in the minds of those who heard the poem. Many years later, when Vitaly Shentalinsky discovered the manuscript of the "Epigram Against Stalin" in the KGB archives, he found no variation at all from the *samizdat* version that had circulated across the USSR. The poem had etched itself faithfully in the memories of those who heard it recited in the distant year of 1934.

ELEVEN

Are We the Folk in This *Lok*?

Translating in the Plural

CHRISTI A. MERRILL

The Riddle

I begin this paper by asking a riddle, but in order for you to appreciate its implications you need to understand that I speak both as a theorist of translation and also as a practitioner. The riddle revolves around a story I myself have translated into English from a Hindi short story Vijay Dan Detha wrote that itself was inspired by a Rajasthani folktale. I call my version "A True Calling" and Detha called his Hindi version *"Rijak ki Maryada,"* while the Rajasthani version(s) have neither title nor name— at least, as far as I know. The riddle, then, is this: If I have written this story in English from a story written in Hindi that in turn was written from a story told (several times, and in several ways) in Rajasthani, then who can be said to have authored the English version?

Convention dictates that as the translator I name Vijay Dan Detha author of "A True Calling," but in doing so I become caught in the same snarl of contradictions Detha himself gets caught in, conforming to modern (European) notions of single authorship when the creative process itself is decidedly plural. In this paper I am going to suggest that a more productive approach to Detha's dilemma and mine would be to create a new category called "storywriter," which can apply equally to author and translator, and be used as the literary equivalent of a "storyteller." In short, I suggest that the truest answer to the riddle "Who authored the English version?" turns out to be: "The folk."

Detha's Short Stories as Folktales,
or Folktales as Short Stories

"*Rijak ki Maryada*" was published in *Kathadesh* in March 1997, but that was not my first encounter with it. I had already translated a yellowed manuscript version of the same tale a decade earlier while working with Vijay Dan Detha and his Hindi translator Kailash Kabir in Jodhpur in 1990, and had included it in my M.F.A. thesis in 1993.[1] If you want to be crassly legalistic, you could argue that since my English translation of "A True Calling" was the first copyrighted version of that tale, then the story can be said to belong to me. Or if you're more conventional, you could argue that since my English version was directly derived from Detha's Hindi version, then the tale should belong to him. Or you could insist that the story should be claimed by the person who originally told it. But I would argue that we need to ask the question a different way. I would argue that the story belongs to Detha and to me, and to anyone else who has told it, will tell it, has heard it, or will hear it. I would even venture to say that the question of ownership when you're discussing translations—especially translations of self-professed *lok-katha* (folktales)—is not just misleading but downright dangerous. Dangerous not just for myself, and for Detha as the "author," but for the storytelling tradition more generally.

It must be said that Detha sits somewhat uncomfortably between the designations "folklorist" and "author." At the beginning of his writing career he unabashedly thought of himself as a folklorist, and made it his life mission to put into print the exceedingly varied and vibrant oral tales he grew up hearing in his native rural Rajasthan. When I met him in 1988, he had already published fourteen fat volumes of tales written in Rajasthani as part of a series called *Batan ri Phulwari* (*A Garden of Tales*),[2] and from those fourteen volumes Kailash Kabir had culled two collections' worth of stories he then translated from Rajasthani into Hindi. Of course we know that writing in a regional—and, it must be admitted, less prestigious—tongue such as Rajasthani does not command the same cultural capital as writing in a national language such as Hindi. While we could talk about the implications of this inequality from many different angles, here I will focus on the vexing question of authorship, since Detha's national—and you could even assert international—reputation as an author has been based primarily on the Hindi versions written by Kailash Kabir.

The contradiction at the heart of my riddle is this: Detha may be considered the author of these stories so many people have read and lauded in Hindi, but he is not their writer. At least, not exclusively. I can testify as one of those many readers that part of what moved me in reading these texts was the way Detha re-created the oral quality of the tales in his written (Rajasthani) versions, and part of what moved me was the way Kabir was able to convey a certain Rajasthani inflection in the Hindi prose. In short, it wasn't simply the tale itself I was responding to, but the way the tale was performed. The problem is that we expect to hold only one person accountable for this artistic success.

It would be easier if we could assume the problem arises from the fact that stories such as "Dohari Zinadgi" or "Anekhon Hitler" are translations, and that we just have to work out more carefully what part is the translator's input and what part the author's. But when we look again we can see that analogous issues arise from reading stories Detha wrote himself—whether in Rajasthani or in Hindi (as is the case with *"Rijak ki Maryada"*). By trying to identify a single person responsible for the creation of a story, we spend much of our time gathering evidence to ascertain whether Detha is a folklorist or an author. The assumption is that if Detha is labeled a folklorist, then he should become a completely transparent conduit for the stories and should name the true creators of the stories as the original authors; or else that if he is an author, then he shouldn't claim any true kinship to the oral culture he evokes in his tales so that we can designate the origin of the stories as his (godly) imagination. What I would like to assert here is that the distinction between the two is somewhat false, and that if our main goal is to keep storytelling (or storywriting) alive and well, it would behoove us to create a new set of criteria whose goal isn't so much to assess ownership as liveliness, eloquence, even emotional, political, or moral relevance. We need to adjust our expectations so that we think of the written text as yet one more performance of a story in a tradition necessarily various and multiple.

What Is an Author?

Part of what I'm calling into question is the definition—you may even say the institution—of the "author." Here I rely on the observations Michel Foucault makes about the (mostly European) history of authorship in his famously provocative 1969 essay, "What Is an Author?" He points out that an author's name begins to be linked to a literary text as copyrightable property when the discourse contained in it is thought to be transgressive—that is, when the work is considered to represent a significant departure from the tradition—and so the individual's name is supplied in order to vouch for the material set forth as a way of holding one person responsible for said transgressions.[3] Of course, we know that the effect of this maneuver has been to romanticize the singular transgressiveness of literary creation to such an extent that we now do not consider a work sufficiently literary unless it is deemed to be a complete departure from previous norms. A writer is not considered a true "author" unless s/he can prove that her/his work is in no way derivative—a significant problem for a storywriter such as Detha whose stories are based on folktales.

Such expectations have not always obtained, however. "Even within our civilization," asserts Foucault via Bouchard and Simon's English,

> the same types of texts have not always required authors; there was a time when those texts which we now call "literary" (stories, folk tales, epics, and tragedies) were accepted, circulated, and valorized without any question about the identity of their author. Their anonymity was ignored because their real or supposed age was a sufficient guarantee of their authenticity.[4]

In this quasi Golden Age of identityless literature, according to Foucault, only scientific texts had to prove their authenticity by stating the author's name. Then in the seventeenth and eighteenth centuries scientific texts began to be "accepted on their own merits and positioned within an anonymous and coherent conceptual system of established truths and methods of verification," while suddenly literary texts were required to carry the author's name, date, place and circumstance of writing to guarantee their authenticity.[5] My point here is not to open up a historical debate on literary versus scientific discourse in Renaissance Europe, but rather to challenge these received notions of authorship as they shape our reading of literary texts today—most specifically our reading of folktales. If, as Foucault concludes, "these aspects of an individual, which we designate as an author . . . are projections, in terms always more or less psychological, of our way of handling texts . . ." then how do these projections onto a single individual shape our reading of a story such as *"Rijak ki Maryada"*?[6] The danger is that reducing an ongoing creative process to the text of a single performance does not fully account for the story's multiple origins—oral or otherwise.

Albert Lord suggests in *The Singer of Tales* that part of the problem lies in our discomfort with multiplicity. In oral tradition, he claims, "the words 'author' and 'original' have either no meaning at all . . . or a meaning quite different from the one usually assigned to them."[7] A folklorist may hear numerous versions of a song, but if he is called upon to single out an author, then he will name the performer before him. After all, explains Lord: "A performance is unique; it is a creation, not a reproduction, and it can therefore only have one author."[8] How is this possible, that a story can be one and many at the same time? Lord replies:

> Actually, only the man with writing seems to worry about this, just as only he looks for the nonexistent, illogical, and irrelevant "original." Singers deny that they are the creators of the song. They learned it from other singers. We know now that *both* are right, each according to his meaning of "song." To attempt to find the first singer of a song is as futile as to try to discover the first singing. And yet, just as the first singing could not be called the "original," so the first man to sing a song cannot be considered its "author," because of the peculiar relationship . . . between his singing and all subsequent singings. From that point of view a song has no "author" but a multiplicity of authors, each singing being a creation, each singing having its own single "author."[9]

What Lord fails to take account of in such a scenario, however, is the role played by the invisible, nameless scribe setting these songs to paper. If Lord can insist that each performance of a song is a creation unique in its own right and not a mere reproduction, then he should consider a written version as yet another performance.

I say this not to disparage Lord's documentary skills, but rather to point out that he himself gets caught in the same impossible demands made on someone trying to re-create the experience of these songs or tales through writing. What do you do if you are a Vijay Dan Detha or one of the brothers Grimm, inspired by the tales you hear as part of your everyday life, because in them you sense something special, something worth preserving, a certain spiritedness you wish to have captured for posterity? You may very well do as the Grimm brothers did—at least according to Jack Zipes—and modify the stories for greater effect. Theirs is an instructive example because we know the outcome: the Grimm brothers succeeded in their goal of popularizing a corpus of stories that might otherwise have dropped out of circulation.

The way Zipes tells it, the Grimm brothers would invite family, friends, and other "educated young women of the middle class or aristocracy" into their drawing room and have these women repeat stories they had heard growing up from their "nursemaids, governesses, and servants, or tales they may have read."[10] Zipes takes care to note that the Grimms' informants would often draw on both "the oral and literary tradition of tale-telling and combined motifs from both sources in their renditions."[11] The brothers did not seem to distinguish authenticity based on oral versus written sources, but rather would write down as many versions as they heard, and then begin the arduous process of refining them in order "to *create* an ideal type for the *literary* fairy tale, one that sought to be as close to the oral tradition as possible, while incorporating stylistic, formal, and substantial thematic changes to appeal to a growing bourgeois audience."[12] In other words, they reworked the various versions they elicited to conform to the ideals they shared, namely:

> . . . the endeavor to make the tales stylistically smoother; the concern for clear sequential structures; the desire to make the stories more lively and pictorial by adding adjectives, old proverbs, and direct dialogue; the reinforcement of motives for action in the plot; the infusion of psychological motifs; and the elimination of elements that might detract from a rustic tone. The model for a good many of their tales was the work of the gifted romantic artist Philipp Otto Runge, whose stories in dialect, *The Fisherman and His Wife* and *The Juniper Tree,* represented in tone, structure, and content the ideal narrative that the Grimms wanted to create.[13]

If you did not know the names of these writers who endeavored to make their stories livelier, stylistically smoother, with clearer sequential structures, but I asked you to categorize them as "author" or "folklorist," I don't imagine you would have chosen "author." But you might also have felt uncomfortable choosing "folklorist," for such aesthetically minded mediations do not fall under the domain we like to think of as folklore. I say this not to disparage the validity of the Grimms' work, but quite the contrary: to point out that they were able to preserve these stories because they paid such careful attention to the ways they wrote. Categories of "author" versus "folklorist" become incidental in the face of their larger success.

What matters to us is that their work as storywriters has become valued. I would therefore like to suggest that instead of investigating *whether* writers like the Grimms or Vijay Dan Detha craft the stories they present, we should look instead at *how*. In order to do this successfully, our job as critical readers should be to develop a more complex language for appraising the writers' work that takes into account the inherent multiplicity of their stories.

Detha's Professional Honor

If we don't, then what's the danger? In Detha's case, we can see that the pressure to fit him into the slot of either folklorist or author has opened him up to criticism, either for improvising too much (and therefore tampering with the "original") or not enough (to call his version an "original"). This demand for a single, singular original forces us to disregard any elements in a story that reveal a dynamic relationship with folk tradition, even if they are the most distinctive and compelling aspects of the story. In short, this demand for a single, singular original forces us to misread, whether the work is attributed to an author, the folk, or both at once, as is the case with Detha's stories.

Detha's particular writing gift lies precisely in the ways in which he plays with and against the storytelling tradition. He retains enough elements of it to create a fuller context for the rhetorical and political transgressions he makes, so that the departures represent a critique of the tradition from within. Such artistry is difficult to appreciate if we cannot tolerate multiplicity. Stories like Detha's are not created in a vacuum and are not meant to be read in a vacuum. They represent a particularly fruitful relationship with the various *lok* brought together in the stories — and here I mean *lok* in the sense of people or folk, but also in the sense of worlds. If we are serious in calling these stories *lok katha*, it behooves us to ask: Who are these *lok*, what, and where?

Alan Dundes asks a similar question in the essay, "Who Are the Folk?" The essay sets out to challenge the stereotype of "folk" as a monolithic, homogeneous mass of illiterate, uncivilized peasants.[14] Instead of a blurry mass of romanticized peasants, he suggests,

The term "folk" can refer to *any group of people whatsoever* who share at least one common factor. It does not matter what the linking factor is—it could be a common occupation, language or religion—but what is important is that a group formed for whatever reason will have some traditions which it calls its own. . . . . A member of the group may not know all other members, but he will probably know the common core of traditions belonging to the group, traditions which help the group have a sense of group identity.[15]

He explains that people may identify as being in a group because they are part of the same family, ethnicity, race, nation; because they are all baseball players, computer programmers, coal miners, cowboys, fishermen, surfers . . . the possible varieties are infinite.[16] He ends the essay by answering the question, "Who are the folk?" by proclaiming cheerfully, "Among others, *we* are!"[17]

The implicit moral to Dundes's story is that folklore functions in part to create a sense of belonging: the answer to his question can be "we are" because lore binds us together, makes us feel part of that particular *lok* (as people, and as world). And yet, the feeling of inclusiveness a performance creates gives rise to a certain attendant anxiety: suddenly we feel we must know exactly who this is performing our identity for us. To know our identity we must know the identity of the singer of this song, the teller of this tale, this single entity who speaks of and for the *lok*. The singing, telling, speaking, performing redefines what and who the *lok* is, and the more acutely we sense the definition of the *lok* shift, the more we insist on holding an individual performer responsible for the collective movement. We crave this shift in the plural, but blame the performer in the singular. It is this gesture toward artistic scapegoating that Detha highlights in his version of the *lok katha* he calls *"Rijak ki Maryada."*

In brief, the story revolves around the plight of a *bhand* or shapeshifter who is said to be so good at his trade that he fools one person after another with his excellent disguises. (A lovely analogy for a storywriter!) By the rules of the game, no one can hold the *bhand* responsible for what he does when he's impersonating another character; he explains that his professional honor (the *"rijak ki maryada"* of the title) requires him to enter fully into whichever persona he adopts for the designated period of time. When he's a mahatma he refuses to let his ascetic vows be compromised by all the riches dangled before him, and when he's a *dayan* he drinks the blood of the queen's own brother when he crosses their path. Of course, the queen has trouble accepting the rules of the game once it has been played to the death and sets out to seek revenge for her brother's horrific murder. But the king and his courtiers realize they can't put the *bhand* to death for a crime he committed while he was in disguise, especially after he had so specifically and publicly warned them. Finally, when there seems to be no way to avenge the murder of the queen's brother, a lowly barber thinks up a way to outwit the *bhand* in his own terms: have the *bhand* assume the guise of a *sati* who must immolate herself on her husband's funeral pyre.

In the version Detha heard—or so I heard from his friend, Komal Kothari—a barber told the tale in such a way that celebrated the cleverness of the fictional barber by showing how he outsmarted not only the *bhand* but the mighty king and all his stumped courtiers as well. In the nameless barber's version, the issue of the *sati*'s sacrifice served as only an instrument to a different kind of justice, but in Detha's version he uses the traditional story form to highlight the atrociousness of such a practice by sympathizing deliberately with the *bhand*, and adopting a sorrowful tone rather than the whimsical delivery common to many folktales:

> तत्पश्चात् उस विचित्र भाँड ने जैसा कहा, वैसा ही किया. हजारों
> मनुष्य सती का स्वाँग देखने के लिए उमड़ पड़े. देखते-देखते चंदन की
> चिता सजी. सती-माता सहज भाव से चिता पर बैठी. उसके सत का
> करिश्मा कि अपने-आप चिता में आग की लपटें धू-धू करके जल उठीं.
> सती का स्वाँग भी सम्पन्न हुआ .

Detha's version treats the *bhand*'s decision to go through with the sacrifice as a tragedy, figuring the *bhand* not so much as a mischievous trickster who must be taught a lesson but as an unparalleled artist with a laudable commitment to his art. The story ends with what at first appears to be a somewhat heavy-handed judgment about the *bhand*'s honor compared to the king's:

> पर राजा की मर्यादा के झूठे अहंकार और भाँड की मर्यादा के सहज
> गौरव में जाने-अनजाने कहीं कोई समानता नहीं थी.

It's only when we read this line in the context of other folktales in the Rajasthani oral tradition that we hear a parodic edge to the narrator's voice. These are the moments when Detha uses traditional storytelling conventions not only to comment on the events within the story, but to comment on the traditions themselves.

After all, Detha himself is an artist who has been so effective at mimicking other people's voices that the line between who he is in play—i.e., a storyteller—and who he is in reality—a writer—becomes irrevocably crossed, and as the performer of that play he runs a greater risk of being singled out as scapegoat for the resulting transgression. We could read the story as a version of "The Death of the Author," Rajasthani folktale style. For just as French theorists such as Michel Foucault and Roland Barthes critique a system that mythologizes the author of the text so that it may sacrifice him, so does *"Rijak ki Maryada"* critique a system that demands a performance to the death.

The remedy, suggests Susan Stewart in her *Nonsense*, which combines folklore and literary studies, is to protect the welfare of the players by protecting the welfare of the play.[20] The main difference between play and reality? According to Stewart, play is repeatable, reversible, intangible, temporary.[21] This is the difference between seeing Detha's version of the story as one performance in a line of many, and regarding it as a definitive and original piece of literature.

By locating a storywriter in the plural—as part of the *lok*—you are allowing there to be play in the re-creation (and here it is important to think of "play" both in the sense of dynamic movement and in the sense of fun). Play for Detha, as well as for the storywriters and storytellers who preceded him and for those who will follow. Thus while logocentricity encourages us to believe the power of the story can be reduced to specific words in a fixed text, *lok*-ocentricity forces us to embrace the ambiguity and temporality inherent in plural play. This isn't a distinction based on oral versus written media, but on the expectations surrounding the performance of a story. If you want to keep not just the individual storyteller or author alive, but the whole tradition, you would then want more people to feel part of a *lok* that has play, has movement. You would want that *lok* to keep re-creating itself through an endless line of performances. You would want the play to continue on through a revolving series of players.

Now, you may ask, what does this have to do with translation?

Part II: The Translator at Work

What Is a Translator?

Some of you may have noticed that I didn't offer my English versions of the passages I just quoted from Detha's story in Hindi. But now I will do my own bit of "A True Calling" and offer my translation:

> After that the incomparable *bhand* did just what he said he would. Thousands gathered to see a man assume the guise of a *sati*. Soon a cremation pyre was laid of sandalwood. She mounted the funeral pyre with the natural bearing of a true *sati*. Such was the power of her conviction that flames leapt up from the pyre of their own accord.
>
> The *sati* disguise had been fully realized.

I refrained quite intentionally from offering my version, not wanting to follow Detha into the allegorical flames already raging. After all, in a world that would sacrifice an author, the translator would be next to go. I'm not ready for a fire test like that.

Sherry Simon has a similar worry. She points out in *Gender in Translation* that the identity of the translator is bound up with the identity of the author as "exclusive proprietor of the text."[22] Her metaphors underscore the tangible and therefore permanent nature of our expectations. Her theory is an easy one to test. When you read the question with which the story concludes—

> How to compare a monarch's false pride with the natural honor of a *bhand*?

—what moral do you draw, and with whom do you imagine sharing it? My hope is that you are able to imagine me, and Detha, and the nameless barber, and a long line of other storytellers and writers who have passed on this tale, each of us offering a version that is repeatable, reversible, intangible, temporary, playful. My hope is that in the moment when you came to the end of the story, you were able to feel part of this *lok* somehow.

For a *lok*-ocentric vision of a story would see translation as less of a tangible carrying across, in the English sense of the word, and more of an intangible telling in turn, as is suggested by the Hindi word for translation, *anuvad*. Such an approach would allow us to embrace the inherent multiplicity of storywriting, in such a way that individual performers wouldn't be placed in the unenviable dilemma of having to demand entire credit for the work or none at all. Just as the relationship between Detha and the nameless barber can be cast as a one-on-one, winner-take-all contest for possession of the (tangible) text, or can be seen as two of many instances in on ongoing line of (an intangible) story performance, so I suggest we recast the author–translator relationship in such a way as to emphasize the creative enterprise we both participate in. I have confined my discussion to the literary re-creation of folktales, but for me these examples simply offer a heightened version of the situation any translators—nay, any storywriters—are in. All of us are potential translators, redefining the *lok* in the way we pass along stories.

I will then end with a beginning, of a story I wrote in English after a story Vijay Dan Detha wrote in Hindi after a story he heard told in Rajasthani. It belongs to us and them and him and you. After all,

> Nothing happens to a story if all you do is listen. Nothing happens if all you do is read, or memorize word for word. What matters is if you make the heart of the story part of your very life. This story is one of those.

Notes

1. A version of my translation of *"Rijak ki Maryada"* has been published on Words Without Borders as "A True Calling" (wordswithoutborders.org/article/a-true-calling/). "Untold Hitlers," another of my translations of Vijay Dan Detha's work, can also be read there.

2. Vijay Dan Detha, *Batan ri Phulwari*, 14 vols. (Borunda: Rupayan Samsthan, 1964–88).

3. Michel Foucault, "What Is an Author?" in *Language, Counter-Memory, Practice,* ed. D. Bouchard, trans. D. Bouchard and S. Simon (Ithaca, N.Y.: Cornell University Press, 1977), 124–25.

4. Foucault, "What Is an Author?" 125.

5. Foucault, "What Is an Author?" 126.

6. Foucault, "What Is an Author?" 127.

7. Albert Lord, *The Singer of Tales* (Cambridge, Mass.: Harvard University Press, 1960), 101.

8. Lord, *The Singer of Tales*, 102.

9. Lord, *The Singer of Tales*, 102.

10. Jack Zipes, *The Brothers Grimm: From Enchanted Forests to the Modern World* (New York and London: Routledge, 1988), 10.

11. Zipes, *The Brothers Grimm*, 11.

12. Zipes, *The Brothers Grimm*, 12.

13. Zipes, *The Brothers Grimm*, 12.

14. Alan Dundes, "Who Are the Folk?" in *Interpreting Folklore* (Bloomington and London: Indiana University Press, 1980), 2.

15. Dundes, "Who Are the Folk?" 7 (italics his).

16. Dundes, "Who Are the Folk?" 7–8.

17. Dundes, "Who Are the Folk?" 19.

18. Vijay Dan Detha, *"Rijak ki Maryada," Kathadesh* (March 1997):15.

19. Detha, *"Rijak ki Maryada,"* 15.

20. Susan Stewart, *Nonsense: Aspects of Intertextuality in Folklore and Literature* (Baltimore and London: Johns Hopkins University Press, 1978), 57–66.

21. Stewart, *Nonsense*, 118–123.

22. Sherry Simon, *Gender in Translation: Cultural Identity and the Politics of Transmission* (London and New York: Routledge, 1996), 46.

TWELVE

Choosing an English for Hindi

JASON GRUNEBAUM

Americans translating into English from, say, French or Spanish don't have to think about all the English speakers, and potential readers, of their English translations in France or Spain—or consider that the English spoken by those people has its own long history, and is different in meaningful ways from North American and UK English idioms. Translators translating from South Asian languages into English do have to consider the 254 million English speakers and potential readers in the countries that are the source of the original work.[1] More importantly, the translator's process of bringing cultural differences and nuances from the source language into English, weighing one strategy against another, might conclude with one choice if the English reader is from North America and quite another if the reader is from South Asia. Translators translating from South Asian languages into English must ask themselves, "Which English?" in a way that raises very interesting questions about the process of translation and the intended audience.

"Can't you imagine the pleasure of serving your friends back home at a tea with well prepared samosas, pakoras, honey filled rolled chaptis, and Indian sweets?" wrote Faye Sollid in her introduction to the bilingual English-Hindi *American-Hindi Cook Book*, published in 1956 by the American Women's Club of New Delhi, after learning new recipes during an overseas stay. Would she serve chai at the tea, and what would she call it? It might depend on the guests.

I'd like to discuss this question of different English-speaking audiences by sketching two readers, one Indian and one American, and looking at the different ways that they might influence translation strategies. Then I will discuss specific translation examples, drawn largely from my English version of Uday Prakash's Hindi novel *The Girl with the Golden Parasol* (Penguin India, 2008; Yale University Press, 2013), and see how two readers might react to different possible choices.

Uday Prakash is one of the most important, daring, original, and funny voices in contemporary Hindi literature over the past twenty-five years. In *The Girl with the Golden Parasol*, Rahul, a non-Brahmin college boy, falls in love with Anjali, a Brahmin girl. One might assume that caste isn't a problem in today's modern India, with its call centers, high tech, and new cars, but in this coming-of-age campus love story, Prakash shows how private lives can still be crushed by the age-old system of caste, a rigid hierarchy further fortified by new forces of globalization. The story is also a stinging satire about abuse of power, corruption, and the question of who owns language.

I'd like to posit a character sketch of one possible reader: Krishna, twenty-two years old, living in South Delhi, who did an M.Sc. in biology at Delhi University, is currently working in human resources for an ad agency, and sends romantic poems to lovers via text message on a new Panasonic smartphone. Krishna eats pizza, parathas, paneer, burgers, papadum, fries, dosas, and Uncle Chipps, in no particular order, and, like many South Asians, is a polyglot, equally comfortable speaking Hindi, English, and Panjabi, often switching among all three languages in the same sentence—though Krishna may prefer to read in English rather than Hindi (more on this later).

Krishna loves to read, mostly fiction written in English or translated into English, and this year has read a John Grisham and a Dan Brown novel, all of Harry Potter, *Two Lives* by Vikram Seth, *The Alchemist* by Paulo Coehlo, *English, August* by Upamanyu Chatterjee, José Saramago's *Blindness*, *Lateral Thinking* by Edward de Bono, *The Kite Runner* by Khaled Hosseini, García Márquez's *No One Writes to the Colonel*, *The Brief Wondrous Life of Oscar Wao* by Junot Díaz, and *The Immortals* by Amit Chaudhuri.

If I decide as a translator that Krishna is my ideal reader, I can leave some Hindi words in the English translation. Words like *dhoti*, *adivasi*, *puja*, *ustad*, *chunni*, and *yaar* won't need to be translated—or even require a "stealth gloss," where I would try to sneak a definition of the word or phrase into the English text, hopefully without the reader realizing he or she is being taught a new word or idea. Krishna will get the significance of names of figures and places like Ravana, Ayodhya, Madhuri Dixit, Naxalites, Sita, and Chanakya without explanations, "equivalents," or footnotes.

In other words, there will likely be many fewer cultural differences I'll be responsible for translating for Krishna, even though Uday Prakash's novel will be read in a different language than it was written in.

Leaving certain words from the Hindi in the English translation won't be the only difference in strategy if I translate for Krishna. I might also decide to write in a more South Asianized English. I might use an idiomatic phrase like, "I am just coming," confident that Krishna would take this to mean what in American English would translate as, "I'll be right back." Sometimes Uday's characters use English words in their Hindi or even speak in complete English sentences, like when the protagonist, Rahul, bursts into tears, and his friend implores him (and this is the Hindi), "Don't be senti, Rahul!" "Senti" comes from the word "sentimental," and here means an excessive public display of emotion: when someone loses it, can't keep a grip on himself, fails to keep a grip on himself or hold it together. Krishna would know what "senti" means, and I could leave this, and many other instances of English-in-the-Hindi, as is.

We will momentarily leave Krishna enjoying a caffe Mexicano and spicy veg puff at the local Barista location, at 15 Defense Colony Market, in South Delhi.

Ten-and-a-half time zones away, sipping a chai iced-tea latte at a Starbucks in Chicago, is Kris, the second possible reader, reading a copy of Jhumpa Lahiri's *The Namesake*. Kris grew up in the suburbs of Detroit, did a B.A. at the University of Michigan at Ann Arbor, majoring in poli sci and minoring in English, then pursued an M.B.A. at DePaul, making many friends who were South Asian, or of South Asian origin. During that time, Kris attended *bhangra* dance parties and was invited to an Indian friend's wedding in Cleveland. Kris has recently taken up yoga.

Kris, like Krishna, also loves to read. Before *The Namesake*, Kris, too, read Vikram Seth's latest book, and *A Fine Balance*, by Rohinton Mistry, is a favorite. This year Kris has read the last Harry Potter, Alice Sebold's *The Lovely Bones*, Bill Bryson's *I'm a Stranger Here Myself*, John Kennedy Toole's *A Confederacy of Dunces*, and Haruki Murakami's *Kafka on the Shore*; Kris reread Ondaatje's *The English Patient*, finally finished

García Márquez's *One Hundred Years of Solitude*, and enjoyed the new Pevear/Volokhonsky translation of *Anna Karenina*.

If Kris turns out to be my reader, I can count on someone who has some exposure to South Asian culture, primarily through food, music, and for lack of a better category, fitness. But the cultural differences between Kris and the Hindi will be far greater, and much more translation will need to be done. Hindi words I might feel justified leaving in Hindi for Krishna will require some kind of explanation for Kris. If I do want to use some of those Hindi words, either because I decide it's important to "give some of the flavor of the original" or because they turn out to be simply the most precise and economical words available, I'll have to stealth gloss in a way that does not cause readers' eyes to glaze over.

What are the pros and cons of choosing either Krishna or Kris as the ideal reader? Translating for Krishna—in other words, for a South Asian English-speaking audience—would have several benefits. Chief among them, perhaps, is that the audience would likely be much larger: more people would read the book. South Asians are accustomed to reading translations, and there is a lot of literary commerce (although, sadly, not nearly enough) among the twenty-two official languages of India. The "associate official language" of India, English, is obviously an extremely important bridge language on the subcontinent. Therefore, *The Girl with the Golden Parasol*, translated with a South Asian audience in mind and published in India, could expect to draw as readers English-literate speakers of Assamese, Bengali, Bodo, Dogri, Gujarati, Kannada, Kashmiri, Konkani, Malayalam, Maithili, Manipuri, Marathi, Nepali, Oriya, Panjabi, Santali, Sindhi, Tamil, Telugu, Urdu, and other modern regional South Asian languages who are curious about Hindi literature.

In addition to this potentially sizable market, the audience would include many fluent Hindi speakers like Krishna, who haven't read any Hindi literature (in Hindi) since their high school days in an English-medium school when they were required to read writers like the father of modern Hindi and Urdu prose, Premchand. Often the Hindi literature curriculum in secondary schools in India is government-prescribed, dry, and lifeless—and generally not a favorite subject among students. In addition, the study of Hindi literature at the university level in India doesn't have a reputation that's commensurate with the genius of the language, and therefore Hindi departments are not considered appropriate homes for the bright and ambitious. This is a tragedy, and one that is dramatized in detail in *The Girl with the Golden Parasol*. But for the purposes of this discussion, the point is that Krishna, and many others fluent in Hindi, would be much more likely to read *The Girl with the Golden Parasol* than पीली छत्री वाली लड़की.

In sum, translated well, marketed properly, this book might have a pretty large audience in South Asia.

And what if the translator decides that Kris is the target reader? One immediate point of comparison is that, given the tiny number of translations into English published annually in the United States, the number of readers might be much smaller than in South Asia for *The Girl with the Golden Parasol*—perhaps an unfair fate for such a funny, relevant, and timely novel. Can marketing play a role? Is it wise for translators to think about marketing before starting a translation? It is undeniable that many South Asian writers and writers of the South Asian diaspora writing in English sell books: Salman Rushdie, Jhumpa Lahiri, Vikram Seth, Michael Ondaatje, Rohinton Mistry, Vikram Chandra, Bharati Mukherjee, Anita Desai, Amitav Ghosh, and others. Would it be cynical or unfair to try to ride the coattails of these writers, and try to market Uday Prakash as the next Jhumpa Lahiri?

But he's not Jhumpa Lahiri. And that's the point. Uday's voice is quite different from Jhumpa's, Salman's, Rohinton's, and the others'. All of the great South Asian and diaspora writers writing in English have their own, distinct voices, and all should be given a chance to be heard. Uday should too. Unfortunately for him, he happens to write in a language far less well-connected than English is. But he has a lot to say about a part of India that's not often depicted in the media or written about, and that I think U.S. readers would be very interested in. It's not just Uday: there is a lot more literary activity on the Indian subcontinent happening in languages other than English. I don't think it's controversial to assert that readers, particularly English-speaking North American readers, would profit immeasurably from exposure to these works. But in order for readers to discover them, good translations must exist.

Though many people in the United States (editors, publishers) may argue that translated books don't sell, cultivating good translations is simply the right thing to do. Kris, the potential American reader, has possibly won me over with, if nothing else, a persuasive need to hear other voices from the subcontinent.

There's another, very practical, reason it makes sense for me to translate this book into American English: it's my mother tongue. Even though I think I could probably do a passable imitation of colloquial Indian

English, I have innumerably more tools at my disposal if I translate into colloquial American English.

So do I forget about Krishna, my potential Indian reader? I don't think I as a translator should give up on any potential reader. Shouldn't it be possible to translate into a distinctly American idiom of English without alienating a South Asian English-speaking audience? Couldn't I still include Hindi words like *dhoti, adivasi, puja, ustad, chunni,* and *yaar* in my English rendition, stealth glossing where necessary for those who might need extra context? Could I still leave those words as-is for South Asians, who will hopefully not find the gloss to be an annoying redundancy, or feel as if the text had been "pre-chewed"? It should be possible to translate with an American audience in mind, but without forgetting everyone else. After all, translation is about enlarging the conversation of literature.

Now that thought has been put into the question of audience, I would like to turn to concrete examples that can be placed under the general category of translating cultural differences. I chose the following examples not because I've done a perfect job negotiating all the complexities of each problem—every translator knows that nagging feeling that there's always a better solution—but because I hope they offer interesting insight into the particular problems posed by Hindi and how I went about tackling them.

Let's begin with जूठन, *juthan.* जूठन is not just leftover food, it's leftover food that has been made ritually impure by someone else's having touched it. At a family dinner in South Asia, you rarely hear "Oh, are you going to finish that potato?" accompanied by a hand reaching across the table. Traditionally, once an eater touches his or her food, that food is off limits for everyone else: it becomes impure and is no longer food; it has become जूठन. A rigid interpretation of the caste system is largely responsible for the notion of "you touch the food, no one else can eat it." Each caste makes its own food and doesn't like to eat food prepared by another caste, particularly one lower down the ladder. In contemporary India, there are countless people who may follow this notion a little, or a lot, or not at all. But it is a concept that is very much alive in the culture.

The first two instances of जूठन occur in back-to-back sentences. Our hero, Rahul, is imagining a fat, rich man who never stops eating. Prior to this sentence, this man's arrogance and gluttony have been described. Retaining only the Hindi word जूठन for the moment, the two sentences translate, "As he eats and eats and begins to get full, he starts to flick off

Choosing an English for Hindi

161

the जूठन from his plate. Millions of hungry people could be fed with his continental, nutritious जूठन."

There's no direct equivalent outside of South Asia for the concept of food rendered ritually impure because it's been touched by someone, or a particular someone. I first thought about segregation in the United States as a potential source of "cultural stuff" to help me with जूठन: after all, it wasn't so long ago that African Americans were forced to eat at separate lunch counters and drink from separate water fountains. But I rejected this possibility, concluding it was too specifically American, and began to think in more general cultural terms: food can go bad, it can be moldy, past its expiration date. When there's something really wrong with food, it's less often because a particular type of person came into casual contact with it, more often because it's spoiled.

So, the first occurrence of जूठन I decided to render as "spoiled morsels." I decided on "morsels" because it seemed to both preserve the satirical tone of the passage and fit nicely with the register of "continental" (which is the same word used in the Hindi). "Spoiled" is about as good and evocative a "bad food" modifier as any other I could think of. In addition, the sentence implies he's been eating and eating for a long time—long enough for some of the food on his plate to become spoiled.

The next जूठन I translated simply as "leftovers." To add an adjective, say, "impure," to "leftovers," as I considered doing, might stop the reader in his or her tracks. The reader might wonder who is it who has adulterated or molested the food, and think about the difference between "pure" and "impure" leftovers (is there one?). I decided leftovers are already crummy enough, and the word provides the same effect of humorous surprise at the end of the sentence that जूठन does in the Hindi.

जूठन is a noun, but particular food items, once impure, are described with the adjective जूठा. Our hero, Rahul, is a non-Brahmin, and his love interest, Anjali, is, of course, a Brahmin—and Brahmins traditionally have the strictest rules about who touches their food. The first time he lays eyes on Anjali, Rahul and his friends are sitting around on a sultry August afternoon eating one of the delicious late-monsoon treats in South Asia, corn on the cob roasted over hot coals, slathered with salt, spices, and lime. Anjali shows up, and a girlfriend of hers kindly offers half of her corn:

"Do you want some corn on the cob? I've only eaten half," offered Renu.

Part II: The Translator at Work

162

Before Anjali can reply, another friend, Seema, jumps in and teases Anjali. The Hindi: "'पंडितानी है। तेरा जूठा भुट्टा खाएगी तो उसका ध र म भ्रष्ट हो जाएगा,' सीमा ने व्यंग्य किया." The fact that Anjali is being teased gave me a certain latitude in translating जूठा, and here I felt comfortable using the precise but otherwise rather heavy and potentially out-of-register "defiled" for जूठा. I translated this sentence as, "'Heaven forbid! She's a strict Brahmin,' Seema said in jest. 'She'll become an outcaste if she eats that defiled piece of corn of yours.'" Actually, it turns out Anjali's not a strict Brahmin at all—she's a modern woman. In the story, she ends up accepting Renu's offer, and munches away on the delicious, defiled corn.

The next example concerns the Hindi word स्वदेशी, which has seen a lot of action over the decades. Literally it means both of one's own country (India) and something made and manufactured in one's own country (India). The word *swadeshi* was a powerful rallying cry during the struggle for independence from the British, and, in that context, referred specifically to the ban of imported textiles. If you've seen the film *Gandhi*, the two images of the huge bonfire of British-manufactured clothing and Gandhi sitting at his spinning wheel give two good guideposts for the emotional impact that स्वदेशी can have. Something *swadeshi* can stir an Indian's emotions and make him or her feel proud in ways few things can.

So when Rahul, our hero, lauds as "स्वदेशी" the gorgeous back of Madhuri Dixit, one of Hindi cinema and India's most beloved actresses, I was in a bind. The *swadeshi*-ness of Madhuri's back, Rahul declared, was one of the things that made her unique, incomparable. Her natural and *swadeshi* back was compared unfavorably to the synthetic-looking and *videshi*—foreign—backs of other Indian actresses.

What can we do for *swadeshi* in English? What about "uniquely Indian," "typically Indian," "inexplicably Indian"? No, these phrases sound as if they belong in an ad for saffron-colored nail polish. "Indian born and bred": that's not right either, a bit too south of the Mason-Dixon line. What about those stickers and labels found on products that say "Made in the USA"? We can borrow this marketing device that appeals to patriotic feelings for the benefit of describing Madhuri's back. Changing "Made in USA" to "Made in India" convinces me I can leave in *swadeshi*, a word I felt was important to retain. The translated sentences read: "Madhuri's back was natural and authentic, and, unexplainably, a *swadeshi* one. Made in India. The others were unnatural, foreign imports, Rahul deduced, and that was why they held no charm."

Holidays can be very culturally specific. "It was two days until Rakshabandhan," the reader is told. This is the literal translation of the sentence. Since Rakshabandhan is not a well-known holiday outside the Indian subcontinent, I felt it needed some context. Rakshabandhan is not the equivalent of Christmas, but how would you translate Christmas—and describe how it is celebrated—for someone who had never heard of Christmas before? (Of course it would depend on whether it was an American Christmas, a German Christmas, or an Indian Christmas.) In any case, if "it was two days until Rakshabandhan," was the first and last mention of the holiday in the text, I might be tempted to translate it as something only slightly more precise and literary than "important Indian holiday," or make up a little English name for the holiday that gave a rough translation. But immediately following the news that Rakshabandhan is coming up is a lovely sentence that makes little sense if you don't know something about the holiday. So, given that I've ruled out footnotes and a glossary,[2] I'm left with little choice. I need to prime the reader with a gloss in the text itself containing the minimal amount of information for him or her to understand enough about this holiday so as to make sense of the next sentence. It's bound to be somewhat, if not very inelegant, and I can only hope that Krishna doesn't feel that the text is being too pre-chewed, or, even worse, that leftovers are being served. The original "It was two days until Rakshabandhan," with the added imperative to add a gloss, has now swelled in my English to, "It was two days until the holiday of Rakshabandan, when sisters tie colorful threads of affection—the *rakhi*—around the wrists of their brothers, or those they consider like brothers." I justify this addition with what I hope is enough of a payoff for the reader in the following sentence. "Talk was thick about which girls, by dint of tying the *rakhi* around the wrist of a boy or a teacher, would cancel once and for all the one-sided soap opera and recast the once aspiring lover as esteemed brother." This wouldn't make much sense to a reader who didn't know the basics of Rakshabandhan.

What happens when spoons start kissing ass? The Hindi word for spoon, चम्मच, can also mean yes-man, ass-kisser, or, to give away the choice I made in this instance, lackey. The चम्मच actively curries favor with some sort of superior to whom he has pledged prolonged servility and for whom acts of self-debasement often know no bounds. Think

Smithers from the Simpsons and you're on the right track. In South Asia, an important person is not an important person unless he or she has a proper flock of चम्मचs.

There are plenty of चम्मचs running around the college campus where *The Girl with the Golden Parasol* takes place. Among them is the clever and cunning hostel warden Upadhyay. The adult from the university who is in charge of the hostels where students live is the hostel warden. In the United States, we have wardens for prisons and little else; but the term "warden" was perfectly appropriate for both the character and the circumstances described in the book, so I decided to keep it instead of giving Upadhyay a bloodless American job title. I did change some Indian English campus terminology into North American English, for example, "transferring" to another university instead of "getting migration papers." Others I did not change: Indian university students live in on-campus "hostels," which I decided to keep, rather than changing it to "dorm," which I thought sounded too American.

In the story, the students begin to keep files—which they call "de facto" files—on their professors and the college administration, chronicling the corruption and cronyism. The deeds and misdeeds of the hostel warden are compiled, including his relationship with the VC—that's Vice Chancellor, or head of a university. The relationship between the VC and the hostel warden is characterized in the following sentence, which, though in Hindi, contains only one Hindi word—चम्मच. The rest are English words transliterated into Hindi. "Solid Stainless Steel चम्मच of V. C. Mister Ashok Agnihotri." The first thing I have to do is let go of the dream of keeping the word चम्मच in my translation, as perfect as it is in the Hindi—I just can't seem to think of any connection in English between spoons and brown-nosing. With चम्मच, sadly, it seems I must also say good-bye to solid stainless steel. But I want to keep as much from the solid stainless steel as possible. Stainless steel in South Asia has the general connotation of high quality, durability, being made to last. And it's shiny. I've chosen "lackey" for चम्मच over yes-man because "lackey" seems more evocative, and more likely to be able to support a couple of adjectives, for example, "loyal" and "lacquered." It's far from perfect, but our solid stainless steel चम्मच has become a loyal lacquered lackey. He's durable because he's loyal, and, being lacquered, he's undergone a special treatment giving him shine and luster. I tried to retain some of the alliteration of the original, even if being lacquered is a bit more baroque than the clean, cold, steely चम्मच.

Choosing an English for Hindi

A चपरासी—a word that seems to come up a lot while translating from Hindi—is somewhat related to a चम्मच, but comes with more job security. चपरासी is routinely translated without a second thought into South Asian English as "peon." "Peon" is not only still a very valid job description in India, but for many is a job they'd be delighted to have: a kind of all-purpose office assistant who serves the functions of errand boy, file fetcher, gossip catcher, chai maker, and often behind-the-scenes power broker.

Say the word "peon" to a North American, however, and he or she will probably picture a Victorian-era indentured hunchback, dressed in rags, doing the most menial of menial tasks. "Office assistant" is the kind of bland, nonevocative American job title I didn't want to give hostel warden Upadhyay. The solution that I think strikes the right balance between maintaining the sense of the servility of the position and still endowing the job holder with agency is "underling." There is also a stickiness in the sound of the word I like. This is the solution for "peon" for now—until a better one comes along.

Finally, the case of the corrupted chai. What follows is an instance of translating cultural difference where perhaps too much thinking about how the reader might receive a certain word might become paralyzing for the translator.

If I'd translated this book fifteen years ago, I'd be translating it before it was written, which would have been very interesting and challenging as a translator, but I'd still have come across the word *chai*—tea—many times in the Hindi, and thought, *Here's an open-and-shut case. I'll just carry the Hindi word* chai *right over into the English. It'll be an easy, if not necessarily meaningful way to keep some of the "color" of the original.* I would have assumed that enough of the American audience had been to South Asia or a South Asian restaurant, or knew the word *chai* from one of the many other languages it occurs in. Or, if all else failed, the word appears enough times in the book itself for any reader to figure out what it is the characters keep drinking.

Then Starbucks and its hot-beverage handmaidens in corporate America ruined the word "chai" by super-sizing it and making it into an expensive specialty drink. If I use the word "chai" in the translation, it is possible that Kris will picture a beverage of double-digit ounces, full of Splenda, topped with soy foam and two shakes of ground cinnamon.

The problem is that the *chai* in *The Girl with the Golden Parasol* comes in something like an oversized shot glass—though it should be sipped and slurped. This *chai* is boiled in a dented aluminum pot—not stainless steel—

over a cow-dung fire and comes with a little layer of something brownish and thick and creamy floating on top that your average Starbucks chai drinker would likely describe as "gross," but which, for the *chai* drinkers in the novel, would be considered the best part.

After all this, might "tea" be the better choice? Or should "chai" still be favored? What kind of advice might Faye Sollid give, if she were to invite us to her gathering? In the "Kitchen Hints" section of her *American-Hindi Cook Book*, she advises cooks that "unpolished rice contains minerals and vitamins which are lacking in polished rice. Use unpolished rice and steam it to save as much nutritional value as possible." A round of chai for Krishna and Kris at Mrs. Sollid's tea!

This is a fascinating cookbook, and it's fun to imagine both American and Indian cooks trying out some of the recipes—say, for Apple Betty or Never Fail Cup Cakes. The point of the book was of course to teach local cooks how to lessen the homesickness pains of their American sahibs. But the point was also to share. "It is hoped that our Indian friends who would like to prepare simple, tasty American dishes will find [the recipes] useful," wrote Sollid, in the introduction.

I wonder how many of Sollid's Indian friends tried their hands at Old Fashioned Rocks or Spiced Vinegar? Sharing goes both ways. Citing the "keen interest" in Indian cooking, presumably among fellow expats, Sollid notes the inclusion of "representative Indian dishes" in the volume. She cautions that "the measurement system differs from ours [and] the Indian recipes may be difficult to follow." But she hopes "that enough enthusiastic women will experiment with the difficult conversion problems for some future edition to include a great expanded section on Indian cooking."

Enthusiasm, above all, is absolutely what is needed to work out "difficult conversion problems." And sometimes even a lowly teaspoon can, and must, be converted into a loyal lackey, stirring in the sugar to make the chai sweeter.

Notes

1. I arrived at this figure by adding the most recent census figures of English speakers (but not "English users," a category requiring only basic competence) in India, Pakistan, Bangladesh, and Sri Lanka.

2. My general rule of thumb with footnotes is that if there were none in the original, I won't use any in my translation. Glossaries I generally object to for two reasons.

One, I suspect that with a bit more work, much of the information contained in glossaries could be incorporated into the text itself with little or no disruption. Two, a glossary's presence divides the readers into two groups: one that needs to use it and the other that doesn't. It's like saying, "If you're not in on things, you have to use the glossary," which is not in the spirit of why I am translating in the first place.

As Translator, as Novelist

The Translator's Afterword

HARUKI MURAKAMI

TRANSLATED BY TED GOOSSEN

To the best of my recollection, I was in my late thirties when I started telling people I was going to translate *The Great Gatsby* when I turned sixty. Having made that pronouncement, I then conducted my daily affairs as if I were moving toward that fixed point, so that much of what I did was pushed along by a kind of reverse calculation. Metaphorically speaking, I had placed *Gatsby* securely on my *kamidana*, the high shelf that serves as a household shrine to the Shinto gods, and then lived my life glancing up at it from time to time.

For some strange reason, however, it became harder and harder to wait till my sixtieth birthday. Restlessly, my eyes sought the book in the shrine more and more often until I finally had to give in. So, three years ahead of schedule, I sat down to work on this translation. Initially I told myself that I would just pick away at it in my spare time, but once I got going I found I couldn't stop, and I finished the whole translation with unanticipated speed, in a single burst of energy. I was like the impatient child who can't wait until his birthday to open his presents. This tendency to jump the gun never seems to change, no matter how old I get.

I had decided to wait until I was sixty to translate *The Great Gatsby* for a number of reasons. For one thing, I figured (or hoped) that by that age my skill would have improved to the point where I could do the job properly. Given *Gatsby*'s importance to me, I wanted my translation to be as precise and thorough as possible so that I would have no regrets. Another reason was the existence of several prior translations, which meant there was no need to rush yet another into print, especially when so many contemporary novels had to be translated as quickly as possible. Finally, there was the picture I had constructed of myself at sixty. By that stage, I thought, life will be more leisurely, and I can enjoy playing with *Gatsby* in the same way that old men enjoy puttering around with bonsai on their verandas. When I was in my thirties, the world of sixty seemed absurdly far away.

Once the reality of the problems and possibilities of that age had come into clear view, however, I became acutely aware that "bonsai on the veranda" wasn't going to fit my situation at all. When I stopped to think about it, I could see clearly that no sudden, drastic change was going to take place when I turned sixty; for better or worse, I would be the same man continuing the same very undramatic life. That being the case, I reconsidered my position and decided there was no need to wait. Moreover, at the risk of sounding presumptuous, I had gained a fair degree—only a degree, mind you—of confidence as a translator. The time had come, I realized, for me to tackle *Gatsby*. I could feel it in my bones.

There was another reason, too, which probably has something to do with my age: the number of current works I felt the urgent need to translate was gradually shrinking. Most of the important books by writers crucial to my generation were already available in Japanese. As for the new crop of younger novelists, well, I could leave their work to a new group of eager young translators. Such a move would allow me the luxury of stepping slightly outside the current of the times to translate works I had long dreamed of putting my hand to. This would not mean that I would forgo contemporary literature altogether. Indeed, I fully expected—or at least hoped for—new works to pop up that I would want to translate. What would certainly change, though, was the ratio between old and new: now classics and semiclassics would come to make up the greater part of my repertoire. These were the texts I had kept close at hand over the years, the books I loved. Most of them, of course, already existed in standard translations; yet if I could refresh them—"wash them anew," as we say—even slightly, my efforts would have been worth it.

My translation of J. D. Salinger's *The Catcher in the Rye*, which I published several years ago, is part of this "rewashed" series, as is, of course, this version of *The Great Gatsby*. I have no desire to take exception with the translations of my predecessors. Each is outstanding in its own way. In fact, if a reader who had grown attached to a novel through one of those translations were to demand to know why I had gone to the trouble of producing yet another version, I would find it hard to justify myself. Nevertheless, it is my conviction that, as I wrote when my version of *Catcher* came out, every translation possesses its own "best before date." Although numerous literary works might properly be called "ageless," no translation belongs in that category. Translation, after all, is a matter of linguistic technique, which naturally ages as the particulars of a language change. Thus, while there are undying works, on principle there can be no undying translations. Just as dictionaries eventually become outdated, so, to some extent, does every translation (including, of course, my own) grow obsolete as times change. I would even go so far as to say that when a specific translation is imprinted too deeply on the minds of its readers for too long, it runs the risk of damaging the original. It is therefore imperative that new versions appear periodically in the same way that computer programs are regularly updated. At the very least this provides a broader spectrum of choices, which can only benefit prospective readers.

In the case of *The Great Gatsby*, I found that none of the translations I looked at satisfied me, regardless of their quality. Inevitably, I would think, *This feels a bit (or a lot!) different from the* Gatsby *I know*. I must hasten to add that this reaction was personal, based on the image I carried in my mind, and had nothing at all to do with objective—or academic— critical assessments of the works at hand, such evaluations being beyond my power anyway. All I could do was scratch my head at how wide the gap was between "my *Gatsby*" and the impression I received from the translations—this again from a purely subjective perspective. I don't normally discuss my reactions to others' work so frankly. But this is *The Great Gatsby* we are talking about, so I am willing to stick my neck out.

Put differently, I translated *Gatsby* at an extremely personal level. I wanted to make my long-standing image of *Gatsby* clear and concrete, so that readers could picture the distinct colors and contours of the novel and feel its textures. To do this, I strove to eliminate anything that was the slightest bit obscure or that might leave the reader feeling as if they had somehow missed something.

I have always felt that translation is fundamentally an act of kindness. It is not enough to find words that match: if images in the translated text are unclear, then the thoughts and feelings of the author are lost. In this particular case, I tried hard to be as kind a translator as possible. As I went over passage after passage, I attempted to clarify the meaning of each in Japanese to the best of my ability. Still, as with everything, there were limits. All I can say is, I tried my best.

I have written of the crucial importance that *The Great Gatsby* holds for me. As a responsible translator, therefore, it behooves me to try to explain that importance in more concrete terms.

When someone asks, "Which three books have meant the most to you?" I can answer without having to think: *The Great Gatsby*, Dostoevsky's *The Brothers Karamazov*, and Raymond Chandler's *The Long Goodbye*. All three have been indispensable to me (both as a reader and as a writer); yet if I were forced to select only one, I would unhesitatingly choose *Gatsby*. Had it not been for Fitzgerald's novel, I would not be writing the kind of literature I am today (indeed, it is possible that I would not be writing at all, although that is neither here nor there).

Whatever the case, you can sense the level of my infatuation with *The Great Gatsby*. It taught me so much and encouraged me so greatly in my own life. Though slender in size for a full-length work, it served as a standard and a fixed point, an axis around which I was able to organize the many coordinates that make up the world of the novel. I read *Gatsby* over and over, poking into every nook and cranny, until I had virtually memorized entire sections.

Remarks such as these are bound to perplex more than a few readers. "Look, Murakami," they'll say, "I read the novel, and I don't get it. Just why do you think it's so great?" My first impulse is to challenge them right back. "Hey, if *The Great Gatsby* isn't great," I am tempted to say, inching closer, "then what the heck is?" Yet at the same time I am not without sympathy for their point of view. *Gatsby* is such a finely wrought novel—its scenes so fully realized, its evocations of sentiment so delicate, its language so layered—that, in the end, one has to study it line by line in English to appreciate its true value. Fitzgerald was a master stylist, and when he wrote *Gatsby* at the age of twenty-eight he was at the absolute peak of his craft. Unavoidably, Japanese translations have stumbled over some of the fine points of his novel, while others have been entirely omitted. As they say, a delicate wine doesn't travel well. Try as one may, it will lose at least a portion of its aroma, mellowness, and texture en route.

The only answer, I guess, is to read a work such as *Gatsby* in the original; yet that is more easily said than done. The beauty of Fitzgerald's fluent, elastic prose lies in his ability to alter tone, pattern, and rhythm to create infinitesimal shifts in atmosphere. To be perfectly honest, a work that achieves this stylistic level is too difficult for a person with limited English to comprehend—only a truly advanced reader is able to see what he is really up to.

This is why, if I may be allowed to exaggerate in a somewhat high-handed manner, it is my impression that Japanese readers have never *truly* appreciated *The Great Gatsby*. At the very least, judging from the overall reaction of those I have exchanged views with (most of whom are, at least to some extent, professionally connected to the literary world), I can only be pessimistic about *Gatsby*'s reception in Japan. And standing behind this pessimism is the imposing barrier of the translation process itself.

I cannot be so presumptuous as to claim that my translation of *Gatsby* clears that barrier entirely. No one is more aware than I am of what a heavy undertaking it is to translate *Gatsby*, so I am not being falsely modest when I concede that my effort, too, is bound to have some faults. Whoever looks hard enough, I fear, can probably locate any number of places where I have failed. Yet is there a way of transferring a work of such beauty and completeness in English into another language without the occasional failure?

Until *Gatsby*, I had always tried to keep the fact that I was a writer far from my mind when translating: I wanted to make myself invisible, like a black-garbed puppet handler on the Bunraku stage. What mattered, I believed, was fidelity to the original. True, my being a writer had to be involved to a certain degree, since it formed part of the context I brought to the work, but that was something that arose naturally, without any conscious intent on my part. *Gatsby*, however, was a different story. From the outset, I set my sights on putting my novel-writing experience to as good a use as possible. This did not mean that I translated loosely or substituted my own phrases for those of the original. Rather, it meant that, at strategic moments, I brought my imaginative powers as a novelist into play. One by one, I dug up the slippery parts of Fitzgerald's novel, those scattered places that had proved elusive, and asked myself, *If I were the author, how would I have written this?* Painstakingly, I examined *Gatsby*'s solid trunk and branches and dissected its beautiful leaves. When necessary, however, I stepped back to take a broader view, forsaking a word-by-word approach. Had I gone about translating *Gatsby* any other way, I wouldn't have been able to convey the power of Fitzgerald's prose. To fully grasp its essence, I had to plunge into its heart—then and only then could his writing burst into bloom.

As Translator, as Novelist: The Translator's Afterword

To put it in extreme terms, I turned *The Great Gatsby* into a final goal of sorts—through focusing on it, I was able to complete one stage of my journey as a translator. In this sense, while my *Gatsby* marked the end of something, a consummation and a conclusion, it also was a step forward into a new and broader realm. This is of course a purely personal concern, a task I set for myself, which has little direct relevance for readers who may pick up this book.

I had several objectives in mind when I set to work on the "Murakami version" of *The Great Gatsby,* what I guess you could call the fundamental principles of this translation.

The first was to make *Gatsby* a modern tale. The work was written in 1924, and set in 1922, so that more than eighty years had elapsed by the time I launched the translation. Long enough, in other words, for the novel to be considered ancient history. Yet I didn't want it lumped with the other classics: whatever else, the story had to live in the present day. Thus I kept only those old-fashioned turns of phrase and descriptions of the period that I considered essential and eliminated the rest, or at the very least toned their colors down. Nick, Gatsby, and Daisy, Jordan and Tom—all had to exist as if they were literally standing beside us, breathing the same air that we do. They had to be our relatives and friends, our acquaintances and neighbors, which meant that their conversations had to come to life. One of the things I had absorbed over the years was an appreciation of just how crucial dialogue can be in the fashioning of a novel, a lesson I had originally picked up from *Gatsby* itself.

As readers will see, each of the characters in this novel is fully formed, with his or her distinctive manner of speech. This does not mean, however, that they are fixed and unmoving. While each character acts within a consistent framework, their feelings and thoughts shift—as do yours and mine—when their environment and circumstances change, and that in turn alters the way they speak. Yes, not only must their words come alive, their every breath must be seen to carry some sort of meaning.

Capturing Fitzgerald's rhythm was another goal. Fitzgerald's prose flows as does a piece of elegant music, and his sentences ride upon this rhythm. Like a fairy-tale beanstalk, they soar endlessly into the air, carrying the reader with them. Each word gives birth to the next in a single, ascending stream. Searching for space to grow, they spread out until they cover the sky. It is a beautiful sight. Principles such as logic and consistency do not rule here; indeed, they may be banished entirely. When that happens, words are sucked upward with their ambiguities and multiple meanings intact, so that they bulge with implications and possibilities. This in turn causes me, as a responsible translator, to shake my head in wonder over why a particular word has seemingly popped up from nowhere. Readers caught in the flow, however, are not discomfited in the slightest—they naturally apprehend what Fitzgerald is doing, for the writing is of unparalleled beauty, and the resonance of his language leaves nothing unsaid. This, I guess, is what literary genius is all about. For the translator, however, rendering such prose into colloquial Japanese is virtually impossible.

Faced with this dilemma, I decided to emphasize the musical rhythm that lies at the heart of Fitzgerald's style. If I could somehow re-create that rhythm in Japanese, then the melody and the lyrics would fall into place. This musical analogy made natural sense when it came to approaching Fitzgerald. I occasionally found myself reading sections of the novel aloud as I worked, sometimes in the original English and sometimes in Japanese. I'm not sure how effective this was. But you should know that I used this technique in carrying out this translation, and that it reflects my fundamental approach to his art. What makes Fitzgerald's prose so striking is that rhythm—once established, the words flow naturally. This is the beauty of the Fitzgerald style as I see it.

I fear I have gone on a little too long talking about my relationship to *The Great Gatsby*, and what it took to translate it. Still more might well be said, but that could go on forever, so I will set it aside and turn to another of my duties as translator: laying out the historical context of Fitzgerald's novel and the circumstances under which he wrote it. By necessity this will be a simple and fairly rough account, a quick trip across an immensely detailed landscape.

The idea of writing *Gatsby* first came to Fitzgerald in 1923. He started serious work on the novel the following spring in France, where he and his wife, Zelda, had gone to live, and completed it by the end of that year; it was then published in the United States in April 1925.

Fitzgerald had become the golden boy of the literary world after his sensational 1920 debut, and had already published two long novels, *This Side of Paradise* (his first novel) and *The Beautiful and the Damned*, as well as two collections of short stories, *Flappers and Philosophers* and *Tales of the*

Jazz Age. Americans had been swept up in the unprecedented economic boom that followed the First World War, and they were looking for a hero who would embody the blossoming new culture. Young, handsome, and utterly fearless, Fitzgerald was precisely the literary icon they required, an elegant and magnanimous voice that could speak on behalf of the new generation. Meanwhile, Zelda, his beautiful young wife, reigned as the princess of the flappers: poised at the cutting edge of fashion and liberated from old-fashioned morality, she indulged herself to her heart's content in a life of carefree consumption.

Even while enmeshed in this flamboyant lifestyle, Fitzgerald raked in the money, turning out one high-priced short story after another for the popular journals. Most were simple, guileless stories with happy endings, designed merely to amuse, but included in the mix were a few that were breathtaking. How a callow young man such as Fitzgerald was able to produce such masterpieces despite his ignorance of the world, and his general lack of stability and self-discipline, remains a mystery. Unless, that is, one chalks it up—as one does with Mozart, Schubert, and their comrades—to that single word, *genius*.

Despite the noisy disorder of his life, Fitzgerald was filled with a burning ambition—to write an epoch-making novel. Certainly, the short stories he kept spinning out meant that he would never want for money. While novels forced one to wait in the hope that royalties would eventually start rolling in, the big magazines were offering fantastic rates for commissioned stories, and they paid right away. Financially, therefore, short stories were by far the better option. Professionally, however, Fitzgerald knew he would never be considered a first-class author until he had bequeathed a solid, weighty novel to posterity. This was the way the literary world worked then—and, with very few exceptions, still does. Fitzgerald was convinced that he was no lightweight; that if he could create just the right circumstances, he was capable of turning out a novel that would become an enduring classic. *This Side of Paradise* and *The Beautiful and Damned* had not been bad efforts, and their critical reception had been reasonably good. They had sold well. Yet his inner voice told him that he was capable of writing a novel with much more depth. Success was within his grasp.

Once the flurry of activity surrounding his literary debut and marriage had subsided, Fitzgerald escaped the hubbub of New York with Zelda for the more peaceful community of Great Neck in suburban Long Island. It was 1922, and he was twenty-six. He was committed to settling down there to do some serious writing; yet there was no way the hyperactive and glamour-loving Zelda could submit to a quiet suburban lifestyle and so, once again, the boisterous parties resumed. It would be a mistake, however, to see them as profitless, for the endless round of revelry they enjoyed in Great Neck paid off later, when it came time for Fitzgerald to craft the scenes we find in *The Great Gatsby*.

Fitzgerald was the type of novelist who could only write about what he had actually experienced or seen, which is why it was imperative that he live near the eye of the typhoon that was Zelda. We can therefore presume that had it not been for their wild nights in Great Neck, the masterpiece that is *Gatsby* would never have been written or, failing that, would have taken a very different shape. Certainly, Fitzgerald could never have described the parties in the book in such a fresh and lively way. One of Fitzgerald's weak points was his difficulty in striking a balance between input and output. When his input passed a certain level, the excess energy reduced his output (this is the story of the first half of his career); conversely, cutting back on his input deprived him of the material he needed to write (this is the story of the second half). In *Gatsby*'s case, miraculously, Fitzgerald was able to hold these two sides in a beautiful, albeit precarious, balance. Such perfect equilibrium, however, would never occur again in his life.

In 1924, seeking a quieter, more relaxing spot that would allow him to concentrate on his novel and enable both of them to cut back on their escalating expenses (a futile goal, however often they might move), the Fitzgeralds changed locations yet again. Putting Great Neck behind them, they steamed across the Atlantic to their new home on the French Riviera. The couple seemed fated to spend their lives restlessly moving from one temporary abode to another (I am hardly one to talk here, by the way). Settling down in one place was quite beyond them. As a result, as long as he lived Fitzgerald never owned his own house, choosing instead to rent. Nor did he try to build up any sort of financial security. One can see these choices as reflecting a kind of purity, I suppose, but the upshot was that Fitzgerald's life lacked any semblance of stability, whether in his home life or in his finances.

In any case, once ensconced in the fabled beauty of southern France, Scott—in what was a rarity for him—threw himself into his work. For Zelda, this was no fun at all. Being left on her own for long periods of time sent her boredom level skyrocketing. For the life of her, she couldn't fathom why her husband was so wrapped up in his project. Why, she would complain, did he have to work like a horse on his damned novel? If he just went back to scribbling his stories during spare moments they would be free to go out and party. They would never have any fun this way—and after having taken so much trouble to find such a gorgeous spot! . . . As Scott resolutely poured his heart and soul into his writing, Zelda, out of boredom and a desire for revenge, entered into an affair with a dashing young French flyer. This was in the summer of that year.

Zelda's fling was a replay of the many flirtations she had enjoyed as a girl with the young officers—including Scott—stationed near her home in Montgomery, Alabama. For better or for worse, she was the type of young woman who needed to be constantly admired by the men around her. Scott had learned to accept the fact that men were crazy for Zelda and to put his trust in the strength of their bond, so much so that when she began stepping out with other men he welcomed it as the elimination of a major distraction from his work. His lighthearted reaction turned to shock, however, when he realized how serious she was about her new beau. Those around Zelda assumed her relationship with the flyer was sexual, although it is impossible, looking back from today's vantage point, to know for certain. We are only left to imagine that in all probability they were right.

At any rate, when Scott heard the rumors, he grilled Zelda about what was going on. Zelda admitted she had fallen in love and raised the possibility of a divorce. This was a devastating blow for Scott. As one might expect, he broke off his writing and confronted the couple with a final ultimatum (much as Tom does to Daisy and Gatsby in the novel). There followed a long series of histrionic exchanges, at the end of which it was decided that Zelda and her French airman would call an end to their brief summer of love. Given time to think the situation over coolly, Zelda had decided (as does Daisy) that it would be a foolish mistake to give up the life she shared with Scott. Nevertheless, the wounds the couple suffered from the affair were deep.

The work-obsessed husband and the wife who looks elsewhere for her pleasure are such common figures that we might dismiss them with a brief word and move on, yet the impact of these events on Scott was incalculable. In a single stroke, his ability to write his novel in peace and his unquestioning trust in his wife had been shattered. To gauge his reaction, we need only look at his portrait of Daisy, which in all likelihood was shaped by his pain and frustration. Or, at a deeper level, how the

novelist in him unconsciously drew from the emotional turmoil generated by the affair to gain the creative "nourishment" he needed to write
Gatsby.

At any rate, Scott was somehow able to right himself, and in late October of that year he sent the completed manuscript to the publisher. His
editor, Maxwell Perkins, sent back a letter full of praise that basically
said, Fabulous! This thrilled Fitzgerald, who anticipated sales on an
unprecedented scale. Yet the book never got off the ground. Although
Fitzgerald had privately embraced the hope that one hundred thousand
copies might be sold (ensuring the financial security he longed for), in fact
barely twenty thousand moved, despite overwhelmingly excellent reviews.
This feeble performance meant that, once his advance was subtracted, he
received almost nothing. Why were sales so low? Probably the reason was
that the young readers who had supported Fitzgerald's popularity up to
that point found *Gatsby*'s content a little too deep, and the novel as a whole
a little too difficult. What they wanted from him were urban novels that
were bright and fashionable, and slightly sad. In a way, Fitzgerald had
outgrown his own audience. Intellectually, and abruptly.

It was not to be until after Fitzgerald's death that *Gatsby* was accorded
the rank of "masterpiece" and placed on high school reading lists, with
hundreds of thousands of copies sold annually. Scott had fulfilled his
goal of creating an undying novel, although, sadly, he was not around to
enjoy the sight. In fact, he had been ignored for many years, a "once-
popular writer" left to languish in the dimly lit margins of history. He
had single-handedly borne the burdens of his dependency on alcohol,
Zelda's mental and physical illnesses, and the care of their only daughter,
all while living under chronically straitened circumstances; yet even so
he had never lost his literary ambition or his literary conscience, pushing
himself to keep writing novels and stories (still well worth reading,
though they lack the sparkle of his heyday) until finally, having whittled
himself down to almost nothing, he passed away at the young age of
forty-four. Toward the end, Fitzgerald often compared his career to that
of Hemingway. Hemingway was a modern literary titan, he lamented,
whereas he himself amounted to no more than a master of technique, a
sort of literary prostitute. In a sense, Fitzgerald *truly* believed this. Many
saw this as an example of his characteristic defeatism, but who could
blame him, given the way events were unfolding? There was a time in
the late 1930s when *The Great Gatsby* was out of print, and one year the

total royalties from Fitzgerald's books amounted to a mere thirty-three dollars. In the meantime, Hemingway had become a culture hero for his times, worshipped by the young and celebrated around the world.

After the Second World War, however, Hemingway's literary reputation steadily declined (or, one could say, returned to its proper, uninflated level) while Fitzgerald's, propelled by the efforts of a handful of critics, rose dramatically, so that by now his fame is virtually unshakable. I am a bit shocked today when rereading Hemingway's novels to see how quickly they have aged while *Gatsby* has managed to cement Fitzgerald's reputation. It stands unblemished, a seamless work of art, clearly a level above *The Sun Also Rises*, my choice as Hemingway's best novel. There is a common saying that one cannot assess a life until the lid to the coffin has been nailed shut; Fitzgerald's case shows just how much time may pass after the coffin is closed without a final appraisal being reached.

In any event, one thing for certain is that, were it not for *The Great Gatsby*, such a reassessment of Fitzgerald's work—had one occurred at all—would have been much less dramatic. That is how central *Gatsby* is to Fitzgerald's legacy. Among his other works, *Tender Is the Night* is a special favorite of mine, an unforgettably beautiful and moving novel; yet there is no getting around the fact that, unlike *Gatsby*, there are a number of places where it fails to cohere. Fitzgerald himself was well aware of this situation. Looking back over his career in 1934, he said that the only time he had been able to sustain a pure state of artistic conscience was several months during the writing of *The Great Gatsby*. Why was such a feat impossible at other times? Clearly, the reasons are complex. Hemingway, who for a time was close friends with Scott, was characteristically forthright on the issue. He had found it impossible to fathom, he said, why a man capable of writing something as good as *The Great Gatsby* would waste his time playing drunken games. Then he met Zelda and it all became clear. In Hemingway's opinion, Zelda was envious of Scott's immense talent and took great satisfaction in preventing him from doing any serious work. In a letter to Maxwell Perkins, Hemingway wrote, "There are only two ways Scott can be saved. Either Zelda dies, or his stomach gets so bad he can't drink another drop." Hemingway also warned Scott that Zelda was crazy and that he should leave her (unsurprisingly, Scott ignored him).

Hemingway hit the bull's eye from one angle; but from another I think he missed the target altogether. Scott intrinsically needed the fiery force that was Zelda, and she for her part intrinsically required the heat he produced. This exchange generated a vital energy, which heightened their inspiration and kept it vivid and fresh. Seen in this way, their choice of life partners could hardly be called mistaken. Nevertheless, the intensity of the heat so exceeded normal bounds that it became impossible to maintain a balance that allowed them to help each other. To make matters even worse, neither had a shred of practical sense when it came to running their lives, and the idea that they might cover for each other's shortcomings seems never to have occurred to them. Even if it had, however, they fatally lacked the strength and patience to turn that awareness into action. Whatever shape their relationship might have taken, its collapse was unavoidable. No one, however, could have foreseen Zelda's tragic and early descent into mental illness.

At all events, we can enjoy the fruit of the rare (once-in-a-lifetime may be more apt) dynamic that was Scott and Zelda in that almost flawless novel ("almost" here being purely rhetorical), *The Great Gatsby*. For this we can only rejoice. Though our hearts may ache at the thought of the strange vicissitudes of fate, so very magnificent and so terribly sad, that they had to endure. Yes, even then.

When I told Americans I was translating *Gatsby*, their first question was invariably: "How are you going to translate Gatsby's pet phrase, 'old sport'?" I suppose this was entirely natural. If I were American, I would probably ask the same thing. "Well," I answered, "I plan to leave it as it is." "But shouldn't you try to find an appropriate expression in Japanese?" they replied, looking perplexed. Of course, I would have happily used "an appropriate Japanese expression," had such a thing existed. But I couldn't find one. Please understand, I have been batting the "old sport" problem around for more than twenty years, trying to come up with something. Nevertheless, when the time to commit myself to paper arrived, I could only shrug and go with the original English. It was not a question of laziness or a failure of nerve. Rather, after all those years, I had reached the conclusion that there could be no other solution. "Old sport" has to be left as "old sport"—there are no substitutes. Such is my thinking on the matter. Or, more hyperbolically, such is the path I have chosen. Had the word occurred just once in a specific situation, of course, there would have been any number of choices. That would have been a mere technical problem. Since it was a key word that occurred throughout the text, though, I could only leave it as it was.

As Translator, as Novelist: The Translator's Afterword

"Old sport" was probably a British expression around that time, somewhat similar to "old chap" today. Americans have used neither of these. If you were to look for an equivalent turn of phrase in American English, you would probably end up with something like "old friend." Gatsby must have picked up "old sport" during the time he was enrolled at Oxford and then made it a habit after his return, a kind of personal affectation. Fitzgerald was able to suggest Gatsby's innate theatricality, at once shady and naïve, through this form of address. Such transparently vulgar taste—also represented by things such as Gatsby's pink suits and yellow sports car—is what grates on the nerves of Tom Buchanan, a true son of the upper class. "Old sport" clearly operates within this context, yet try as I might, I could find no Japanese word with similar associations. Even after twenty-odd years!

I also racked my brains over the opening and concluding sections of the novel. Why? For the very reason that both are lauded as examples of superb writing. Even after countless rereadings, they still take my breath away. Every word is filled with meaning and substance, laden with implication yet as light as ether; and when you reach out to grasp one, it slips through your fingers. It was my lack of confidence that I could handle these sections, I must confess, that led me to put off translating *Gatsby* for two decades. Instead, I placed it up on my *kamidana* and left it there. To be honest (and I should whisper this, or ask the publisher to print it in smaller type), I am still not entirely confident. All I can say is, once again, I gave it my best shot.

It is my sincere desire that you will enjoy *The Great Gatsby*, the sad, beautiful tale of a single summer, in whatever way you see fit. And that you will understand why I have treasured it for more than forty years. If I have been able to communicate even a portion of those feelings, and you are able to share my love of Fitzgerald's novel, then I am happy. That is my one and only wish. I have written a great deal here, but, in the end, it seems that is really all that needs to be said.

FOURTEEN

Haruki Murakami and the Culture of Translation

TED GOOSSEN

Japanese culture is often characterized as a culture of translation. In fact, the Japanese language of today is the result of centuries of effort by translators struggling to match Chinese characters and Japanese words, affixing native pronunciation in some cases, adopting approximations of Chinese pronunciation in others, and developing two different syllabaries: one—*katakana*—initially used by men; the other—*hiragana*—by women (the eleventh-century *Tale of Genji* was written in the latter). At no time, however, was translation more crucial to the Japanese than in the second half of the nineteenth century, when Western colonial pressure was most intense. At first it was young samurai, handpicked by their feudal lords, who labored over foreign documents (often written in Dutch) to try to ferret out what was required to defend and develop their fiefs. Later, when the Meiji period (1868–1912) was under way and the national system of education established, "modern" learning necessarily focused on the mastery of Western texts and their transmission to a broader public. At the outset, the goal was purely practical—to strengthen the country militarily, technologically, and institutionally—but by the 1880s the focus had broadened to include European literature, philosophy, and the arts, now seen as key to the construction of an advanced society on a par with the West.

It was no accident that the founders of Japanese modern literature tended to be either scholars of Western literature or translators. Ogai Mori, for example, is known outside Japan for his stories and novels, but at home he is also revered for his translations of Goethe and Hans Christian Andersen; Japan's first great novelist, Soseki Natsume, wrote essays on Shakespeare and modern literary theory before giving up his prestigious day job as Professor of English at Tokyo's Imperial University to concentrate on his fiction. Although Soseki's novels, the most famous of which is *Kokoro* (a word that means both "heart" and "mind"), were profoundly influenced by his study of English literature, they were hardly derivative. In fact, *Kokoro,* an elegiac romance whose latter half is comprised of an apparent suicide letter from the hero to the young narrator, anticipates an authorial strategy (the reader never learns the narrator's reaction) that had not yet been used in the West.

Novelist/translators are not a uniquely Japanese phenomenon, of course—similar figures are common throughout the world, although much more rare in French and English literary cultures. Even so, however, the number of modern Japanese novelists who have turned their hand to translation (or vice versa, since many translators eventually turn to fiction) is striking, no case being more remarkable than Haruki Murakami. Murakami is an internationally successful novelist, with legions of readers in places as far-flung as China, Russia, Europe, and South Korea. Yet in Japan he is equally celebrated as the translator of American writers such as Carver, Chandler, Fitzgerald, Capote, and Salinger. His translations are best-sellers too, since Japanese readers tend to select books based on their translators, something hard to imagine in a culture such as ours in which the name of the translator seldom registers in a reader's mind. A few years ago, for example, when Murakami's version of Carver's complete works was just out, I saw red banners flying in front of the Kinokuniya bookstore in Shinjuku promoting the series; not surprisingly, perhaps, Murakami's name was placed above Carver's and printed in larger characters.

The Japanese profile of American authors whom Murakami translates thus soars the moment his translation appears—even the original English texts are snapped up, though few can read them easily. That Murakami is aware that this affects the reputations, and the pocketbooks, of previous translators of the same work can be seen from his afterword, which takes pains to commend their efforts on the one hand while lamenting their inability to capture "his *Gatsby*" on the other. Indeed, beneath the modulated modesty (*de rigueur* in the Japanese afterword genre), Murakami's announcement that all of American literature is fair game hurls down a literary gauntlet. In the process, he also raises the bar for his fellow translators by stressing the importance of being able to reenact the creative process itself—that is, "how we would have written it, had we been the author." Tackling *The Great Gatsby*, and by implication any other good novel, means occasionally stepping back from the surface meaning of words to try to capture the bigger picture in a style that sings.

The problem facing his fellow translators is that no one sings quite like Murakami, whose distinctive rhythms—drawn from his lifelong love of jazz—characterize all that he writes, including his translations. As Jay Rubin puts it in *Haruki Murakami and the Music of Words*, "It is a wonder that he did not become a musician himself—though, in a way, he did. Rhythm is perhaps the most important element of his prose." Fitzgerald and Murakami are thus beautifully matched: just as Fitzgerald established a style for his times by giving his writing a jazz swing, so has Murakami drawn from Stan Getz, Billie Holiday, and other jazz greats from a later era—as well as from American novels such as *The Great Gatsby*—to fashion his literary voice.

The influence of jazz and American literature on Murakami has led some Japanese critics to call his writing "unnatural" (read "un-Japanese"), especially in the 1980s when he first became popular. Today, though, such criticisms seem rather moot—having been read by so many for so long, the "Murakami style" now feels quite normal, especially for those raised on it (I include myself in this group). Still, some continue to lament its effects on today's readers, whose view of literature has been narrowed, so the argument runs, by the likes and dislikes of people such as Murakami and his occasional collaborator, Motoyuki Shibata, another star translator of American fiction. Given America's postwar military occupation and the decades of American influence that followed, the impact of American culture on Japan (and the rest of the globe) is bound to remain a heated issue, and Murakami's writing is placed squarely in the middle of it.

Nevertheless, thanks to this deep and long-standing tie with America, Japanese readers come to a work such as *The Great Gatsby* with considerable background knowledge. Although few can speak the language very well, many are comfortable reading English at some level, and almost everyone has a basic vocabulary. They are also likely to have a vague image—formed primarily through films—of what the Roaring Twenties looked like. Murakami can count on this experience, which means that when he comes to a crucial yet untranslatable phrase such as "old sport," he has the option—which he takes—of leaving it in English, and then discussing it in the afterword. Far better, he insists, to stick with the original than replace it with a Japanese phrase whose associations are markedly different.

Translators of Murakami's books into Western languages face similar problems, but have no recourse to a similar solution. The word *kokoro* (mind/heart), for example, which was the title of Soseki's masterpiece, also plays a central role in my favorite Murakami novel, *The Hard-Boiled Wonderland and the End of the World*. There, the hero loses his *kokoro* when his shadow is forcibly detached from his body and spends the rest of the narrative trying to reunite with it. In English, however, the hero is trying to save his *mind*, a word that subtly alters the emotional and spiritual aspects of his dilemma. Had translator Alfred Birnbaum been given the option, you can bet he would have left *kokoro* in the original and then explained his choice in a translator's preface. It is hard to imagine a Western publisher going along with such an arrangement, however, since translators here are kept tucked safely out of sight to perpetuate the illusion of "seamlessness." For English readers, it appears, books need to be dubbed, not subtitled.

Translating Jacopone da Todi

Archaic Poetries and Modern Audiences

LAWRENCE VENUTI

I write here as a literary translator, prefacing my own work, but I do not
intend to offer yet another belletristic commentary on translation. My
aim is also to challenge the prevailing tendency among contemporary
translators to make fairly impressionistic remarks on their practice, on
its literary and cultural values, on the equivalence they believe to have
established between their translations and the foreign texts. In adopting
this approach, translators actually avoid addressing the conceptual problems posed by translation and so inadvertently raise the question of
whether any translation practice can ever take into account these
problems without a sustained theoretical reflection. Such a reflection, I
believe, can enrich practice in ways that have yet to be fully explored.

My starting point is a skepticism as to whether cross-cultural understanding is possible in literary translation, particularly when the foreign
text to be translated was produced in a remote historical period. Maintaining a strict semantic correspondence to the foreign text, a correspondence based on dictionary definitions, cannot obviate the irreparable loss
of the foreign context. Translation radically decontextualizes a foreign
text by uprooting it from the literary traditions and practices that not
only give rise to it, but make it meaningful to foreign readers who have
read widely in the foreign language and literature. This context of production and reception can never be restored so as to provide the reader
of the translation with a response that is equivalent to the informed

foreign-language reader's response to the foreign text (I dissent from the widely held notion of "equivalent effect," particularly as formulated by Nida[1]). For foreign traditions and practices, their cultural meanings and historical weight, can rarely (if ever) be signified in the translation itself, at any textual level, whether linguistic or stylistic, discursive or thematic, prosodic or generic.

Of course, a scholarly apparatus might help immensely in compensating for the loss of context. But any such compensation, however much learning it incorporates, can never enable the translation to elicit an equivalent response: the very term "scholarly" means, not only that the audience of the translation has been narrowed to readers seeking specialized knowledge in the form of historical scholarship, but that the foreign audiences for which the foreign text was originally written have been displaced. These audiences were never limited to scholars or other professional readers. And historical scholarship, notwithstanding its enormous value in understanding past moments, always asks questions of those moments that they did not ask of themselves, questions that issue from the moment of historical research and the historian's particular methods. This fundamental anachronism in historical scholarship is exacerbated in the translation of archaic literatures. Because translation is decontextualizing, it inevitably opens up a historical difference from the foreign text through the very linguistic choices that the translator makes to overcome that difference. For these choices expose the translator's address to audiences in another culture at a later moment.

Archaic poetries bring the added difficulty of generic and prosodic features that, even when they have been revived by modern poets, continue to signify a historical remoteness to modern readers. During the twentieth century, the practice that came to dominate English-language poetry translation was to avoid developing comparable prosodic features, especially rhyme schemes and stanzaic structures, and rather assimilate the foreign text to the forms that dominated English-language poetry: varieties of unrhymed metrical verse and free verse. Indeed, the dominance of these forms has been so decisive that many modern readers take them as the distinguishing feature of "modern" vs. "archaic" poetry. In the case of translation, this dominance has created a set of reader expectations that have undoubtedly limited the translator's choices, but that can be strategically frustrated to produce a range of effects in the translating language and culture. These effects might be designed to evoke the form of an archaic foreign poetry. But insofar as they violate a modern poetic norm, they might also defamiliarize prevailing translation practices.

Archaic poetic forms cannot be easily imitated in English. Prosody, in particular, is a repository of literary traditions and practices, so that the translator's effort to imitate somehow the meter or rhythm of an archaic foreign poem cannot simply restore past sounds and listening experiences for readers who do not have sufficient access to the foreign context. On the contrary, such efforts risk the infiltration of later sounds and listening experiences—which is to say the inevitable problem of anachronism in translation.

The translator, however, might admit this inevitability and turn it to advantage. Ezra Pound's translations and his commentary on them can prove exemplary here. Pound showed how an archaic foreign poem might be rendered through the imitation of an analogous poetry in the translating language or, in other words, through a calculated recontextualization. Nonetheless, he was acutely aware that the analogy was never a perfect stylistic or temporal fit and could not control every reader's response. In "Guido's Relations" (1929), for instance, Pound describes his effort to translate Cavalcanti's poetry by drawing on "pre-Elizabethan English," the language used by poets such as Wyatt and Surrey. And he anticipates two

> objections to such a method: the doubt as to whether one has the right to take a serious poem and turn it into a mere exercise in quaintness; the "misrepresentation" not of the poem's antiquity, but of the proportionate feel of that antiquity, by which I mean that Guido's thirteenth-century language is to twentieth-century Italian sense much less archaic than any fourteenth-, fifteenth-, or early sixteenth-century English is for us.[2]

By "quaintness," the first objection, Pound seems to be referring to a superficial appearance of historical difference, a pastiche, say, whereby the translation does not offer readers a compelling depth of engagement as a historically situated foreign poem might do. Avoiding this appearance depends much on the translator's skills, not only as a writer of the translating language, but as a literary imitator with a wide stylistic repertoire. Two kinds of imitation are at stake. In addition to maintaining a semantic correspondence, the translator mimics distinctive features of the foreign poem by mimicking an analogous style drawn from the poetic traditions in the translating language. The stylistic analogue does not supply the loss of the foreign context, nor does it enable an equivalent effect; it rather provides another context in the receiving culture, a context of production and reception in which the translator inscribes the foreign poem with an interpretation that is both illuminating and convincing, that does not seem merely a literary prank.

The second objection to Pound's method is perhaps more consequential: creating an analogue from literary traditions and practices in the translating language can distort the historical difference that an archaic foreign poetry signifies in its own language. Here Pound has run up against the inevitable anachronism in translation, which occurs whether the translator relies on current usage or resorts to the imitation of an archaic poetry. To object that Pound's poetic analogue is historically distorting assumes that a literary translation can establish a relation of historical adequacy to the foreign text, regardless of the fact that languages and literatures develop disjunctively, at different speeds, establishing different relations to other languages and literatures. The objection, then, does not recognize the radical decontextualization at work in every literary translation.

Yet Pound's response also remains questionable. He does not insist on the inevitable anachronism that accompanies the loss of context in translating, but rather assumes that a degree of historical adequacy is possible between the foreign and translated texts. Thus he suggests that his pre-Elizabethan English versions of Cavalcanti "can show where the treasure lies" to the modern reader who cannot read the Italian.[3] Yet he describes that "treasure" with such terms as "clarity and explicitness," as opposed to "magniloquence and the thundering phrase," and thereby reveals his preference for poetries that reflect his modernist concern for linguistic precision, excluding the work of Marlowe and Milton, among other poets.[4] Pound assumes that his reading of archaic foreign poetries is true to the texts themselves, to their essential values, not one possible interpretation determined by his own modernist poetics and underwritten by a modernist canon of English-language poets.[5] And he does not admit that he is translating for like-minded readers, modernists, or at least for readers whom the very power of his translating might persuade to accept a modernist aesthetic in a translation.

Despite these problems, Pound's translation method remains an advance over widely adopted approaches (namely, maintaining a semantic correspondence in current usage), and it should not be rejected by modern translators of archaic foreign poetries. Yet it does require greater self-consciousness on the translator's part, greater attention, on the one hand, to the relation between the translation and the foreign text and, on the other, to the relation between the translation and the literary traditions and practices from which an analogue is fashioned in the translating language. These two relations are both interpretations, enacted in the translation process, and so they are provisional, directed to specific audiences, engaged in the reproduction of forms and meanings in a particular cultural situation at a particular historical moment. And because both interpretive relations are culturally and historically variable, neither leaves its object—the foreign text and the literature in the translating language—entirely unaffected or intact. To a certain extent, both objects are transformed, at once imitated and inscribed with an interpretive difference, trusted as meaningful yet submitted to a revisionary manipulation. As a result, the translator's creation of a stylistic analogue signals the linguistic and literary features of the foreign text in a disjunctive and indirect manner, through the interpretive differences that transform the foreign forms and themes as well as the receiving literature.

Yet the problem of modern audiences still looms in the background. For which readers will both the foreign text and the receiving literature be transformed? Can a translation of an archaic foreign poem be appreciated by readerships who do not necessarily share the interpretation that the translator has inscribed in the text through a stylistic analogue? Is the translation necessarily directed to a readership that possesses specialized knowledge of literature in the translating language or can it cross the boundaries between readerships, appealing to readers who have limited or no access to that knowledge?

These reflections have increasingly shaped my approach to translating poetry, including a recent project in which I attempted versions of the medieval Italian poet Jacopone da Todi. What follows is a set of introductory comments on the poet and his work, on some previous translations, and on my own versions, two of which are reproduced here. None of this commentary constitutes the contextualization that the materials deserve. I rather present them with two aims: to stimulate further consideration of the problems posed by translating archaic poetries and to encourage experimentation with the methods used in translating them.

Compared to other European poetries, poetry in Italian languages developed late, not emerging till the twelfth century. At first it was dominated by the chivalric romances of northern France and the love lyrics of the Provençal troubadours, but the Bible was also a strong influence. The *Ritmo Laurenziano* ("Laurentian Verse," named after the Biblioteca Laurenziana in Florence where it was discovered) is the oldest surviving poetic composition in an Italian language. Written between 1150 and 1170 in the Tuscan dialect, it is the work of a troubadour who requests the gift of a horse from a bishop. Between 1224 and 1226, St. Francis of Assisi wrote his hymn, *Laudes creaturarum*, "Canticle of the Creatures," in the Umbrian dialect, modeling it on the Psalms and the Book of Daniel.

During the thirteenth century, Italian poetry was a mixture of secular and religious genres in various dialects, northern and southern. Among the most striking of the early poets is Jacopone da Todi, who wrote in Umbrian. Jacopone produced more than a hundred poems in a genre called the *lauda*, a religious song or hymn, designed for a soloist with a chorus and framed in different meters and verse structures.

Although Jacopone's themes were fundamentally religious, his poetry was unique in giving them a distinctly personal cast. He used the *lauda* not only to explore theological concepts, but to express his psychological state during mystical experiences. He also used the form to petition a pope for pardon and even to satirize him and his supporters. Appreciating Jacopone's poetry, then, requires some knowledge of pertinent events in his life, even if the power and popularity of his work soon inspired biographical legends that overlay the incomplete historical record and complicate any attempts to separate fact from fiction.

Jacopone was born Jacopo dei Benedetti in Todi around 1230, a member of a noble family. He was trained as a *notaio*, an office that combined the functions of a notary and an attorney, and he argued cases in Bologna, amassing great wealth. In 1267, he married a pious noblewoman named Vanna di Bernardino di Guidone, in whose judgment he dwelt too much on earthly things. In 1268, at her husband's insistence, she attended a ball and met her death when the platform on which she stood suddenly collapsed and crushed her. Stricken with guilt as well as grief, Jacopone noticed that she was wearing a hair shirt. Thus he became painfully aware that she had led a penitent life on his behalf.

This sequence of events motivated his abrupt conversion to a rigorous asceticism. He abandoned the legal profession, distributed his wealth and possessions among the poor, and pursued a penitential course of self-denial in poverty. He became a humble Franciscan tertiary. His piety sometimes took the form of mysticism, bouts of ecstatic madness that cast doubt on his mental stability. His poetry suggests that he was familiar with the mystical works of such authors as Hugh of St. Victor and St. Bonaventure.

In 1278, Jacopone attempted to become a Franciscan brother, but was rejected because of rumors concerning his sanity. That same year, however, he was admitted to the Order of Friars Minor on the strength of a poem he had written: it deplored the vanity of worldly values. He gravitated toward a faction known as the *Spirituali*, the Spirituals, who wished to return the order to the extreme poverty espoused by St. Francis.

By the end of the thirteenth century, Jacopone assumed a position of leadership in the Spiritual faction, which mired him in the political struggles surrounding the newly elected pope, Boniface VIII. The Spirituals' bid for clerical autonomy had been denied by Boniface, whom Jacopone opposed in 1297 by signing a manifesto that declared the pope's election invalid. In 1298, Boniface retaliated by excommunicating Jacopone and sentencing him to life imprisonment. The pope's death in 1303 brought Jacopone's release, whereupon he retired to the monastery in the Umbrian town of Collazzone and died three years later.

The first printed edition of Jacopone's poetry appeared in 1490. Yet by that time it had already enjoyed wide circulation. Many manuscript copies were made, stretching into the seventeenth century. Individual texts were enthusiastically sung by confraternities or guilds who performed *laude* in processions and dramatic recitations. The intensity of Jacopone's poems also appealed to heretical sects such as the wandering flagellants who sang them as devotional hymns. These diverse performances show that his writing, although influenced by both religious and secular literature, made an important contribution to popular piety in Umbrian towns.

The poems I have chosen to translate are representative of Jacopone's forms and themes. In "O papa Bonifazio," an epistolary poem evidently written during his imprisonment, he addresses the papal retaliation against the Spirituals by questioning it even as he appeals for Boniface's mercy. The Umbrian text is written in couplets that vary from seven to eight syllables, and the meter is fairly singsong, despite the variations. As scholars have shown,[6] the language is extremely heterogeneous: although generally simple, it employs the extended metaphor of the shield for theological concepts and mixes doctrinal and liturgical terms ("scommunicazione," "assoluzione") with a Latin phrase and a vernacular Latinism ("per secula infinita" and "Absolveto," which was a popular form for *absolvetur*).

In "O iubelo del core," Jacopone addresses a recurrent theme in mystical literature, the inexpressibility of the ecstatic experience. Here too the meter is irregular, with lines varying from seven to eight syllables, but the verse structure is much more intricate: the opening couplet (xx) is followed by five six-line strophes with an alternating rhyme scheme (ababbx) and an incremental repetition of the key word "iubelo." The language is also marked by heterogeneity: the simple lexicon contains dialectal forms (the repeated assimilation of -*nd*- to -*nn*- in "quanno" for "quando," "granne" for "grande," "pensanno" for "pensando") and vernacular forms of Latin words and phrases ("iubelo" from "iubilo," "'n deriso" from "in derisum"). A couple of words that have since become archaic in Italian point to a French or even Provençal influence ("dolzore" for "dolcezza," "convenente" for "conveniente").

The formal features of the Umbrian texts, notably their prosody and language, clearly pose difficulties to the modern English-language translator who wishes not only to establish a semantic correspondence, but to compensate somehow for the loss of the medieval context. Because of this loss, the form cannot be reproduced so as to enable a response that is equivalent to the responses of Jacopone's contemporaries. Consequently, modern translators have been forced to develop strategies that answer primarily to the function which the translations were designed to serve. Two translations produced during the twentieth century are particularly worth examining because they exemplify very different approaches.

The first consists of a selection of Jacopone's poetry included in Evelyn Underhill's 1919 biography. The translator is identified on the title page as Mrs. Theodore Beck. The function of the translations, as Underhill stated in her preface, was "to illustrate the most important points of his mystical growth and outward career."[7] She viewed the literary dimension of Jacopone's "career" as combining two contemporary influences: "secular poetry" represented by the philosophical love lyrics of the *dolcestilnovisti* and "that popular demand for vernacular moral and devotional songs which the penitential movements of the thirteenth century—especially the Franciscan revival—had created and developed."[8]

Interestingly, Underhill's interpretation of Jacopone's poetry can be glimpsed in Beck's translations, although only very indirectly, through the translator's decision to develop a resonant stylistic analogue. Here are the opening lines from her version of "O iubelo del core":

> Thou, Jubilus, the heart dost move;
> And makst us sing for very love.
>
> The Jubilus in fire awakes,
>   And straight the man must sing and pray,
> His tongue in childish stammering shakes,
>   Nor knows he what his lips may say;
>   He cannot quench nor hide away
>   That Sweetness pure and infinite.[9]

Beck obviously tried to evoke the meter and rhyme scheme of Jacopone's six-line strophes. Yet the fluent regularity of her tetrameter lines, combined with her reliance on standard usage mixed with poetical archaisms, suggests that her model was the eighteenth-century hymn. A similar six-line stanza frequently recurs in John Wesley's collection of Methodist hymns (this analogy was proposed by an anonymous reader who evaluated my essay for the journal, *Translation and Literature*, but who cannot be held responsible for what I made of it). The following example is typical:

> Come, Holy Ghost, all-quick'ning fire,
> My consecrated heart inspire,
>   Sprinkled with the atoning blood;
> Still to my soul thyself reveal,
> Thy mighty working may I feel,
>   And know that I am one with God![10]

In translating Jacopone's poem "O papa Bonifazio," Beck likewise imitated his couplets. Here too the analogue with the hymn can be perceived, along with her use of poetical archaisms. Her version breaks the Umbrian text into four-line stanzas, another form that appears in Wesley's collection. I print one of Beck's stanzas followed by a stanza from another hymn:

> Though fierce and sharp be thine attack,
> By Love I'll beat thine onslaught back;
> I'll speak to thee with right good will,
> And gladly shalt thou listen still.[11]

> When rising floods my soul o'erflow,
> When sinks my heart in waves of woe,
> Jesu, thy timely air impart,
> And raise my head, and cheer my heart.[12]

If Beck's translations are compared only to the Umbrian texts, her work can easily provoke criticisms. It might be objected, not just that she translates too expansively, adding words to fill out her lines, but that her meters are too regular, her diction too smoothly poetical, to mimick Jacopone's irregular rhythms and heterogeneous language. And indeed a contemporary reviewer complained that Beck's translations are "stilted, artificial, unpleasantly anthropomorphic, and appallingly flat."[13] Such criticisms, however, ignore the irreparable loss of the medieval context at the level of the poetic line and the interpretive relation that the translator created with English-language poetry to compensate for that loss. At her later moment, Beck does create a convincing stylistic analogue that gives a glimpse of the formal features of the Umbrian texts, and the various archaisms do signal the historical remoteness of the poems. This historicizing effect is produced by the archaic lexical and syntactical items in her English (other examples include "fray," "foeman," and "If thou canst pink me openly"), as well as the use of a medieval Latin word, "Jubilus," signifying an exultant shout.

The analogy with the eighteenth-century hymn, once perceived by the reader, results in a translation that possesses greater historical depth than a quaint pastiche. In effect, Beck's stylistic analogue invests Jacopone's poetry with considerable cultural value in English: it positions him in a popular poetic tradition that has long supported religious worship. At the same time, however, the formal and thematic differences between Jacopone's *laude* and the hymns remain sufficiently clear in the translations to invite the reader to think differently, more searchingly, of both poetries. Because Wesley's hymns contain so many phrases taken from canonical poets such as Milton, Dryden, and Pope, because he expressed his own literary aspirations in claiming that his hymns reveal "the true spirit of poetry,"[14] the stylistic analogue can point to the secular influence on Jacopone's poems, the *dolcestilnovisti*, leading the informed reader to ask whether those poems seemed more literary to the uneducated segment of his contemporary readership than they do today. A reader sensitive to the stylistic analogue might also wonder about the extent to which the extreme states depicted in Jacopone's poetry, whether the physical coarseness of his asceticism or the psychological imbalance of his mysticism, overshadow the devotional advance offered by the plain, direct language of Wesley's hymns while calling attention to the fact that their theological content did not deviate from Anglican doctrine. The interpretation enacted by Beck's translations can be doubly interrogative, posing questions about Jacopone's poems and about the English-language poetry on which she draws to fashion an analogue.

Her work differs markedly from the first complete version of Jacopone's *laude* published in 1982 by Serge and Elizabeth Hughes. Able to benefit from a century of historical scholarship, these translators are more aware of the sheer hybridity of the poetry: in his introduction, Serge Hughes calls it "a rough-textured coat of many colors, with nothing in it of the ideal of seamless beauty."[15] Hughes's interpretation, however, foregrounds the religious themes, which he describes as "the mottled word of Jacopone, his multifaceted meanings, the twists and turns of his descent into the self, his wrestling with God," arguing that "the place of music in the *Lauds* as a whole is that of a humble handmaiden."[16] In accordance with this theme-oriented interpretation, the translation makes no attempt to re-create the formal features of the poems. Hughes in fact feels that Jacopone's prosody is not consistently effective:

> The *Lauds* are not well served by making rhyme and meter the primary considerations. Indeed, all too often in the original those considerations become the tail that wags the dog. A translation that concentrates on the strength of Jacopone, by contrast, the mottled word, can bring out the muscular texture of that utterance.[17]

The result of this approach is generally a prosaic rendering in current standard usage. Here are the Hughes versions of the opening lines from the two poems we have examined:

O heart's jubilation, love and song
Joy and joy unceasing,
The stuttering of the unutterable—
How can the heart but sing?
O Pope Boniface, I bear the marks of your preface—
Anathema, and excommunication.[18]

These extracts show that the stress on theme doesn't entirely rule out sound effects, but it does lead the translators to depart from the lineation of the Umbrian texts. It is also clear that they have avoided the creation of a stylistic analogue or any comparable English-language poetry and have chosen an English that is not marked in any distinctive way.

It might be objected, then, that the translation does not reproduce the "muscular texture" of Jacopone's Umbrian texts, that the English versions lack the linguistic heterogeneity characteristic of his work. In the second extract, moreover, the weakness of the translation is evident in the misleading literalism "preface" to render "prefazio," an Italian calque for *Praefatio*, a part of the Mass where the celebrant makes a solemn invocation to introduce the Eucharistic prayer. Jacopone's use of the liturgical term initiates the satire of his poem: it ironically refers to Boniface's harsh sentence. The English rendering is obscure and actually exposes rather than compensates for the loss of the medieval context.

Nonetheless, the translators have succeeded in realizing their main intention: to communicate to the late twentieth-century reader the main themes of all the poems attributed with certainty to Jacopone. Their imagined reader does not possess any specialized knowledge of Italian medieval literature and culture, nor does he or she wish more than the basic information about Jacopone's life and work. As Serge Hughes states, "since this translation is principally an introduction to the *Lauds*, it has not been weighed down with a detailed commentary."[19] The translation presents Jacopone's poetry, not as a body of literature that reflects Italian literary traditions and practices at a particular historical moment, but as a document in the history of Christianity which reveals the author's personal experiences. This presentation was also determined by the conditions under which the translation was published: it was issued by the Paulist Press, an American Catholic publisher operated by an order of missionary priests, and was included in their series, the Classics of Western Spirituality, which contains more than 130 works from various religious traditions. In this context, religious theme is assigned much greater value than literary form.

Today the Beck and Hughes translations, even if effective in their own terms, have come to seem limited, and their very existence has led me to experiment in retranslating Jacopone's poetry for a different audience at a later moment. Like Beck, I tried to cultivate a stylistic analogue, but mine aimed to suggest precisely the heterogeneity of his language while re-creating his loose, jogtrot meters and his rhyme schemes. This sort of analogue, attuned to formal features but avoiding the plainness and metrical regularity of the eighteenth-century hymn, was designed to inscribe my interpretation of the Umbrian texts as at once literary and popular.

English-language poetic traditions contain useful models in which Jacopone's work can be recast. I have imagined him partly along the lines of the early Tudor poet John Skelton, who, following medieval literary genres, wrote satires and ballads in language that mixes learned and oral forms. I was particularly attracted to Skelton's remarkable prosody, in which short, irregularly metered lines are joined to rhyme schemes that vary from stanzaic structures to unpatterned repetitions of sounds. Skelton's poetry, like Jacopone's, sometimes adopts a typically medieval attitude of *contemptus mundi*, pointing to the transitory nature of human life. Here is an extract from a poem "uppon a deedmans head" (c. 1498):

It is generall
To be mortall:
I have well espyde
No man may hym hyde
From deth holow-eyed
With synnews wyderyd [withered]
With bonys shyderyd [shattered]
With hys worme-eatyn maw
And hys gastly jaw
Gapyng asyde
Nakyd of hyde,
Neyther flesh nor fell [skin].[20]

Skelton's satires on Tudor courtiers and statesmen were immediately suggestive of Jacopone's wry epistles to Boniface VIII. Here is an extract from Skelton's attack on Cardinal Wolsey, "Collyn Clout" (1519):

> And yf ye stande in doute
> Who brought this ryme aboute,
> My name is Collyn Cloute.
> I purpose to shake oute
> All my connynge bagge,
> Lyke a clerkely hagge.
> For though my ryme be ragged,
> Tattered and jagged,
> Rudely rayn-beaten,
> Rusty and mothe-eaten,
> Yf ye take well therwith,
> It hath in it some pyth.[21]

Skelton's writing is so strongly marked that a limited imitation might go a long way in a modern translation, might be easily noticeable for readers who have read widely in English poetic traditions. With other, less informed readers, his early modern English and "ragged" prosody, although useful in creating a stylistic analogue for Jacopone's poems, could not be followed closely without risking unintelligibility. The effect I wanted, moreover, was not merely an archaism that signaled the historical difference of the Umbrian texts, but a heterogeneity through which their various influences and audiences might be perceived. Hence, I also incorporated current usage, both standard and colloquial forms, including clichés.

Translating an archaic poetry, however, is always more complicated than inventing a stylistic analogue because of the inevitable anachronism entailed by the address to a later audience. The task for the translator is perhaps how to control this inevitability, how to turn it to effect in supporting and developing the analogue. Because I am translating Jacopone's poems at the beginning of the twenty-first century, the infiltration of popular music seems pertinent and unavoidable. Indeed, when I read the Umbrian texts, I often hear not only Skelton, but a rap artist like Eminem, with echoes of his endlessly played hit, "The Real Slim Shady" (2000). Here is an extract:

> We ain't nothing but mammals; well, some of us cannibals
> who cut other people open like cantaloupes.

But if we can hump dead camels and antelopes
then there's no reason that a man and another man can't elope.
But if you feel like I feel I got the antidote.
Women wave your panty hose, sing the chorus and it goes . . .
        I'm Slim Shady
        Yes I'm the real Slim Shady[22]

In combining colloquial language with varying rhythms and rhymes, rap music offered me another poetic form that can prove helpful in signifying the popular dimension of Jacopone's poetry.

Still, nothing remains unchanged in fashioning a stylistic analogue. The hybrid I sought also redounds upon the various forms that compose it, exposing and interrogating the differences among them and the cultural situations in which they emerged. The extreme individualism of much rap music, the focus on the typically male singer who is given to chest-thumping machismo, can only be questioned by Jacopone's mystical asceticism which extols the virtues of penance and self-denial. Similarly, Jacopone's rejection of the world, his fearless criticisms of a pope, his harsh imprisonment reveal the considerable extent to which Skelton's privileged position allowed him to mount satiric attacks on government officials. Although at Wolsey's order Skelton was once imprisoned for a short time, the poet enjoyed a number of distinguished offices and appointments: after serving as rector of a Norfolk parish church, he became tutor to Henry VIII, Poet Laureate, and King's Orator. Yet Skelton can also come back to worry Jacopone by pointing to his aristocratic status, especially the education and wealth that enabled the Italian poet to write with a knowledge of both secular and religious literary traditions. And when juxtaposed to Jacopone's poetry, rap, performed by so many artists who began in working-class situations, might pose the question of how many medieval poets were lost to poverty and the absence of patronage.

Of course, these implications can be pursued only by an informed reader who also brings an understanding of the translation method that I have sketched here. This reader was not in the audience for which I first translated Jacopone's poems: a group of American students who were spending a junior year at the Rome campus of Temple University. This campus attracts a student body from as many as fifty American schools, ranging from elite private institutions to small liberal arts colleges to large public universities. Each semester begins with an outing to Umbria that includes a stop at Todi, where students can visit the church of San Fortunato, the site of Jacopone's grave. On one such outing I read my translations, along with a brief sketch of Jacopone's life and my translation method. Very few members of this audience were students of Italian or English literature; none, as I recall, had heard of Jacopone or his poetry. Yet they were all able to grasp the affiliations that the translations tried to construct with rap music.

Will the translations work for an audience of literary scholars and translators who not only have some familiarity with the traditional materials I have used, but can understand (if not accept) the theoretical rationale for my method? This is precisely the question I wish to pose to you, my informed reader, who alone are in a position to answer it.

TWO LAUDE BY JACOPONE DA TODI
TRANSLATED FROM THE UMBRIAN BY LAWRENCE VENUTI
LVI

O papa Bonifazio,
eo porto el tuo prefazio
e la maledezzone
e scommmunicazione.
Co le lengua forcuta
M'hai fatta esta feruta;
che co la lengua ligne
e la plaga ne stigne;
ca questa mia ferita
non pò esser guarita
per altra condezione
senza assoluzïone.
Per grazia te peto
che mi dichi: "Absolveto,"
l'altre pene me lassi
finch'io del mondo passi.
Puoi, se te vol' provare
e meco essercetare,
non de questa materia,
ma d'altro modo prelia.
Si tu sai sì schirmire
che me sacci ferire,
tengote ben esparto,
sì me fieri a scoperto:

c'aio dui scudi a collo,
e s'io no i me ne tollo,
per secula infinita
mai non temo ferita.
El primo scudo, sinistro,
l'altro sede al deritto.
Lo sinistro scudato,
un diamante aprovato:
nullo ferro ci aponta,
tanto c'è dura pronta:
e quest'è l'odïo mio,
ionto a l'onor de Dio.
Lo deritto scudone,
d'una preta en carbone,
ignita como foco
d'un amoroso ioco:
lo prossimo en amore
d'uno enfocato ardore.
Si te vòi fare ennante,
puo'lo provar 'n estante;
e quanto vol' t'abrenca,
ch'e' co l'amar non venca.
Volentier te parlara:
credo che te iovara.
Vale, vale, vale,
Deo te tolla onne male
e dielome per grazia,
ch'io el porto en leta fazia.
Finisco la trattato
En questo loco lassato.[23]

LXXVI

O iubelo de core,
che fai cantar d'amore!

Quanno iubel se scalda,
sì fa l'omo cantare,
e la lengua barbaglia

non sa que se parlare:
dentro non pò celare,
tant'è granne 'l dolzore.

Quanno iubel è acceso,
sì fa l'omo clamare;
lo cor d'amor è appreso,
che nol pò comportare:
stridenno el fa gridare,
e non virgogna allore.

Quanno iubelo ha preso
lo core ennamorato,
la gente l'ha 'n deriso,
pensanno el suo parlato,
parlanno esmesurato
de che sente calore.

O iubel, dolce gaudio
che dentri ne la mente,
lo cor deventa savior
celar suo convenente:
non pò esser soffrente
che non faccia clamore.

Chi non ha costumanza
te repute 'mpazzito,
vedenno esvalïanza
com'om ch'è desvanito;
dentr'ha lo cor ferito,
non se sente de fore.[24]

O PAPA BONIFAZIO

My dear Pope Boniface,
I suffer your disgrace,
the dreaded malediction
of excommunication.

You spoke with forkéd tongue
and deeply I was stung:
it has to lick my sore
to show the plague the door;
because I'm sure my grief
can't find the least relief
without the execution
of your absolution.
Out of grace I beg you,
say, "Ego te absolvo,"
leaving my other fears
till past this vale of tears.
You can test your might
and meet me for a fight—
without the self-same arm
that did me all this harm.
Should you draw the blade
that drove me to this shade,
able I can deem you
but then you must strike true:
the two shields that I bear
will banish every care
if I make them mine
until the end of time.
The shield that's on the left
never will be cleft:
a diamond truly tested,
it never will be bested:
thus is my self-hate,
to God's glory conjugate.
The shield that's on the right,
made of carbuncle bright,
is burning like a flame
of an amorous game:
the same is love thy neighbor
filled with a kindled ardor.
If you wish t'advance,
you're free to take a chance;

Translating Jacopone da Todi

but try howe'er you might,
love won't lose the fight.
I'd talk when you have leisure:
I think you'll get some pleasure.
So, fare thee well, fare well,
may God take all your evil
and grant it me for grace,
in pain with a smiling face.
This rhyme I've shaken out
and now I'm heading out.

O IUBELO DEL CORE

Heartstruck jubilation,
erotic incantation!
          Whenever joy enkindles,
the soul begins to sing,
the tongue is tied in mumbles,
speech doesn't know a thing:
you can't keep on hiding
such immense delectation.
          Whenever joy is burning,
the soul begins to shout;
with love your heart is yearning
much more it can't stick out:
you scream, you shriek without
the slightest humiliation.
          Whenever joy takes hold
of the heart enamored,
people turn so bold,
mocking how it stammered,
they utter things unmeasured
when it feels the calefaction.
          Joy, sweet blissfulness,
the mind is penetrate,
the heart would be sagacious
to conceal its estate:
you can't hardly obviate

such clamorous exclamation.
     Lacking this experience,
people judge you insane,
seeing your divergence
like a man grown vain;
but within your heart is pain,
undetected by observation.

Notes

1. Eugene A. Nida, *Toward a Science of Translating, With Special Reference to Principles and Procedures Involved in Bible Translating* (Leiden: Brill, 1964), 158.

2. David Anderson, *Pound's Cavalcanti: An Edition of the Translations, Notes, and Essays* (Princeton: Princeton University Press, 1983), 250.

3. Anderson, *Pound's Cavalcanti*, 251.

4. Anderson, *Pound's Cavalcanti*, 250.

5. See Lawrence Venuti, *The Translator's Invisibility*, 2nd ed. (London and New York: Routledge, 2008), 165–78.

6. Rosanna Bettarini, "Jacopone da Todi e le laude," in Cesare Segre and Carlo Ossola, eds., *Antologia dela poesia italiana: Duecento* (Torino: Einaudi, 1997), 284–90.

7. Evelyn Underhill, *Jacopone da Todi, Poet and Mystic—1228–1306: A Spiritual Biography* (London: J. M. Dent, 1919), vi.

8. Underhill, *Jacopone da Todi*, 212, 217.

9. Underhill, *Jacopone da Todi*, 279.

10. John Wesley, *A Collection of Hymns for the Use of the People Called Methodists*, ed. Franz Hildebrandt, Oliver A. Beckerlegge, and James Dale, vol. 7 in *The Works of John Wesley* (Oxford: Clarendon Press, 1983), 503.

11. Underhill, *Jacopone da Todi*, 441.

12. Wesley, *A Collection of Hymns*, 487.

13. L. C. Willcox, "A Famous Mystic of the 13th Century," *New York Times* (April 11, 1920), BR166.

14. Wesley, *A Collection of Hymns*, 74.

15. Serge Hughes and Elizabeth Hughes, eds. and trans., *Jacopone da Todi: The Lauds* (New York: Paulist Press, 1982), 3.

16. Hughes, *Jacopone da Todi*, 4, 3.

17. Hughes, *Jacopone da Todi*, 64.

18. Hughes, *Jacopone da Todi*, 227, 177.

19. Hughes, *Jacopone da Todi*, 65.

20. John Skelton, *The Complete English Poems*, ed. V. J. Scattergood (Harmondsworth: Penguin, 1983), 39.

21. Skelton, *The Complete English Poems*, 248.

22. Eminem, *The Marshall Mathers LP* (Interscope Records, 2000).

23. Gianfranco Contini, ed., *Poeti del Duecento*, vol. 2 (Milano-Napoli: Ricciardi, 1960), 69–70.

24. Contini, *Poeti del Duecento*, 105–107.

SIXTEEN

"Ensemble discords"

Translating the Music of Scève's Délie

RICHARD SIEBURTH

As John Hollander observes in his classic study, *The Untuning of the Sky: Ideas of Music in English Poetry, 1500–1700*, for nearly a millennium Boethius's *De Institutione Musica* set the terms for the Western imagination of music. This sixth-century treatise influentially divided music into three parts: *musica mundana, musica humana,* and *musica instrumentalis.* By *musica mundana* Boethius intended the overall harmony of the universe, ultimately grounded in the Pythagorian music of the spheres but also perceptible (or rather, intelligible) in the cosmological order of elements, astral bodies, and seasons. Boethius in turn described *musica humana* as "that which unites the incorporeal activity of the reason with the body . . . a certain mutual adaptation and as it were a tempering of high and low sounds into a single consonance"—with the crucial notion of "temperament," as Hollander points out, here referring not only to the tuning of strings but to the proportionate tempering of the various parts of the human whole (body and soul, thought and feeling, etc.). Boethius's third category, *musica instrumentalis*, refers to what Hollander terms "practical" (as opposed to "speculative") music, that is, the actual singing or playing of music (flute, lyre, harp, or, as we move into the Renaissance, viol or lute).[1] In the following pages, I would like to briefly address the music of Scève's *Délie* (and the possibilities of its translation) in terms of this tripartite Boethian model, still very influential in mid sixteenth-century Lyons through its more recent reformulation by Ficino.

Composed of 449 *dizains* interspersed with 50 emblematic woodcuts, the *Délie* is commonly acknowledged to be the first illustrated *canzoniere* of its kind. Unlike Petrarch's *Rime sparse*, whose "vario stile" included sonnets, ballads, and sestinas, Scève's lyric sequence of 1544 is devoted to the manic (depressive) hammering home of a single chord 449 times in succession, each of its *dizains* composed of 10 lines of 10 syllables and each observing the identical claustrophobic rhyme scheme: ABABBCCDCD. A first challenge to the translator: how maintain what John Ashbery has called the "fruitful monotony" of this kind of grid composition while at the same time allowing for all its minute variations and overtones?[2] Or: how, within the compact ambit of each of these 10 x 10 matrices, produce an *harmonia* that would be faithful both to the original Greek meaning of the term (that is, the ratios of scales or horizontal melodic schemata taking place in time) and to its more modern polyphonic developments (that is, the blending of simultaneously sounding musical tones in a vertical all-at-onceness)?[3] Given the importance of the visual emblems to the overall rhythm of the *Délie*, these two kinds of harmonies—the temporal and spatial—also inform the ways in which the text speaks both to the reader's (or lover's) eye and ear, for Délie, the obscure object of desire, is experienced throughout the sequence both melodically and chordally, that is, both as a gradual disclosure of fetishized partial objects and as a kind of sudden and overwhelming *jouissance* that strikes her lover blind or dumb.

True to Boethius's tripartite schema, the microcosm of the lover's *musica humana* in the *Délie* (i.e., the whole agon of inarticulate sobs, sighs, cries, and "silentes clameurs" that constitutes the ground tone of Scèvian song) is frequently situated vis-à-vis the *musica mundana* of the macrocosm. Délie, "Object de plus haulte vertu" (as she is described in the subtitle), may be an anagrammatic embodiment of the Platonic *Idée* (like Samuel Daniel's *Delia*), but she is also, as the following *dizain* rather programmatically declares, a mythical sky-goddess and cosmic instance of the interdependence of *eros* and *thanatos*, day and night. Bearing within her name the solar radiance of the Delian Apollo, she is also his sister Diana, goddess of the moon and—in her more archaic Greek guises—Artemis the virgin huntress, Hecate the witch, and Persephone, queen of the Underworld:

Comme Hecaté tu me feras errer
Et vif, & mort cent ans parmy les Vmbres:

Comme Diane au Ciel me resserer,
D'ou descendis en ces mortelz encombres:
Comme regnante aux infernalles vmbres
Amoindriras, ou accroistras mes peines.
　　　Mais comme Lune infuse dans mes veines
Celle tu fus, es, & seras DELIE,
Qu'Amour a ioinct a mes pensées vaines
Si fort, que Mort iamais ne l'en deslie.

As Hecate, you will doom me to wander
Among the Shades, alive & dead a hundred years:
As Diana, you will confine me to the Sky
Whence you descended to this vale of tears:
As Queen of Hell in your dark domain,
You will increase or diminish my pains.
　　　But as Moon infused into my veins,
You were, & are, & shall be DELIE,
So knotted by Love to my idle thoughts
That Death itself could never untie us.

(D 22)[4]

How translate the overtones of proper names? In the original, lines 8 and 10 wittily exploit the homophony of the name DELIE and the verb "deslie" (here rhymed as "untie"). *Lier* in turn derives from the Latin *ligare* (to bind or gather, as in *religio*, the bond between man and gods)—which provides one of the most crucial vocables in the entire work, namely the word *lien* (not unrelated to the city of *Lyon*, another metonym of Délie), at once the bitter bondage that sadomasochistically links master to slave and the musical legato that provides the sweetest ligature of love. Given the paranomastic poetics of the *Délie*—where letters, words, and semes continuously tie and untie themselves into different knots—the verb "délier" can occasion a veritable "délire," a hermeneutic delirium in which reading, like dreamwork, forever unravels into a mis- or dis-reading ("délire") that is never far from . . . translation.[5]

The masculine subject in the above-quoted *dizain* plays a rather passive role vis-à-vis the all-powerful cosmic Object of his desires. As the unquiet shade of an unburied body, he is condemned by Hecate to wander—still "alive," not yet fully "dead"—through the Underworld for a hundred years before he can reach the Place of Eternal Rest. Or, like the hunter Orion who offended Artemis/Diana, he has been "confined" or "restrained" to the Sky in the shape of a constellation, condemned to revolve endlessly through the heavens. And finally, like the sick man under the influence of the moon, his fevers merely increase or decrease according to her waxings or wanings. The medical metaphor is made even more explicit in D 383:

Plus croit la Lune, & ses cornes r'enforce,
Plus allegeante est le febricitant:
Plus s'amoindrit diminuant sa force,
Plus l'affoiblit, son mal luy suscitant.

The more the Moon waxes, & extends her horns,
The more she soothes the sick man's ague:
The more she wanes, & loses force,
The more he ails, & wastes away.

As one can hear, the anaphoric "plus . . . plus" ("the more . . . the more," with the caesura falling after the fourth syllable both in the French and the English) serves to establish the rhythmic and causal link (or *lien*) between the *musica mundana* of the phases of the moon and the *musica humana* of unruly temperatures. The period between the recurrences of this kind of intermittent fever was called an "interval" during the Renaissance. This space in between, this respite from pain, this caesura, provides a duration of time—ranging from the shortest of moments to the longest of years—in which the sufferer is promised (erroneously, it turns out) some sort of solace:

O ans, ô moys, sepmaines, iours, & heures
O *interualle*, ô minute, ô moment,
Qui consumez les durtez, voire seures . . .

O years, O months, weeks, days & hours,
O *intervals*, O minutes, O moments
Who swallow up the pain, however sour . . .

(D 114)

This conception of time as made up of a series of salvific gaps (or feast-days, as in the "intervalle" defined by Cotgrave's dictionary as "the flesh-daies between Christmas and Ashwednesday") in turn prepares for the more musical definition of the term "interval"—the distance separating two sounds in harmony or in melody—that is beginning to make its way into French via the Italian around the time that Scève publishes the *Délie*.[6] This new usage makes it possible to read the "interval" of the following *dizain* below as referring not only to the measurement of geographical features, but to the more traditional figure of the *musica mundana*. Here the challenge to the translator was how rhythmically to convey Scève's condensation of the whirling *energeia* of an entire Renaissance *mappemonde* into the microcosm of a mere hundred syllables:

De toute Mer tout long, & large espace,
De terre aussi tout tournoyant circuit
Des Montz tout terme en forme haulte, & basse,
Tout lieu distant, du iour et de la nuict,
Tout *interualle*, ô qui par trop me nuyt,
Seroa rempliz de doulce rigueur.
   Ainsi passant des Siecles la longeur,
Surmonteras la haulteur des Estoilles
Par ton sainct nom, qui vif en ma langueur
Pourra par tout nager a plaines voiles.

Every long, & wide expanse of Sea,
Every whirling tract of solid land,
Every Mountain ridge both low, & high,
Every distant site of day, & night,
Every *interval*, O you who unsettle me,
Will be filled by your sweet severity.
Thus surpassing the spans of Time,
You will climb beyond the spheres of Stars,
Your sacred name, sped by my misery,
Traversing all creation at full sail.

(D 259)

These are a but a few examples of how Scève attunes the music of the spheres to the private tempers of the scorned lover's body and soul. Boethius's third category of music, *musica instrumentalis*, makes itself felt less through the occasional references to lyre or lute (in D 158, D 316, D 344) than through the traditional wordplay (which Hollander informs us goes back to Cassidorus) on the possible homophonic confusion between the Latin *chorda* (string or catgut) and *cor, cordis* (heart)—which gives us the expression "heartstrings."[7] As the Concordance to the *Délie* reveals, Scève's *canzoniere* contains a relatively high incidence of the terms "accordes" (2), "accordz" (5), "discord" (1), "discords" (1), "discordz" (3), "concordes" (1) and "cordes" (2), all resonating within (and against) the sounds of two of the most frequent words in the book, "Coeur" / "coeurs" (114) and "corps" (59).[8] In D 376, the *dizain* moves from an initial "Corps" to a terminal "discords" (or "dis-corps"?) as the lover, no longer an infernal shade doomed to errancy by Hecate, now becomes the "shadow" of the body of the beloved, a male moon reflective of the dark light of his female sun. The suggestion of celestial bodies, in any event, encouraged me to (liberally) translate "En me mouant au doulx contournement / De tous tes faictz" as "As you move me to assume my orbit / Around all you do or say"—with the rotations of this *musica munda* in turn leading me to register the final "discords" not simply as "discordant" (etymologically from *dis* + *cor*, apart + heart) but rather as the more explicitly musical "out of tune" (*dis* + *chorda*):

Tu es le Corps, Dame, & ie suis ton vmbre,
Qui en ce mien continuel silence
Me fais mouuoir, non comme Hecate l'Vmbre,
Par ennuieuse, & grande violence,
Mais par pouoir de ta haulte excellence,
En me mouant au doulx contournement
De tous tes faictz, & plus soubdainement,
Que lon ne veoit l'vmbre suyure le corps,
Fors que ie sens trop inhumainement
Noz sainctz vouloirs estre ensemble discords.

You are the Body, & I your shadow, lady,
In my abiding silence, you govern
My motion, not as Hecate holds sway
Over the Shades by violence, & disarray,
But by the attraction of your excellence,
As you move me to assume my orbit
Around all you do or say, far swifter
Than a shadow chasing after its body,

Were it not for something inhuman
When our two wills fall out of tune.

(D 376)

Behind the oxymoronic "ensemble discords" of the last line of this poem
lies the rich tradition of *concordia discors*—the term Horace used to describe Empedocles's vision of a world shaped by the perpetual strife between the four elements, yet ordered by love into a higher "discordant
harmony." Scève's deployment of the topos in the above *dizain* is far more
bitter, however, for the beloved's indifference or willfulness produces
not the ultimate harmony of *musica humana*, but a note "trop inhumainement" jarring to the poet's well-being—"something inhuman / When our
two wills fall out of tune."

   D 344, "Leuth resonnant, & le doulx son des cordes," the sole *dizain* in
the collection that actually mentions a lute—even though seven poems of
the *Délie* were set to music during Scève's lifetime—provides one of the
most achieved examples of Scève's wryly ironic music of discordance.[9]
This lyric has often been compared to Louise Labé's celebrated Sonnet
12, "Lut, compagnon de ma calamité"—the authenticity of which, however, has been recently cast into doubt by Mireille Huchon, who argues
that the work of La Belle Cordière was mostly written by Scève and his
circle of male poet friends.[10] In Labé's sonnet (so its witty conceit runs),
the lute has not only been her faithful "companion" in calamity, but also
the "témoin irreprochable" (irreproachable witness) of all of her sighs
and the "controlleur véritable" (accurate observer or secretary) of all her
sorrows. But the problem is: so often has the lute accompanied her in her
complaints, so deeply has it been touched by her piteous tears that even
should she try to make some sort of more pleasing noise ("quelque son
delectable"), the instrument, grown so accustomed to her sad songs, simply renders back all her joys as laments:

   Et si te veus efforcer au contraire,
   Tu te destens & si me contreins taire

To paraphrase: no matter how I try to force you [to play] otherwise [i.e.,
to respond to my joy], you come unstrung and reduce me to silence.

   This discordance between performer and instrument, between the
lyric "I" and the conventions of the poetry of complaint to which it must

submit—a theme also treated by Wyatt's nearly contemporaneous "Blame not my lute"[11]—is brilliantly explored in Scève's D 344, a brief song that again turns on the crucial wordplay of "cordes," "accordes," and "accordz":

> Leuth resonnant, & le doulx son des cordes,
> Et le concent de mon affection,
> Comment ensemble vnyment tu accordes
> Ton harmonie auec ma passion!

The initial apostrophe to the lute delicately attunes the vibrating sibilance of the s's to the more guttural pluckings of the hard c's, both of which resonate across the nasalized sequence of the /ã/ or the / / sounds. The caesurae within each line establish a slight pause, allowing for internal rhyme ("resonnant" / "concent" / "Comment" / "vniment") to play itself off against the alternating masculine and feminine endings of the lines. As in Labé's sonnet, however, this initial statement of harmony, wherein the lute seems to act in unanimous concert with the poet's own passion, swiftly gives way (by a transitional "lors" which echoes "cordes" and "accordes") to its opposite:

> Lors que ie suis sans occupation
> Si viuement l'esprit tu m'exercites,
> Qu'ores a ioye, ore a dueil tu m'incites
> Par tes accorz, non aux miens ressemblantz.

The symmetrical syntax of line seven ("ores a ioye, ore a dueil") underscores a typically Scèvian moment of cyclothimia (now joy, now grief)—here incited, paradoxically, by the chords/strings of the lute which leave him no respite in his "unoccupied" state of even-temperedness or equanimity and instead "excite" his spirits into discord. One more turn (via a crucial "car"), and the end of the poem screws down like a vise:

> Car plus, que moy, mes maulx tu luy recites,
> Correspondant a mes souspirs tremblantz.

The soft s's and hard c's of the opening lines here return, but voice a significant reversal of the initial situation. If at the outset of the poem the lute's "harmony" was in unanimous "accord" with the speaker's "passion," here the instrument (or again, the poetic genre of complaint itself) seems to betray the poet—precisely because of its articulateness (that is, its capacity to "recite" his pains to his lady) and its mellifluousness, to which the deep, sincere *alogos* of his own "souspirs tremblantz" (trembling sighs) proves capable only of a distant "correspondance."[12]

Of the following English translation of this *dizain* I can only say that like the lute (or lover) in both Labé's and Scève's poems, it tries to provide companionship to the original, aware that its acts of faithful witnessing or accurate observation will inevitably cause it to waver between harmonious accord and outright dissonance. Like the unresembling "accorz" of Scève's D 344, the "discord" of a translation vis-à-vis its original almost always lies in the various ways in which it is forced to become more explicit, more articulate, more "clear" (and more disincarnate) than the trembling sighs it tries to body forth in another language—even if it manages (as here below) to provide a "sympathic vibration"[13] in response to the original's rhyme scheme, the patterns of its caesurae, and the swift skitter of its tetrameters:

> Resounding lute, & sweet pluck of strings,
> And the concert of my affection,
> How you accord into a single song
> Your harmony and my passion!
> > Yet when I am without occupation,
> You put my mind through so many paces
> That from joy to sorrow it now races
> In your chords, so unresembling mine.
> > For you speak to her with such graces
> Of the pain I only tremble forth in sighs.

D 17, the final *dizain* I would like to address in this quick survey of Scèvian musics—be they *mundana*, *humana*, or *instrumentalis*—is a lyric that ecstatically celebrates the *harmonia* that obtains between the poet and his beloved. Although the precise term "harmonie" (used on several occasions in the *Délie*) does not occur here, it is nonetheless present through the double negative of line 10, "Qu'auecques nous aulcun discord s'assemble" (literally, "than no discord assemble itself among [or between] the two of us")—which, seeking to foreground the theme of "sympathetic vibration" that runs throughout the *canzoniere*, I have translated as "Than any discord throw us out of tune." Like the anaphoric "plus . . . plus" of D 383 previously discussed, this *dizain* is governed by a similar trope based in the mathematical (or musical) notion of proportion, here expressed through the temporal figure (repeated three times) of "plus tost . . . que"—an adynaton that expresses the counter-factual condition of *impossibilia* (e.g., before our love could change, the unthinkable would have to happen). Whereas in the previous poems we have examined the *musica humana* composed by the two lovers was often related to the *musica mundana* made by the turnings of celestial bodies (earth, sun, moon, constellations), here Scève fuses an implicit allegory of cosmic harmony with the literal features of the landscape around Lyons—the river Rhône roiling down from the Alps and flowing into the more placid waters of the Saône while the two large hills of the Mont Fourvière and Mont de la Croix-Rousse overlook this convergence from on high:

> Plus tost seront Rhosne, & Saone desioinctz
> Que d'auec toy mon Coeur se desassemble:
> Plus tost serons l'vn, & l'aultre Mont ioinctz,
> Qu'auecques nous aulcun discord s'assemble:
> Plus tost verrons & toy, & moy ensemble
> Le Rhosne aller contremont lentement,
> Saone monter tresuiolentement,
> Que ce mien feu, tant soit peu, diminue,
> Ny que ma foy descroisse aulcunement.
> Car ferme amour sans eulx est plus, que nue.

This is a poem of conjunctions and disjunctions, of gatherings and dispersals—as played out in the rich rhymes of the first five lines: "desioinctz," "ioinctz," "desassemble," "s'assemble" "ensemble." As Defaux points out in his recent edition of the *Délie*, Scève lifts all these rhymes directly from a poem by his master, Clément Marot, who here, at the concrete level of *sound*, plays the Rhône that flows into Scève's Saône just as much as does Petrarch—whose Sonnet 208 popularized the *figura etymologica* of *Rhodanus rodens*: "Rapido fiume, che d'alpestra vena / rodendo intorno (onde 'l tuo nome prendi)" ("Swift river, from your Alpine spring gnawing a way for yourself, whence you take your name"), which Scève in turn translates in D 417, "Fleuve rongeant pour t'attiltrer le nom / De la roideur en ton cours dangereuse."[14] The dramatic confluence of the Rhône (male, violently "gnawing" its course down from the Alps) and the Saône (peacefully female) at Lyons provides Scève not just with a metaphor for erotic harmony, but also, given the explicit intertextual echoes that resound through this poem, allows him to locate his own Lyonese *Délie* as the intersection where his great precursors, Petrarch and Marot, receive their most achieved *translatio*.

Translation, like love (or music)—as I have been trying to suggest with Scève—involves being apart together, mutually ingathered by an interval or caesura that, as he puts it in D 376, renders us "ensemble discords." One of the particular typographical features of the original 1544 printing of the *Délie* which I was anxious to maintain in my edition was the productive dissonance of its spelling and its pronunciation—that is, the disjunction between how Scève's words *look* on the page and how they *sound* (even though, like so much poetry from the distant past, it may be well-nigh impossible to accurately reconstruct its actual music— veni, vidi, vici or weni, widi, wiki?). In D 17 and elsewhere, the rivers Rhosne and Saone (as Scève spells them, though I use the modern French spellings Rhône and Saône in my translation) indeed chime perfectly to the ear, even if they do not exactly rhyme to the eye. This disparity—this *différance*?—between pronunciation and orthography opens a gap, an aporia, in which the temporality of the proper name—its history, its etymology—makes itself felt. Thus the "s" in Scève's "Rhosne" becomes a placeholder for the river's evolution from its Latin Rhodanus into Renaissance French, just as the circumflex on the modern Saône roofs over its Latin onomastic origins as the river Segona or Saucona—all these consonants and syllables that have been lost in the course of the etymological river-run now contracted into the rich vowelly O's of RhOWne and SOWne, so clearly audible when the two enter into rhyme at Lyons and then flow south together where they eventually spill into the Mediterranean Sea in a final *Liebestod*:

> N'apperçoy tu de l'occident le Rhosne
> Se destourner, & vers Midy courir,
> Pour seulement se conioindre a sa Saone
> Iusqu'a leur Mer, ou tous deux vont mourir?

> (D 346)

In my English version, I have tried to capture the *concordia discors* of Rhosne/Saone by avoiding the obvious end rhymes and instead displacing them to the inside of the line ("Don't you *see*," "From the *east*," "And die in their *sea*"). I then close the *dizain* with a purely anagrammatical eye-rhyme ("Saône" / "as one"):

"Ensemble discords": Translating the Music of Scève's Délie

Don't you see the Rhône turn
From the East, & rush South,
To conjoin with its Saône
And die in their Sea as one?

To conclude, I would like to call attention to a further typographical feature of the original printing of Scève's *Délie*, a feature which only I. D. MacFarlane's 1966 edition of the poem retains but which almost every subsequent French edition (including Defaux's) omits—namely Scève's eloquent use of the ampersand (which is "normalized" into an "et" by all of his French editors). To return to D 7, here is how the harmony between the Rhône and Sâone is typographically expressed:

Plus tost seront Rhosne, & Saone desioinctz

This pattern of disjunctive conjugation, which involves two terms at once linked by an ampersand yet separated by a comma, is repeated two more times in the poem (with the same interplay of a metrical caesura after the fourth syllable and an optical blink of the eye after the fifth or sixth):

Plus tost seront | l'vn, & l'aultre Mont ioinctz

. . .

Plus tost verrons | & toy, & moy ensemble

In adopting this rather idiosyncratic form of punctuation—"x comma and y," or "both x comma and y"—Scève (or his printer in Sulpice Sapon's shop) followed the rules laid down by yet another of his mentors, the humanist, publisher, and translator Etienne Dolet. Dolet published his treatise on punctuation, *De la punctuation de la langue Francoyse*, as part of his *La maniere de bien traduire d'une langue en aultre* in Lyons in 1540, four years before Scève's *Délie*.[15] It is perhaps no accident that it took a *traducteur* of Dolet's eminence to understand that the minute visual and rhythmic interval defined by the tmetic comma preceding an ampersand provides a perfect *punctum* for the music of Scève's poetry and . . . its translation:

Rhône, & Saône shall sooner be disjoined
Than my heart tear itself away from you:
The two Mounts shall sooner be conjoined

Than any discord throw us out of tune:
Together, we shall sooner see, I, & you,
The Rhône tarry, & reverse its course,
The Saône roil, & return to source
Than this my fire ever die down
Or my fidelity ever lose its force.
True love, without these, is but a cloud.

Notes

1. John Hollander, *The Untuning of the Sky* (Princeton: Princeton University Press, 1961), 24–25, 42, 45.

2. Ashbery's comments on Scève (which are related to his own Scève-inspired "Fragment" of 1968) are quoted in John Shoptaw, *On the Outside Looking Out: John Ashbery's Poetry* (Cambridge, Mass.: Harvard University Press, 1994), 111.

3. See Hollander, *The Untuning of the Sky*, 26–28.

4. The originals and translations of the *Délie* are quoted from my *Emblems of Desire: Selections from the* Délie *of Maurice Scève* (Philadelphia: University of Pennsylvania Press, 2003).

5. Randle Cotgrave's *Dictionarie of the French and English Tongues* (1611), an essential anatomy of mid sixteenth-century French, in turn defines the verb "delire" as "to chuse, cull, select, gather, picke out" and "delirer" as "to doat, rave, do things against reason."

6. According to the *Trésor de la langue française* (Paris: Editions du CNRS, 1983), IV, 467, the Italian term *intervallo* begins taking on this musical sense in 1546.

7. Hollander, *The Untuning of the Sky*, 42.

8. Jerry C. Nash, ed., *Maurice Scève: Concordance de la* Délie (Chapel Hill: North Carolina Studies in the Romance Languages and Literatures, 1976), 2 vols.

9. Three poems (D 41, D 82, D 89) were set by composers before the actual publication of the *Délie* and four (D 5, D 131, D 256, D 364) afterward; four of the settings were polyphonic (for four voices), three homophonic. For more detail, see V.-L. Saulnier, "Maurice Scève et la musique," in *Musique et poésie au XVIe siècle* (Paris: CNRS, 1954), 89–103.

10. Mireille Huchon, *Louise Labé: Une Créature de papier* (Geneva: Droz, 2006). The following quotes from Labé are taken from Huchon's facsimile reproduction of the *Euvres de Louïze Labé Lionnoize* published by Scève's publisher friend Jean de Tournes in 1555.

11. Hollander, *The Untuning of the Sky*, 130–131.

12. Pascal Quignard, *La Parole de la* Délie (Paris: Mercure de France, 1974), 65–70.

13. See Hollander, *The Untuning of the Sky*, 137 for a discussion of the phenomenon of "sympathic vibration"—the production of a tone by a free string if another one,

placed at some distance, but tuned to exactly the same frequency, is struck. A 1618 emblem of "Love as Sympathetic Vibration" is reproduced on page 242.

14. For Marot and Scève see Gérard Defaux, ed., *Délie* (Geneva: Droz, 2004), vol. 1, xliv–li. For Petrarch's Rhône and Scève's, see Jacqueline Risset, *L'Anagramme du désir* (Paris: Fourbis, 1995), 53–57.

15 Dolet's treatise on punctuation is reprinted in Nina Catach, *L'Orthographe française à l'époque de la Renaissance* (Geneva: Droz, 1968), 305–309. My colleague John Hamilton informs me that various musicologists of antiquity introduced what was known as a "komma"—a small interval (about a quarter-tone)—in order to even out or temper the distance between the tonic and the fourth and hence justify some of the inconsistencies in the musical scale. Later musical theorists from the Renaissance on adopted kommas of varying sizes (barely perceptible intervals such as a quarter-tone, a fifth-tone, a sixth-tone) to align the imperfections of *musica instrumentalis* with the mathematical purity of *musica mundana*. It would be extremely tempting to connect these intervals to Dolet's system of punctuation—except that what we call "comma" he calls "point à queue," and what he calls "comma" we would call a colon (or, "deux points").

SEVENTEEN

Translation and the Art of Revision

SUSAN BERNOFSKY

Revision isn't the first thing that comes to mind when we think about creativity and artistic production, but it is nonetheless a crucial part of the writing process. Occasionally a revision radically alters a book's conceptual framework (as when Franz Kafka decided to have his protagonist Josef K. "arrested" rather than "captured" in the opening sentence of *The Trial*); more often, it's a matter of fine-tuning a work's nuances and voice. Many authors known for the richness of their style rework virtually every sentence: The manuscripts of Flaubert and Proust are thickly crabbed with excised and inserted lines of text, and Nabokov is famous for the index cards he belabored with both ends of the pencil. Shirley Hazzard, to cite a more recent master of the perfectly chiseled sentence, did such extensive revisions on her novel *The Great Fire* that only about one-third of the published text was original to the first draft. That effortless-sounding prose, those spot-on rhythms came about through sustained labor.

In translation, similar principles apply. Although we strive to produce translations that look as though they hatched perfectly formed from the translator's skull, generally a great deal of reworking is required. Before I explore some of the issues involved in revising translations and techniques for addressing them, let me provide a quick overview of what the revision process looks like in my case. I tend to revise quite extensively, putting my translations through what usually winds up being at least four drafts. The first of these is intentionally sloppy and quickly executed; it is meant to be discarded but at the same time to serve as a seedbed for ideas worth preserving. This "sketch" of the text gets typed into the computer as quickly and with as little thought as I can manage. After this, I produce a painstakingly meticulous second draft, still working at the computer, but with frequent pauses to consult multiple bilingual and German-language dictionaries. I google German phrases to confirm their usage and look up English words too, in both *Webster's* and the *Oxford English Dictionary*, to make sure a word's range of meaning makes it the best choice in a given context. *Roget's International Thesaurus* (indexed, not in dictionary form) helpfully sorts words by categories, grouping together associated nouns, verbs, and adjectives; and the new historical thesaurus embedded in each of the *OED*'s entries provides first-usage dates for each synonym given. When translating an older author like Robert Walser, I make a point of verifying the senses in which a word was used a hundred years ago—if it was in use at all. Recently I resisted the temptation to use the word "brinkmanship," which would have fit handily in one particular Walser sentence, because when I looked it up I found it was coined only in 1956 (when Adlai Stevenson used it in reference to then Secretary of State John Foster Dulles). It just wouldn't have made sense to invoke that bit of history in a story dating from 1905.

When I finish the second draft of my translation, I print it out, because the next round of revision involves paper and pencil. I've found that no matter how carefully I revise onscreen, sentences look different on the page. At this third-draft stage, I try to avoid looking at the original text as much as possible—the point of this draft is to ensure the English-language text works on its own terms. I read the text aloud to myself, since a surprisingly large number of problems that the eye overlooks reveal themselves to the ear. Inevitably I wind up referring to the original, because trouble spots in the English can often be explained by some difficulty in or with the original text. The fourth, and with any luck final, draft is mainly a last read-through to check for any bits that stick out as unpolished, unclear, or stylistically discordant.

This is a procedural road map for revision; it describes the form the work takes, not the work itself. The word "revision" derives from the Latin *revisere* ("to look again"), and it's important to remember that revision is about looking: scrutiny and inspection, a critical looking. The problem I most often encounter when coaching younger translators is a willingness to be too easily satisfied with a solution to a problem, too quickly convinced that a line is "good enough." In this deadline-driven world, the temptation to accept a line and move on is enormous. In literary terms, however, a line is almost never good enough, and often even a line that *is* good enough might be made even better. The true translator is a person who sees this circumstance as a cause for celebration rather than despair. There is rarely a single perfect solution to any given translation problem, and so the process of revising involves trying out dozens of potential solutions until one of them begins to shimmer in that peculiar way that marks it as the best possible choice.

The art of revision is generally learned through trial and error; in other words, through practice. Another way to study it is to examine how truly great translators revise their work. Unfortunately, it isn't so easy to find examples without heading to the archives to study translators' papers. One of my favorite examples of a beautifully revised translation happens to be in German. It comes from August Wilhelm Schlegel's 1799 translation of *The Merchant of Venice*, *Der Kaufmann von Venedig*. Schlegel was one of the greatest German translators of all time, and his translations of seventeen of Shakespeare's plays were instrumental in laying the foundations for German Romanticism. This master of rhythm, tone, and nuance revised his translations so heavily that his manuscripts contain, for example, five completely different versions of this one simple line: "Sir, I would speak with you" (IV.ii.12, spoken by Portia's handmaid Nerissa disguised as a man). It doesn't sound like a line that would give its translator much trouble. But Schlegel seems to have found it quite troublesome.

Here are Schlegel's five versions of the line:

Herr, ich muß mit euch sprechen. (Sir, I must with you speak.)
Ich muß euch sprechen, Herr. (I must [to] you speak, sir.)
Herr, laßt euch etwas sagen. (Sir, let [to] you something be said.)
Ich wollt' euch etwas sagen, Herr. (I would like [to] you something to say.)
Herr, noch ein Wort mit euch. (Sir, a word with you.)[1]

All of these are perfectly correct translations of Shakespeare's line. The first two are both pretty good, the third and fourth somewhat less so, and the fifth is splendid. To begin with, Schlegel translates the line following the path of least resistance: "Herr, ich muß mit euch sprechen" (Sir, I must speak with you). He follows the structure of the original line as precisely as the German language allows, putting the verb "sprechen" (to speak) at the end only because of standard German syntactical conventions. With this "muß" (must), Schlegel gives the verb "would" an emphatic reading: I *would* speak with you, I must. That works fine, and Schlegel could have declared himself satisfied with this version. But there is something not quite satisfying about the rhythms of the line. *Sir*, I would *speak* with *you*. *Herr*, ich muß mit euch *sprech*en. The line has shrunk from three to two stressed syllables, Shakespeare's iambs are now trochees, and the German line gets mumbly around the middle, trailing off into a weak feminine ending in "sprechen." In fact, after "Herr," the only naturally accented syllable of the line is the first syllable of "sprechen."

Next Schlegel tries putting the "Herr" at the end of the sentence and cutting the grammatically optional "mit" (with), giving him: "Ich *muß* euch *sprech*en, *Herr*" (I must speak [to] you, sir). This is already quite an improvement. Starting the line with "ich muß" (I must) gives the "muß" an accent it didn't have in his first version. Suddenly the line has three real stresses again, making it sound stronger. It's pretty good, good enough. Schlegel could have stopped here. But there's still something not quite perfect about the line. The new stolidly iambic rhythm means there's no caesura to set off the "Herr" at the end: the line just rolls from one end to the other without a rhetorically appropriate pause, and shifting the "sir" to the end makes the request less polite.

Schlegel's next attempt is the version *"Herr, laßt euch etwas sagen"*—literally "Sir, let something be said [to] you," but really meaning "allow me to say something to you." Rhythmically, this is an improvement over the version Schlegel started with: the "laßt euch" sharpens the caesura after "Herr." But the line is now too long—it's gained a syllable—and the speaker is no longer explicitly present. In place of the speaker's stated desire to converse, we are left with the notion of allowing the message to be uttered, which is semantically weaker.

Looking at this series of revisions up to here, it would appear that Schlegel is getting frustrated with the difficulty of the line and has started trying out experimental solutions (such as dropping the subject); this doesn't quite work. Nor does his fourth version ("Ich wollt' euch etwas sagen, Herr"—I would like to say something [to] you, sir): the line is still too long, the "sir" impolitely at the end. But having experimented with various rhythms and the possibility of a sentence without an "I" prepares Schlegel to pull off a sort of quantum leap of revision when he writes: *"Herr*, noch ein *Wort* mit *euch"* (Sir, a word with you). The rhythm of this line perfectly captures the cadence of the original, matching it stress for stress, and the tone of the request is also appropriate. By allowing himself flexibility in the line's semantic content and above all by listening to the rhythm of the words, Schlegel became able to hear the line in German.

The shift of approach that gives Schlegel's final version of the line its strength involves the addition of a word that has no direct antecedent anywhere in the original: the flavoring particle "noch." This specifically German part of speech is a variety of adverb we don't have in English. The function of German flavoring particles in their sentences is less semantic than tonal, though all these words do have individual meanings of their own ("noch," for example, means "in addition," "still," or "yet"). But here the main role of the word "noch" is to "soften" the sentence, making the demand for "a word" sound a bit less forceful, a bit more respectful. It also, as it happens, fills out the rhythm of the line, providing just the unstressed syllable Schlegel needs to match Shakespeare's rhythm beat for beat. The key to this successful revision, then, involves falling back on a strength of the German language to express in both sense and tone something that was said quite differently in the English original.

What can be learned from watching Schlegel revise? Often it is only by revisiting a sentence again and again that we can get our brains to stop repeating the thought patterns that brought us to solutions previously tried and rejected, opening up access to a new set of possibilities. I found myself remembering Schlegel's revision process last year when I was faced with the particularly difficult—though on the surface simple— concluding sentence of the story "New Year's Page" by Robert Walser. Since "New Year's Page" was also the final piece in the collection *Microscripts*, the sentence had to be strong enough to end a book on.

"New Year's Page" concludes with an observation on the relationship between endings and beginnings. In my third or fourth draft, the final sentences looked like this: "When a year stops, another instantly commences, as if one were turning the page. The story keeps on going, and we see the beauty that lies in connectedness." The final phrase of the last sentence was my attempt to render the line "und man sieht die Schönheit eines Zusammenhangs." The word "Zusammenhang"—literally "context," or "connection" in a sense *not* involving human relationships—proved surprisingly recalcitrant. For the very first draft I had tried "and we see the beauty of a context," a quite literal rendering of the original, but it didn't make rhythmical sense as the ending of a sentence, much less of a story or book. What I wanted was a phrase that would work in the manner of

Wallace Stevens's lines "I do not know which to prefer, / The beauty of inflections / Or the beauty of innuendoes, / The blackbird whistling / Or just after." For a long time I played with variations on this theme, such "the beauty of contextuality" and "the beauty of contiguity." But all these variants sounded too academic and tricky. So I tried other approaches: "the beauty of having a context"; "the beauty given us by context"; "the beauty of things in context"; "the beauty of things in their contexts." None of these phrases was right; it just didn't seem plausible that some-one would have chosen to write them in this way. So I let go of the word "context" and tried out other possibilities: "and we see what is beautiful about contiguity"; "and we see what is so beautiful about contiguity"; "and we experience the loveliness/beauty of contiguity." But "contiguity" wasn't really the right choice, since it refers more to the continuousness or close proximity of objects to one another, and not so much to the fact that, taken together, they form a context or whole. So I tried "and we experi-ence the beauty of continuation" (similarly problematic). And then: "the beauty of connection." But the problem with "connection" is the same as with "the beauty of connectedness": in each case, human connection is implied, rather than the things that make up a world joining together to constitute a context within which humans exist and act. So I tried yet another approach, one that would refocus attention on the *things*: "the beauty of linking things together"; "contextual beauty"; "the beauty of putting things in context"; "the beauty of things linked together"; "the beauty of things conjoined." I liked these a bit better, but they all ended too abruptly; none felt dramatic enough to serve as a final phrase for the story.

It wasn't until I'd puttered about in this sentence for several weeks that it occurred to me I could solve the problem by recasting the sen-tence entirely. This was like the moment of inspiration that prompted Schlegel to insert a German flavoring particle into a line of Shake-speare. I realized that the main difficulty with the word "context" was that it wasn't a rhythmically appropriate word to *end* the sentence on; if I could rearrange the final part of the sentence, I thought, maybe the ca-dence might be differently balanced. So I decided to try translating the "man sieht" ("one sees"—which I'd rendered without much forethought as "we see") differently so as to turn "context" into the subject rather than the object of its phrase; then it would no longer have to conclude the English sentence. I tried "The story keeps on going, and the beauty of a context appears to us" and "the beauty of a context reveals itself." These were all near misses. Then it occurred to me to try the passive voice: "and the beauty of a context is revealed." Immediately it was obvious how much better this version was. For one thing, the story (and book) now ended on the suggestive, luminous word "revealed," with a stress on the final syllable to underscore the finality. For another, the phrase was now ambiguous in the same way as Walser's German, with the words "a context" referring both to contexts in general and to the particular context at hand.

Both Schlegel's translation of the line by Shakespeare and mine of a sentence by Robert Walser aspire to the same thing: achieving that unity of sense and sound that characterizes all good writing. This doesn't necessarily mean matching the original author's work syllable for syllable, rhythmically or otherwise. But the translation does have to find a rhythmical identity and integrity that will convince readers they are encountering a genuine piece of writing. When we experience a text as "well written," it will never be with the thought that the author first decided what she wanted to say and then looked around for the words to express it. Ideally, the "what" of a statement arrives on the page together with the words to embody it—sense accompanies sound, sound accompanies sense. This is what Walter Benjamin describes in his essay "The Task of the Translator" as an organic relationship: the language of an original text, he writes, is like the skin of a fruit that has grown together with it, while that of the translation is like royal robes draped about it. When people complain about "translationese," it's generally because they feel this sound/sense unity has not been achieved.

In my translations, this unity tends to arise during the process of revision, which is where the real work of writing occurs. Blocking out the rough contours of a sentence or a paragraph is a preparatory exercise to hearing the text's heartbeat in the cadences of its phrases. To immerse oneself fully in the work of translation is to become a medium, transcribing a text that exists only as a sort of phantasm in the translator's imagination: the text that is just like the original but written in a different language. Revising means listening to a potential text, hearing it amid all the rhythmical detritus of inadequate versions. With each successive draft, the text draws closer to the ideal form it will inhabit when its transformation is complete. The process of repeatedly subtracting whatever isn't working, replacing it with stronger material, is difficult to grasp, describe, and teach. In the end, it is a matter of learning to calibrate dissatisfaction, to judge when a sentence can still be improved on and when a solution—perfect or imperfect—should be left to stand. The best translators are particularly suspicious of the intermediate drafts of their work, of their own ability to produce "good enough" translations.

And the point of all this dogged labor and persistence? To give the impression of effortless-sounding rightness. Although the *vision* in revision implies something visual, revising has less to do with something seen than with something heard: the text's voice. Voice is the crux of all translating. Hearing it happens on a noncognitive level, but approaching the text cognitively while listening can help. Are the dominant vowels in a passage bright, soft, or dark? What about the consonants? Sharp and jagged, or sonorous and smooth?

Syntax too requires attention, as different languages have different ways of assembling sentences. Sometimes the best translation is one whose syntactical structure bears little resemblance to that of the original. At the same time, it is important to be conscious of the *order* in which information arrives. Every sentence is a journey that begins with a particular phrase or image and takes the reader somewhere. So what does the itinerary of a particular sentence look like, and where does it lead? When I am revising, I pay particular attention to endings: the endings of phrases, sentences, and paragraphs. In writing poetry, it goes without saying that a line's final word carries particular weight; the same holds true in prose. I often work to sharpen my sentences by ending them on a strong note, even if this means deviating from the syntax of the original.

Style can go soggy in translation. It is important to counteract this softening trend whenever feasible. This might involve exaggerating certain stylistic features—in fact, I believe that emphasizing and underscoring a text's characteristic attributes is crucial to good translation, a way of turning up the volume on a key aspect of a sentence or phrase to solidify the writer's voice in the translation. I put this technique into practice in the final sentence of my translation of Hermann Hesse's novel *Siddhartha* (Modern Library, 2006), concluding a scene in which Siddhartha's companion Govinda realizes that Siddhartha has attained enlightenment. My first draft of the sentence looked like this:

Deeply he [Govinda] bowed, down to the earth (ground), before the one motionlessly sitting there, whose smile reminded him of everything that he had ever loved in all his life, everything that had ever in all his life been dear and holy to him.

Tief verneigte er sich, bis zur Erde, vor dem regungslos Sitzenden, dessen Lächeln ihn an alles erinnerte, was er in seinem Leben jemals geliebt hatte, was jemals in seinem Leben ihm wert und heilig gewesen war.

This sentence in German has a feeling of balance and suspension, in large part thanks to the chiasmus at its center that unfortunately doesn't work so well in English (Hesse writes the equivalent of: "in his life ever . . . ever in his life"). In revising the sentence, I looked for ways to compensate for the weakened chiasmus and create the sense that all the searching and frantic motion we have seen throughout the novel has given way to stillness and peace. "Holy" is not the final word of the German text. Because of German syntactical rules, the last words of Hesse's book are the equivalent of "had been." But it seemed to me that ending the sentence (and book) on the resonant word "holy" would underscore the peace that lies at the end of Siddhartha's quest. I chose to make "holy" more emphatic by attaching "to him" only to "dear" and not to the unit "dear and holy." In addition, when I revised I doubled the verb "bowed" to give the sentence a slower cadence and air of finality. Revised, the novel's last sentence reads: "Deeply he bowed, bowed to the very earth, before the one sitting there motionless, whose smile reminded him of everything he had ever loved in all his life, everything that had ever, in all his life, been dear to him and holy."

A more dramatic example of turning up the volume in the revision process can be seen in my various revisions of Robert Walser's 1925 story "Letter to Edith." This story takes the form of a letter that the narrator is writing to his ladylove, and eventually it becomes clear that he is drinking as he narrates, his sentences becoming loopier and loopier. By story's end, he sounds thoroughly inebriated: "Ich wankte in eine Konditorei und trank im Wanken sogar noch Kognak. Zwei Musiker spielten mir zuliebe Grieg, aber der Gastwirt erklärte mir den Krieg." When I was first starting out as a translator twenty-five years ago, I translated draft after draft of this dizzying sentence. One of the early ones sounded like this: "I swayed now into a pastry shop and while reeling drank even more cognac. Two musicians played Grieg for my sake, but the proprietor declared war on me." Even this imperfect version of the sentence is already somewhat humorous—the narrator is swaying and reeling, drinking, listening to music, and having war declared on him. I puzzled over this war for quite some time. I did understand that part of the reason

Walser used the word "war" in the sentence was that the word "Krieg" rhymed with the name of the composer Grieg, but I wasn't so happy with how the words "declared war" sounded. When I revised the story a year or two later for publication in the volume *Masquerade and Other Stories* (Johns Hopkins University Press, 1990), I inserted an extra phrase to make the passage "rhymier": "I swayed now into a pastry shop café and, reeling, if I may, put away some cognac. For my benefit two musicians played Grieg, but the proprietor declared war on me." Even after the book was published, this passage continued to bother me; I knew it wasn't quite good enough, and when I wound up writing about this story in an article on Walser's style several years later,[2] I took advantage of the opportunity to revise the sentence one last time.

I had learned some things as a translator meanwhile—including a great deal about just how much freedom a translator really is required to take in order to translate in a way that deserves to be thought of as "faithful." Revisiting Walser's drunken sentence, I began to think about the extent to which the rhyme is actually *constitutive* to the sentence; the semantic value of the word "war" is less important than the fact that the narrator has suddenly started speaking in rhymes in the middle of a prose text. The rhymes exist to provide an index of his drunkenness, and that's where the humor comes from: he's so drunk he can hardly walk, and since the way you walk on the page is by writing, the rhymes represent a sort of spinning in circles. So I looked harder at this war declaration—what did it mean? Probably what the proprietor was actually doing in the scene described was taking the soused narrator off to one side and asking him to either pipe down or leave. That might be described, with paranoid exaggeration, as a war declaration, but was the word "war" itself crucial? Maybe not.

Time is the best medicine for translations. If you are able to lay a text aside long enough to forget exactly what you wrote and what the original looked like in the first place, you can revise with a fresh eye. This is what my fresh eye came up with: "I swayed now into a pastry shop café and reeling, if I may, put some cognac away. To please me, Grieg was played by two musicians, but the proprietor now brought out his munitions." I am delighted with the word "munitions," even though it took me literally years to come up with it. It isn't a synonym for "war," but it comes from the same semantic field and it also, even more importantly, captures the drunken rhyme. It's helpful that "munitions" is a polysyllabic word with a two-syllable rhyme; this makes it stand out in its sentence, which helps produce the sense of comic emphasis.

In the end, all translation is transformation. It just isn't possible for a text to work in its new language and context in exactly the same way it worked in the original. When you create a translation of a literary work, you are creating a new set of rules for the text to operate by. This is what revision is for. Only by revisiting a text again and again, doubting and testing the strength of each of its sentences, can we produce translations that merit consideration as works of literature. And yes, somewhere along the line the original text must be forgotten. It takes a certain amount of pluck—not to mention aesthetic sense and the ability to write well in English—to let go of an original long enough to allow oneself to fully imagine the English words that will take its place, but without this no fully realized translation is possible.

Notes

An earlier version of "Translation and the Art of Revision" was delivered as the keynote address at the Fourth Biannual Graduate Student Translation Conference at the University of Michigan in Ann Arbor, April 24, 2010.

1. The drafts showing Schlegel's revisions are quoted in Michael Bernays, *Zur Entstehungsgeschichte des Schlegelschen Shakespeare* (Leipzig: Hirzel, 1872), 238.

2. Susan Bernofsky, "Unrelenting Tact: Elements of Style in Walser's Late Prose," in Tamara S. Evans, ed., *Robert Walser and the Visual Arts*, Pro Helvetia Swiss Lectureship 9 (New York: City University of New York, 1996), 80–89.

Translation and the Art of Revision

EIGHTEEN

The Art of Losing

Polish Poetry and Translation

CLARE CAVANAGH

I've called my essay "The Art of Losing" for obvious reasons: according to many critics, losing things is what translators do best. And it seems to me—although this may just be my personal bias—that translators of poetry generally get the worst of it. "Why isn't your translation faithful? Why isn't it literal?" we're asked—as if "faithful" and "literal" were synonyms, and as if one of poetry's tasks weren't to shake us loose from the fetters of literal-mindedness. "Why did you keep the form and mangle the meaning, or vice versa?" we're queried—as if poetry weren't forever inviting us to consider the forms of meaning and the meaning of forms. Translating poetry, we're often reminded, is impossible. Well, apparently so is bees' flying—but the bees who translate poetry have been busy for a long while now, so perhaps it's time to reconsider this particular brand of impossibility. What people really mean when they say this, I suspect, is that it's impossible to translate poetry perfectly. Fair enough. But what are the other activities that we human beings perform so flawlessly against which the translation of poetry is being measured and found wanting?

My title is meant to suggest a more humane vision of translation. It implies, I hope, that the losses and gains that make up the art of translation are intertwined, and further, that in the case of poetry, the translator's "art of loss," in John Felstiner's phrase, may perhaps be akin to what Elizabeth Bishop calls the "art of losing," in her glorious villanelle "One Art." I want to examine not how translation violates lyric art so much as the kinship I see between the force that impels some people to write lyric poetry—the force that Osip Mandelstam calls "the craving for form creation"—and the drive that pushes others to translate it. And I'd also like to take a look at what is lost and found when you try to follow the poet's form-creating impulse by re-creating, however imperfectly, the original poem's rhyme and meter.

Bishop's villanelle is a perfect starting point for what I have in mind not only because it's one of the loveliest poems in the English language. It's also been re-created—marvelously—in Polish by my sometime cotranslator Stanislaw Baranczak, who is perhaps the most gifted and prolific translator from English in the history of Polish literature. And Bishop's poem served, in turn, to create a new form in Polish poetry. It inspired Baranczak's own villanelle *"Plakala w nocy,"* from his most recent collection, *Chirurgiczna precyzja* (*Surgical Precision*, 1998), which we have since translated into English as "She Cried That Night." I'll turn to that poem in a moment. But first, Bishop's villanelle:

The art of losing isn't hard to master;
so many things seem filled with the intent
to be lost that their loss is no disaster.

Lose something every day. Accept the fluster
of lost door keys, the hour badly spent.
The art of losing isn't hard to master.

Then practice losing farther, losing faster:
places, and names, and where it was you meant
to travel. None of these will bring disaster.

I lost my mother's watch. And look! my last,
or next-to-last, of three loved houses went.
The art of losing isn't hard to master.

I lost two cities, lovely ones. And, vaster,
some realms I owned, two rivers, a continent.
I miss them, but it wasn't a disaster.

—Even losing you (the joking voice, a gesture
I love) I shan't have lied. It's evident

The Art of Losing: Polish Poetry and Translation

the art of losing's not too hard to master
though it may look like (*Write* it!) like disaster.

Modern poetry, Jean-Paul Sartre remarks, "is the case of the loser winning." And the tug-of-war between mastery and loss that structures Bishop's poem would seem to lend weight to Sartre's paradox. But let me turn here to another poem, whose title appears to contradict my argument. I have in mind one of Wislawa Szymborska's best-known lyrics, "The Joy of Writing" ("*Radość pisania*"). The kind of creation Szymborska celebrates might initially seem directly opposed to the "one art" that shapes Bishop's poem. Szymborska's joy of writing, though, derives by necessity from the limitations that circumscribe and define all human existence: this joy, she writes, is "the revenge of a *mortal* hand" (my italics). "The twinkling of an eye," she exults, "will take as long as I say, / and will, if I wish, divide into tiny eternities, / full of bullets stopped in midflight." But "what's here isn't life," she reminds us: the poet's temporary revenge makes sense only against the backdrop of a world in which bullets can't be halted by rhymes and poetry's "tiny eternities" are quickly gobbled up by greedy time. Szymborska's ephemeral triumphs are tied to defeat in the same way that Bishop's shaky efforts to master loss are trailed by their inescapable rhyme word, "disaster."

If poetry itself can effect only momentary "stays against confusion," then what can possibly be gained by its parasitical in-law, translation? Let's turn here briefly to Baranczak's version of Bishop's "One Art," and take a look at what's been lost and found in translation. First things first: Baranczak keeps the form, and he keeps it beautifully. He even manages, miraculously enough, to retain some of Bishop's key enjambments. Polish doesn't permit him to imitate the eloquent series of rhymes and half-rhymes that Bishop builds around "master" and "disaster": "fluster," "faster," "last, or," "vaster," "gesture." He compensates, though, with a sequence of movingly imperfect rhymes in the stanzas' second lines: "*przeczucie*," "*klucze*," "*uciec*," "*uklucie*," "*nie wroce*," "*w sztuce*." Even a rough translation of these phrases is enough to show how closely he sticks to the original poem's sense: "foreboding," "keys," "to flee," "pang," "won't return," "in art." He can't salvage the seemingly crucial rhyme of "master / disaster" in his Polish text—and it's a loss, but it isn't a disaster. And this is largely because he manages to retain the exquisite villanelle form of the original lyric. The poem's structuring patterns of continuity and slippage, repetition and change, form a perfect analogue to its concern with what is lost through time and what may be retained. Without these, the poem would indeed be lost in translation.

Let me turn now to what Baranczak makes of this form within his own work. Two of *Chirurgiczna precyzja*'s most moving lyrics are villanelles, and the poems not only share the form of "One Art"; they also mirror its concern with mastery and loss, with time's inevitable depredations as partly countered by art. In "She Cried That Night" particularly, Baranczak draws upon Bishop's psychologizing of the villanelle form, as repetition, recognition, and resistance intertwine to dramatize the psyche's efforts to both evade and accept knowledge almost past bearing. (She turns another inherited form to similar ends in her glorious "Sestina.") The poetic form is crucial to the forms of knowing and loss that the poem enacts, which is why we worked to retain it, at a cost, in our English version.

SHE CRIED THAT NIGHT, BUT NOT FOR HIM TO HEAR

To Ania, the only one

She cried that night, but not for him to hear.
In fact her crying wasn't why he woke.
It was some other sound; that much was clear.

And this half-waking shame. No trace of tears
all day, and still at night she works to choke
the sobs; she cries, but not for him to hear.

And all those other nights: she lay so near,
but he had only caught the breeze's joke,
the branch that tapped the roof. That much was clear.

The outside dark revolved in its own sphere:
no wind, no window pane, no creaking oak
had said: "She's crying, not for you to hear."

Untouchable are those tangibly dear,
so close, they're closed, too far to reach and stroke
a quaking shoulder-blade. This much is clear.

And he did not reach out—for shame, for fear
of spoiling the tears' tenderness that spoke:
"Go back to sleep. What woke you isn't here.
It was the wind outside, indifferent, clear."
                    —tr. Stanislaw Baranczak and Clare Cavanagh

There is no equivalent to the villanelle in the Polish tradition; in fact, Baranczak's use of the form was seen by Polish critics as his personal contribution to Polish versification. The poetics of loss thus produce a clear gain for Polish poetry as well as giving a suggestive example of ways the translator's art, or at least this particular translator's art, both resembles and nourishes the lyric impulse.

In Wordsworth's *Prelude*, Stephen Gill remarks, "all loss is converted into gain." My hunch is that this holds true not just for *The Prelude* but for much of modern poetry generally (and perhaps even at times for translation). Certainly the Polish tradition confirms Gill's comment with a vengeance. Since the time of the great Romantics—Adam Mickiewicz, Juliusz Slowacki, Zygmunt Krasinski—Polish poets have apparently wielded precisely the power that Shelley covets in his famous "Defense of Poetry." After Poland vanished from the map of Europe following the partitions of the late eighteenth century, these writers became their battered nation's acknowledged legislators. But if modern Polish history is any example, the losses that foster acknowledged bards and prophets may not offset the gains. Poets took the place of the state when Prussia, Austria, and Russia divided Poland among them, erasing it from the map of Europe for over a century. Poets fought and died in the Home Army that opposed the Nazi invaders during World War II. And poets served as the moral "second government," in Solzhenitsyn's phrase, that countered the illegitimate regime imported from Soviet Russia following the war. They enjoyed a prestige and popularity that their Western counterparts could only dream of.

Not surprisingly, modern Polish poetry has produced a spectacular series of poems demonstrating the possibilities of creation from loss, as poets struggled to infuse a bleak postwar reality with what Mandelstam calls "teleological warmth" by creating lyric forms to take the place of the domestic shapes and human habitations shattered by one atrocity or another. Two of the poems I'll quote here come from Czeslaw Milosz's translations in his anthology *Postwar Polish Poetry*. The first is Leopold Staff's "Foundations":

I built on the sand
And it tumbled down
I built on a rock
And it tumbled down.
Now when I build, I shall begin
With the smoke from the chimney.

The next is Miron Bialoszewski's "And Even, Even if They Take Away the Stove," which he subtitles "My Inexhaustible Ode to Joy":

I have a stove
similar to a triumphal arch!

They take away my stove
similar to a triumphal arch!!

Give me back my stove
similar to a triumphal arch!!!

They took it away
What remains is
a grey
        naked
                hole.

And this is enough for me;
grey naked hole
grey naked hole.
greynakedhole.

Finally, I want to quote a stanza from Milosz's exquisite "Song on Porcelain," in the splendid translation that Milosz himself produced in collaboration with Robert Pinsky:

Rose-colored cup and saucer,
Flowery demitasses:
You lie beside the river
Where an armored column passes.
Winds from across the meadow

Sprinkle the banks with down;
A torn apple tree's shadow
Falls on the muddy path;
The ground everywhere is strewn
With bits of brittle froth—
Of all things broken and lost
Porcelain troubles me most.

The "small sad cry / Of cups and saucers cracking," Milosz tells us in the English variant, bespeaks the end of their "masters' precious dream / Of roses, of mowers raking, / And shepherds on the lawn." Milosz violates his own translatorly preference for preserving sense at the expense of form here. This poem about the fragility of both human-made forms and the human form itself retains its pathos in English precisely because Milosz and Pinsky have managed to reproduce so movingly the stanzas and rhymes of the original. (I first heard the Polish original sung in a student cabaret in Krakow in 1981, and the melody I heard fits the English version as neatly as it did the Polish original, a tribute to the translators' gifts.)

Broken teacups and shattered pastorals: this would seem to be the landscape occupied by the lyric generally, according to many recent theorists. I have in mind critics from every point on the theoretical spectrum, from enemies of the lyric to its defenders, from Adorno, Bakhtin, and de Man to Sharon Cameron or Jerome McGann. The lyric, as the ideological critics in particular would have it, plays host to a panoply of enticing pipe dreams conjured up by benighted idealists whose visions are doomed in advance to frustration as reality fails, time and again, to ratify their various Xanadus and Byzantiums. Terry Eagleton, to give one particularly egregious example, sees it as a chief culprit in art's alleged "refusal of life actually conducted in actual society," which amounts to "complicity with class-interested strategies of smoothing over historical conflict and contradictions with claims of natural and innate organization."

But it's not simply the ideologists who see the lyric as aiming toward a sort of aesthetic isolationism. As Sharon Cameron puts it in *Lyric Time*, the poet strives to evade "the hesitations and ambiguities of a difficult reality" in his quest for "radical sameness" and the "transcendence of mortal vision." He thus becomes the literary equivalent of Sisyphus, as his inevitable failure to attain a definitive reprieve from the limits of mortality plunges him time and again into a kind of lyric inferno, in which he is subjected to every imaginable form of "failure," "pain," "despair," "exhaustion," "grief," and "terror."

What do we make in this context of Bialoszewski's little poem on his vanished stove, with its puzzling subtitle: "My Inexhaustible Ode to Joy"? We could, of course, read this as simple, even simple-minded irony. But I think we would be wrong. The world may well offer only, as Cameron writes, "a landscape of lost things." But Bialoszewski demonstrates that each loss also offers a new way of seeing and something new to see, even if what comes into view is only a "grey naked hole." He manages to generate a new form from absence and emptiness as the "grey-nakedhole" takes on a life of its own. Seen this way, the world's inescapable losses generate not only pain but also creative possibility, and even perhaps "inexhaustible joy." (The poem's final lines in the original Polish read as follows: "*szara naga jama / szara naga jama / sza-ra-na-ga-ja-ma / szaranagajama*." They thus provide an exuberantly Bialoszewskian twist on the art of losing, as the writers Dariusz Sosnicki and Piotr Sommer have suggested to me: this is the closest a Polish poet can come to speaking Japanese.)

I've mentioned the rich Polish tradition of poetic creation from loss. But Bialoszewski's lyric with its unexpected subtitle suggests a different direction taken by some of postwar Poland's greatest poets. This is what I will call the tradition of "joyful failure," in which the poet is plagued not so much by the world's emptiness as by its unplumbable abundance. "You can't have everything. Where would you put it?" the comedian Steven Wright asks. Certainly not in a single poem, or even in a single human life. This is the dilemma shared by poets like Czeslaw Milosz, Adam Zagajewski, and Wislawa Szymborska, whose lyrics are linked by their endlessly resourceful, invariably thwarted efforts to achieve at last what Milosz calls the "unattainable" or, in Polish, "unembraced" or "unembraceable earth" (*nieobjeta ziemia*).

"There was too much / of Lvov, it brimmed the container / it burst glasses, overflowed / each pond, lake, smoked through every / chimney," Zagajewski writes in "To Go to Lvov" ("*Jechac do Lwowa*"), a poem that is at once both a stirring elegy to a vanished world and a paean to its inextinguishable presence: "[Lvov] is everywhere," the poem ends. No merely human vessel can hope to contain once and for all a world that precedes us, exceeds us, and will finally outlast us: Lvov "burst glasses . . . smoked through every chimney." (I'm quoting here from Renata Gorczynska's splendid English version of the poem.) The lyric form, with its built-in limitations, can't pretend to comprehensiveness in the way a novel or an epic poem might. It can serve, though, as a perfect embodiment or enactment of the individual's ceaselessly renewed, joyous struggle to come to terms with a world that always lies slightly beyond his or her reach.

Here I want to turn to two poems, or rather two translations, in which I attempted to keep up with two poets working to keep up with the world itself. The first is Szymborska's "Birthday" ("*Urodziny*"):

> So much world all at once—how it rustles and bustles!
> Moraines and morays and morasses and mussels,
> the flame, the flamingo, the flounder, the feather—
> how to line them all up, how to put them together?
> All the thickets and crickets and creepers and creeks!
> The beeches and leeches alone could take weeks.
> Chinchillas, gorillas, and sarsaparillas—
> thanks so much, but this excess of kindness could kill us.
> Where's the jar for this burgeoning burdock, brooks' babble,
> rooks' squabble, snakes' squiggle, abundance, and trouble?
> How to plug up the gold mines and pin down the fox,
> how to cope with the lynx, bobolinks, streptococs!
> Take dioxide: a lightweight, but mighty in deeds:
> what about octopodes, what about centipedes?
> I could look into prices, but don't have the nerve:
> these are products I just can't afford, don't deserve.
> Isn't sunset a little too much for two eyes
> that, who knows, may not open to see the sun rise?
> I am just passing through, it's a five-minute stop.
> I won't catch what is distant; what's too close, I'll mix up.
> While trying to plumb what the void's inner sense is,
> I'm bound to pass by all these poppies and pansies.
> What a loss when you think how much effort was spent
> perfecting this petal, this pistil, this scent
> for the one-time appearance that is all they're allowed,
> so aloofly precise and so fragilely proud.
>
> —tr. Stanislaw Baranczak and Clare Cavanagh

In the poem, Szymborska sends language scrambling, by way of her frantic wordplay, rhythm, and rhymes, to keep pace with the relentless form-creation that animates nature itself. (She also provides, if we needed one, a perfect defense against the myth that literalness equals fidelity when translating poetry. What ham-handed translator would render the poem's fifth and sixth lines as follows: "These thickets and muzzles and breams and rains, / geraniums and praying mantises, where will I put them?" The Polish text is clearly calling out for translators doing their damnedest to channel Gilbert and Sullivan, or maybe Ogden Nash: "All the thickets and crickets and creepers and creeks! / The beeches and leeches alone could take weeks.")

The second poem I want to quote is Adam Zagajewski's beautiful "Mysticism for Beginners" (*Mistyka dia poczatkujacych*):

The day was mild, the light was generous.
The German on the cafe terrace
held a small book on his lap.
I caught sight of the title:
Mysticism for Beginners.
Suddenly I understood that the swallows
patrolling the streets of Montepulciano
with their shrill whistles,
and the hushed talk of timid travelers
from Eastern, so-called Central Europe,
and the white herons standing—yesterday? the day before?—
like nuns in fields of rice,
and the dusk, slow and systematic,
erasing the outlines of medieval houses,
and olive trees on little hills,
abandoned to the wind and heat,
and the head of the Unknown Princess
that I saw and admired in the Louvre,
and stained-glass windows like butterfly wings
sprinkled with pollen,
and the little nightingale practicing
its speech beside the highway,
and any journey, any kind of trip,
are only mysticism for beginners,
the elementary course, prelude
to a test that's been
postponed.

—tr. Clare Cavanagh

It is another demonstration of the capacity to create lyric joy through apparent failure as Zagajewski, in a characteristic syntactic tour de force, breathlessly stretches one sentence out for the space of twenty-odd lines, only to conclude with the anticlimactic postponed examination that takes the place of the revelation—"suddenly I understood"—we've been waiting for.

In my own conclusion, I want to turn to a distinctly nonpoetic analogy for what I see as perhaps the chief affinity between the poet's joyful frustration and that of the translator. A few years back, when my son was first learning to walk, he started playing a game that scared the hell out of us. He would take a blanket, put it over his head, run down the hallway, bang into the walls at full speed, and fall down on the floor laughing his head off. "Oh my God," we thought, "he's going to be a quarterback."

But then I happened to be talking to a friend who's a child psychologist, and I told her about Marty's game. "It's a philosophical experiment," she said. "He wants to find out if the world still exists even when he can't see it, and he laughs when he hits the wall because it's still there."

Form, substance, and joyful failure: these are defining elements not just in my son's game but also, it strikes me, both in lyric poetry and in poetic translation. Of course translating poetry is impossible: all the best things are. But the impulse that drives one to try is not so far removed, I think, from the force that sends the lyric poet out time after time to master the world in a few lines of verse. You see a wonderful thing in front of you, and you want it. You try reading it over and over, you see if you can memorize it, or copy it out line by line. And nothing works; it's still there. So if it doesn't already exist in English, you turn to translation; you try remaking it in your own language, in your own words, in the vain hope of getting it once and for all, of finally making it your own. And sometimes you even feel, for a while at least, for a day or two or even a couple of weeks, that you've got it, it's worked, the poem's yours. But then you turn back to the poem itself at some point, and you have to hit your head against the wall and laugh: it's still there.

Permissions

Contributors

ESTHER ALLEN translated, edited, and annotated the Penguin Classics anthology *The Selected Writings of José Martí* (2002) and has translated a number of other works from Spanish and French, including, most recently, Antonio Di Benedetto's *Zama* (NYRB Classics, 2014). Editor of the 2007 report on translation and globalization *To Be Translated or Not to Be*, she has twice received fellowships from the NEA (1995, 2010), was named a Chevalier de l'ordre des arts et des lettres in 2006, and was a 2009 Fellow at the New York Public Library's Cullman Center for Scholars and Writers. She teaches at Baruch College, City University of New York.

DAVID BELLOS is the director of the Program in Translation and Intercultural Communication at Princeton University, where he is also a professor of French and comparative literature. He has won many awards for his translations, including the Man Booker International Prize for translation. He received the Prix Goncourt for his biography of Georges Perec and has also written biographies of Jacques Tati and Romain Gary. He is most recently the author of *Is That a Fish in Your Ear?: Translation and the Meaning of Everything* (Faber, 2011).

SUSAN BERNOFSKY is the translator of books by Robert Walser, Jenny Erpenbeck, Yoko Tawada, Hermann Hesse, Gregor von Rezzori, and others, and the author of *Foreign Words: Translator-Authors in the Age of Goethe* (Kritik Series, Wayne State University Press, 2005). She received the 2006 Helen and Kurt Wolff Translation Prize and the 2012 Hermann Hesse Translation Prize as well as awards and fellowships from the NEH, the NEA, the Alexander von Humboldt Foundation, the American Council of Learned Societies, the Leon Levy Center for Biography, and the Lannan Foundation. She chairs the PEN Translation Committee and is the director of Literary Translation at Columbia in Columbia University's School of the Arts, where she teaches in the M.F.A. writing program.

Scholar and translator CLARE CAVANAGH is the author of *Lyric Poetry and Modern Politics: Russia, Poland, and the West* (2010), winner of the National Book Critics Circle Award in Criticism. She is also the author of *Osip Mandelstam and the Modernist Creation of Tradition* (1995) and is at work on the authorized biography of Polish poet Czeslaw Milosz. She has translated numerous collections from poets including Milosz, Wislawa Szymborska, and Adam Zagajewski. Cavanagh's many awards for translation include the John Frederick Nims Memorial Prize in Translation and the PEN/Book-of-the-Month Club Prize for Outstanding Literary Translation. Her translation of Wislawa Szymborska's latest volume, *Here* (2010), won the Found in Translation Award. The recipient of fellowships from the Guggenheim Foundation, the National Endowment for the Humanities, the Social Science Research Council, and the American Council of Learned Societies, she teaches Slavic and comparative literatures at Northwestern University.

PETER COLE is the author of three books of poems, most recently *Things on Which I've Stumbled* (New Directions). His many volumes of translations from Hebrew and Arabic include *The Poetry of Kabbalah: Mystical Verse from the Jewish Tradition* (Yale), *The Dream of the Poem: Hebrew Poetry from Muslim and Christian Spain, 950–1492* (Princeton), Aharon Shabtai's *War and Love, Love and War: New & Selected Poems* (New Directions), and Taha Muhammad Ali's *So What: New & Selected Poems 1973–2005* (Copper Canyon). With Adina Hoffman, he has also published a volume of nonfiction, *Sacred Trash: The Lost and Found World of the Cairo Geniza* (Schocken/Nextbook). Cole has received numerous honors for his work, including an American Academy of Arts and Letters Award in Literature; fellowships from the NEA, the NEH, and the Guggenheim Foundation; and the PEN Translation Award for Poetry. In 2007 he was named a MacArthur Fellow.

MICHAEL EMMERICH teaches Japanese literature at the University of California, Santa Barbara. He has translated numerous books from Japanese, including Yasunari Kawabata's *First Snow on Fuji*; Gen'ichirō Takahashi's *Sayonara, Gangsters*; Banana Yoshimoto's *The Lake*; and Hiromi Kawakami's *Manazuru*, which was awarded the 2010 Japan-U.S. Friendship Commission Prize for the Translation of Japanese Literature. He is the editor of *Read Real Japanese Fiction* and *New Penguin Parallel Texts: Short Stories in Japanese*, and the author of *The Tale of Genji: Translation, Canonization, and World Literature*, forthcoming from Columbia University Press.

MAUREEN FREELY is the author of six novels (*Mother's Helper, The Life of the Party, The Stork Club, Under the Vulcania, The Other Rebecca,* and most recently *Enlightenment*) as well as three works of nonfiction (*Pandora's Clock, What About Us? An Open Letter to the Mothers Feminism Forgot,* and *The Parent Trap*). The translator of five

Contributors

books by the Turkish Nobel laureate Orhan Pamuk (*Snow*, *The Black Book*, *Istanbul: Memories of a City*, *Other Colours*, and *The Museum of Innocence*), she is active in various campaigns to champion free expression. She also works with campaigns to promote world literature in English translation. She has been a regular contributor to the *Guardian*, the *Observer*, the *Independent*, and the *Sunday Times* for two decades, writing on feminism, family and social policy, Turkish culture and politics, and contemporary writing.

FORREST GANDER has degrees in geology and English literature. His recent books include the novel *As a Friend* and the book of *haibun* and poems *Core Samples from the World*, both from New Directions. *Watchword*, Gander's translation of Pura López Colomé's Villaurrutia Award-winning book of poems, came out in 2012. His other recent translations include *Firefly Under the Tongue: Selected Poems of Coral Bracho* (PEN Translation Prize Finalist), and (with Kyoko Yoshida) *Spectacle & Pigsty: Selected Poems of Kiwao Nomura*, awarded the 2012 Best Translated Book Award for poetry. A United States Artists Rockefeller Fellow, Gander is the recipient of fellowships from the NEA and the Guggenheim, Howard, and Whiting foundations. He is the Adele Kellenberg Seaver Professor of Literary Arts and Comparative Literature at Brown University.

THEODORE (TED) GOOSSEN is professor of humanities at York University in Toronto, Canada, and a founding member of the Department of Contemporary Literary Studies at the University of Tokyo. He has written extensively on Japanese literature and film, and has published translations by numerous authors including Hiromi Kawakami, Yoko Ogawa, Masuji Ibuse, Naoya Shiga, Yukio Mishima, and Haruki Murakami. He is editor of *The Oxford Book of Japanese Short Stories* and is presently coeditor, with Motoyuki Shibata, of *Monkey Business International*, the first Japanese literary magazine to be made available in an English version. His translations of Haruki Murakami's first two major works, *Kaze no Uta o Kike* (*Hear the Wind Sing*, 1979) and *1973-Nen no Piboru* (*Pinball, 1973*, 1980), will be published by Alfred A. Knopf.

JASON GRUNEBAUM is a senior lecturer in Hindi at the University of Chicago. He is the translator of Uday Prakash's novel *The Girl with the Golden Parasol* (Penguin India, 2008; Yale University Press, 2013) and Manzoor Ahtesham's *The Tale of the Missing Man* (with Ulrike Stark). His translation of Prakash's story "The Walls of Delhi" was included in *Delhi Noir* (Akashic Books, 2009) and will be published along with two other novellas by Prakash in a collection entitled *The Walls of Delhi* in early 2012 by University of Western Australia Press. Grunebaum has been awarded a PEN Translation Fund grant, an NEA Literature fellowship, and an ALTA fellowship for his translation work, as well as residencies at the Blue Mountain Center for the Arts and the Djerassi Foundation. He has a B.A. from Brown University and a M.F.A. in fiction from Columbia University. His fiction has been published in the magazines *One Story*, Web *Conjunctions*, *Southwest Review*, and *Third*

Contributors

Coast. Salman Rushdie selected his "Maria Ximenes da Costa de Carvalho Perreira" as a distinguished short story of 2007.

ALICE KAPLAN is the John M. Musser Professor of French at Yale University. Before her arrival at Yale, she was the Gilbert, Louis and Edward Lehrman Professor of Romance Studies and Professor of Literature and History and founding director of the Center for French and Francophone Studies at Duke University. She is the author of *Reproductions of Banality: Fascism, Literature, and French Intellectual Life* (1986); *French Lessons: A Memoir* (1993); *The Collaborator: The Trial and Execution of Robert Brasillach* (2000); and, most recently, *The Interpreter* (2005), about racial injustice in the American army witnessed by Louis Guilloux. Kaplan is also the translator into English of Lous Guilloux's novel *OK, Joe*; Evelyne Bloch-Dano's *Madame Proust: A Biography*; and three books by Roger Grenier: *Piano Music for Four Hands*, *Another November*, and *The Difficulty of Being a Dog*.

CHRISTI ANN MERRILL is an associate professor of South Asian literature and postcolonial theory at the University of Michigan, and author of *Riddles of Belonging: India in Translation and Other Tales of Possession*. Her translation of the stories of Rajasthani writer Vijay Dan Detha, *Chouboli and Other Stories*, has recently been published by Katha (New Delhi) and Fordham University Press (New York).

HARUKI MURAKAMI is an internationally acclaimed writer whose awards include the Franz Kafka Prize (2006), the Jerusalem Prize (2009), and the International Catalunya Prize (2011). Among his novels are *Hard-Boiled Wonderland and the End of the World* (1985; English, 1991), *Norwegian Wood* (1987; English, 2000), *The Wind-Up Bird Chronicle* (1995, English, 1997), *Kafka on the Shore* (2002; English, 2005), and *1Q84* (2009; English, 2011). His work has been translated into forty-two languages. He is also a prolific and best-selling translator of American fiction into Japanese. Authors and works he has translated include C. D. B. Bryan, Truman Capote (*Breakfast at Tiffany's*), Raymond Carver (*Complete Works*), Raymond Chandler (*The Long Goodbye*), Bill Crow, Terry Farish, F. Scott Fitzgerald, Jim Fusilli, Mark Helprin, John Irving, Ursula K. Le Guin, Tim O'Brien, Grace Paley (*Enormous Changes at the Last Minute*), J. D. Salinger (*The Catcher in the Rye*), Mark Strand, Paul Theroux, and Chris Van Allsburg.

CATHERINE PORTER, 2009 President of the Modern Language Association, is visiting professor, Society for the Humanities, Cornell University, and professor of French emerita, State University of New York, Cortland, where she served as chair of the Department of International Communications and Culture, 1985–1991 and 1997–2001. She has translated some three dozen books in the humanities and the social sciences, most recently Patrick Weil, *How to Be French* (2008); Maurice Sartre, *Histoires Grecques: Snapshots from Antiquity* (2009); Avital Ronell, *Fighting Theory* (2010); and Jean-Christophe Bailly (*The Animal Side*, 2011). Recent articles include

Contributors

"Presidential Address 2009: English Is Not Enough" (*PMLA* 125, no. 3). She received her doctorate in French literature from Yale University in 1972.

JOSÉ MANUEL PRIETO is the author of several works of fiction and nonfiction, including the internationally acclaimed trilogy of novels *Enciclopedia de una vida en Rusia* (*Encyclopedia of a Life in Russia*), *Livadia* (published in English as *Nocturnal Butterflies of the Russian Empire*), and *Rex*. His novel *Voz humana* (*Human Voice*) is forthcoming. He has translated into Spanish works by Anna Akhmatova, Vladimir Mayakovsky, Andrei Platonov, Gennady Aygi, and many others. Prieto earned his Ph.D. in history at the Universidad Autónoma de México. He has been a fellow at the New York Public Library's Cullman Center for Scholars and Writers and received a Guggenheim Fellowship. He has taught at the Centro de Investigación y Docencia Económica (CIDE) in Mexico City, Cornell University as a visiting professor, and Princeton University as a distinguished lecturer. He currently teaches at Seton Hall University.

In addition to his various editions of Pound for the Library of America and New Directions, RICHARD SIEBURTH has published translations of works by Hölderlin (*Hymns and Fragments*), Büchner (*Lenz*), Benjamin (*Moscow Diary*), Scholem (*The Fullness of Time: Poems*), Nostradamus (*The Prophecies*), Scève (*Emblems of Desire*), Nerval (*Selected Writings* [PEN Book-of-the-Month Prize]; *The Salt Smugglers*), Michaux (*Emergences-Resurgences*; *Stroke by Stroke*), Leiris (*Nights as Day, Days as Night*), and Guillevic (*Geometries*). He is currently working on a translation/edition of late Baudelaire, for which he was awarded a Guggenheim Fellowship. He is a fellow of the American Academy of Arts and Sciences and a Chevalier de l'ordre des palmes académiques. He teaches French and comparative literature at New York University.

Professor of English at Temple University, LAWRENCE VENUTI is a translation theorist and historian as well as a translator from Italian, French, and Catalan. He is the author of *The Translator's Invisibility: A History of Translation* (2nd ed., 2008), *The Scandals of Translation: Towards an Ethics of Difference* (1998), and *Translation Changes Everything: Theory and Practice* (2012), as well as the editor of *The Translation Studies Reader* (3rd ed., 2012). His translations include the anthology *Italy: A Traveler's Literary Companion* (2003), Massimo Carlotto's crime novel *The Goodbye Kiss* (2006), and Ernest Farrés's *Edward Hopper: Poems* (2009), for which he won the Robert Fagles Translation Prize.

ELIOT WEINBERGER's books of literary essays include *Karmic Traces*, *An Elemental Thing*, and *Oranges & Peanuts for Sale*. His political articles are collected in *What I Heard About Iraq* and *What Happened Here: Bush Chronicles*. The author of a study of Chinese poetry translation, *19 Ways of Looking at Wang Wei*, he translates the poetry of Bei Dao and is editor of *The New Directions Anthology of Classical Chinese*

Contributors

Poetry and a forthcoming series of classics from Chinese University Press of Hong Kong. Among his translations and editions of Latin American poetry and prose are *The Poems of Octavio Paz*, Jorge Luis Borges's *Selected Non-Fictions* (winner of the National Book Critics Circle Award in Criticism), Xavier Villaurrutia's *Nostalgia for Death*, and Vicente Huidobro's *Altazor*. His work has been translated into thirty languages.

Index

Index

Index

Helft, Miguel, 100
Hemingway, Ernest, 79, 179–80
Herbert, George, 110
Herder, Johann Gottfried, 19
Heredia, José María, 90
Hesse, Hermann, 230–31
Hillman, Brenda, 109
Hindi language and literature, xviii; and authorship question in the case of folktales, 144–45; choice of English-speaking audience for translations from, 156–68; and "foreign-soundingness," 39–40; Hindi literature curriculum in schools, 159–60
Hispanic American Historical Review, 93
history of translation: attempts to defend or improve "small" languages through translations, 40–41; and authorship question in the case of folktales, 146–49; and educated English speakers' knowledge of French phrases, 35, 37; historically significant translations, 76; and ideology of fluency and transparency in Anglo-American tradition, 61; influence of foreign works on English authors, 110; Japanese translations, 52–53, 183–84; Latin American literature translated in New York City, 83–104; and national purposes, 41; 19th-century conventions for preserving common phrases in the original language, 34–35; and religious texts, 60–61; 16th-century French translations of Italian works, 40; translation booms, 17–21, 96–99; and U.S.'s "good neighbor" policy, 93, 96; and words imported into target language, 42
Hofstadter, Douglas, 58–59
Hollander, John, 209
Hollander, Robert and Jean, xiii
Homer, 110
Hoover, Paul, 109

Hopkins, Gerard Manley, 110
Hopkins, Sarah Winnemucca, 88–89
Hopscotch (Cortázar), 97
House of Mist (Bombal), 92
How to Be French (Weil), 64
Huchon, Mireille, 215
Hughes, Serge and Elizabeth, 197–99
Hurd and Houghton (publisher), 83
Husserl, Edmund, 48
Hyesoon, Kim, 109

Igarashi, Hitoshi, 29
India, 19, 156–68. *See also* Hindi language and literature; Rajasthani language and literature; Sanskrit language and literature
Inferno (Dante), xiii–xiv
intellectual property rights, 73–77; and authorship question in the case of folktales, 144–54
Internet, xix, 100
intertextuality, xxi, 28, 218
Irving, Washington, 84
Isaacs, Jorge, 89, 90
Italian language and literature: Dante's *Commedia*, xiii–xv; earliest poems, 192; and "foreign-soundingness," 37; 16th-century French translations of Italian works, 40; translations of Jacopone da Todi's poetry, 191–207

Jackson, Helen Hunt, 85
Jacopone da Todi, 191–207; Beck's translation, 194–97; biographical sketch, 192–93; Hughes's translation, 197–99; Venuti's translation, 199–207
James, Henry, 79
Japanese language and literature, 53–56; Murakami and the culture of translation, 183–86; Murakami's translation of *The Great Gatsby*, 169–82, 185–96; printing and *The Tale of Genji*, 52–53; words for and meanings of translation, 45–47, 55; writing systems, 55, 183

Index

257

Index

Philcox, Richard, 77, 81n10
Philippi, Donald, 48
Piano Music for Four Hands (Grenier), 79
Le Pierrot noir (Grenier), 78–79
Pindar, 110
Pinsky, Robert, 239–40
Pnin (Nabokov), 68
poetry translations: and Bly's leaping poetry, 107–8; Cavanagh on, 234–44; and choice of English-language form for translation, 188–207; Gander on, 112–16; and goals of translation, 115–16; Hall's warning on, 11–12; impulse to translate, 235, 244; influence of translations on U.S. poetry, 108–10; issues in translations of archaic poetry, 187–221; Polish poetry, 234–44; Pound and, 189–91; Sieburth's translation of Scève's *Délie*, 209–21; time required for, 6; translations of Jacopone da Todi's poetry, 191–207; translator's need for knowledge of the literature of the translation language, 23–26; Venuti on, 187–208. *See also specific poets*
Polish poetry, 234–44
politics, 110; and choice of texts to translate, 9, 97–99, 101; Italian religious politics and Jacopone's poems, 193–94; and Mandelstam's "Epigram against Stalin," 130–42; Turkish politics and translations of Orhan Pamuk's work, 118–26
Pollock, Sheldon, xv
Porter, Catherine, xxi, 58–66, 250–51
Porter, Katherine Anne, 93
Postwar Polish Poetry (Milosz), 238–39
Pound, Ezra, 11, 23–24, 108, 112
Prakash, Uday, 157–67
Preobrazhensky, Yevgeni, 140
Prescott, William H., 90
Pressly, Eugene, 93
Prieto, José Manuel, xx, xxi, 127–42, 251

prosody, 113, 116, 188, 189, 194, 199, 200
publishing industry, xx, 9, 63–64, 73–77, 121–22

Qu'est-ce qu'un Français? (Weil), 64

Rabassa, Gregory, 96–100
Rajasthani language and literature, 144–45
Ramona (Jackson), 85
Ramsey, Albert C., 85
rap music, 200–202
Roscommon, Earl of, 7
Razgon, Lev, 141
Reid, Alistair, 97
religion, 12–13, 28–29, 60–61, 193–94
retranslation, 6, 30, 34, 36, 46, 68, 73–76, 108, 170–71, 199
revision process, 223–33
rhyme, 24–25, 188, 194, 195, 197, 199, 201, 210, 211, 216–19, 232–33, 235–36, 240, 242
"Rijak ki Maryada" (Detha), 143–44, 146, 150–54
Rivera y Rio, José, 86, 91, 103n16
Robinson, Douglas, 60–61
Robinson, James Alexander, 93
Roosevelt, Franklin Delano, 93
Rosa, João Guimarães, 98
Rosenzweig, Franz, 13, 15
Roussin, Philippe, 78
Rubin, Jay, 184
Runge, Philipp Otto, 148
Rushdie, Salman, 28–29
Russian language and literature: and "foreign-soundingness," 35–36; Prieto's translation of Mandelstam's "Epigram against Stalin," 127–42

Sacks, Peter, 109
Saenz, Jaime, 112–13
Sagan, Françoise, 58
Salamun, Tomaz, 109
Salinger, J. D., 170
Sanskrit language and literature, 19

Index

women: translation as a safe way for 19th- and early 20th-century women to channel intellectual and creative impulses, 92

Woolf, Virginia, 75

word choice, 14, 64–65; and cultural differences, 161–67; dangers of mistranslation, 28–29; and different English-speaking audiences for translations from Hindi, 157–67; and Gatsby's pet phrase "old sport," 181–82, 186; input from translator, author, and editor, 95; and location of agency in Spanish, 111–12; and Prieto's commentary on Mandelstam's "Epigram against Stalin," 130–42; and revision process, 223–33; and sound/sense unity, 229–30; and tenses and degrees of evidential investment in Aymara language, 112–13. *See also* poetry translations; translation, issues in; *specific authors and translators*

World Trade Center bombing of 1993, 29

World War I, 19

Wright, C. D., 109

Wright, Steven, 241

writing, material forms of, 53–55

writing, translation as excellent practice for, 28, 80

Wuthering Heights (Brontë), 73–75

Wycliffe, John, 12

Young, Marguerite, 107

Yourcenar, Marguerite, 77

Zagajewski, Adam, 241, 243–44

Zamyatin, Yevgeny, 137

Zipes, Jack, 147–48

Zukofsky, Louis, 109

Index

CPSIA information can be obtained
at www.ICGtesting.com
Printed in the USA
JSHW051306170222
23033JS00001B/30